IMAGES
of America

SAVANNAH'S DAFFIN PARK AND PARKSIDE PLACE

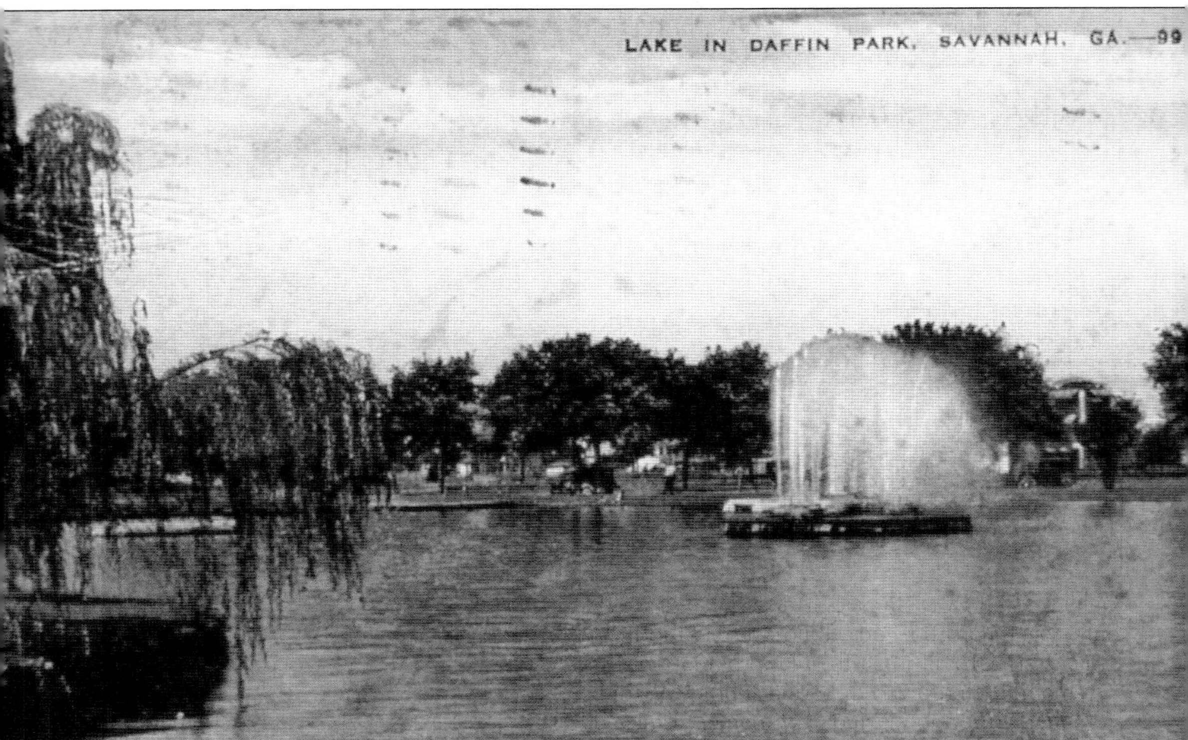

This vintage postcard shows the Daffin Park lake as it looked after it was dug in the 1920s. Many years later, in preparation for the park's 2007 centennial observance, civic leader Herb Traub and the local Rotary Clubs donated more than $200,000 to refurbish the park, including the installation of new lighted fountains in the lake, benches, a pathway along the landscaped shore, picnic tables, and more. (Author's collection.)

ON THE COVER: The Tiger Athletic Club was organized in the early 1930s and directed for years by Fred Garis, the gray-haired man behind the football players pictured here. By the time this photograph was taken in 1963 at Daffin Park, Garis was coaching a second generation of Tigers. (Courtesy of the Garis family.)

IMAGES

of America

SAVANNAH'S DAFFIN PARK AND PARKSIDE PLACE

Polly Powers Stramm

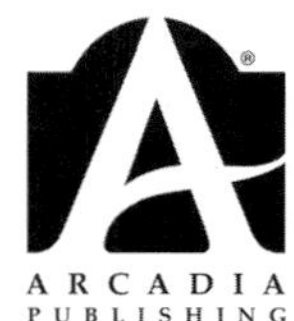

ARCADIA
PUBLISHING

Copyright © 2020 by Polly Powers Stramm
ISBN 978-1-4671-0586-6

Published by Arcadia Publishing
Charleston, South Carolina

Printed in the United States of America

Library of Congress Control Number: 2020937565

For all general information, please contact Arcadia Publishing:
Telephone 843-853-2070
Fax 843-853-0044
E-mail sales@arcadiapublishing.com
For customer service and orders:
Toll-Free 1-888-313-2665

Visit us on the Internet at www.arcadiapublishing.com

This book is dedicated to my family: my husband, Steve; daughters Polly and Mary; and my late parents, Dr. and Mrs. L.K. Powers, both of whom visited Daffin Park in their youth. My father was a fabulous storyteller and fancied himself somewhat of an amateur historian. I sincerely hope I have inherited those traits from him.

CONTENTS

ACKNOWLEDGMENTS

Putting this book together was akin to matching the pieces of a jigsaw puzzle and playing dominoes. While researching the history of Daffin and Parkside, I would talk to one or two people who shared the names of five or six former neighbors. Those folks suggested others to track down and so on.

I contacted as many residents and former Parkside folks as I could, although I'm certain plenty of others will flip through the pages of this book and say, 'That's where I grew up and I have tons of pictures." Nevertheless, I did the best I could do and could not have completed this book without the generosity and cooperation of both Parkside residents and those who considered Daffin Park to be their backyard. Even today, Daffin is much more than a park where people play or watch football, soccer, tennis, and other sports. It's a community gathering place and one of the city's premier green spaces. Residents from throughout the city go there by vehicle, bicycle, or on foot to swim, picnic, run or walk, or to enjoy the playgrounds.

Many thanks to those people who searched treasured family scrapbooks and plundered boxes and attics looking for photographs to share with me. More than a few folks entertained me with memories of their neighborhood experiences. Coaches from long ago, relatives of coaches, team members, and cheerleaders offered stories of victory and defeat, and pictures of teams that practiced and competed in Daffin. Legions of folks helped identify team members and cheerleaders, and my fingers are crossed that the names and spellings are correct.

I also would like to thank Caroline Anderson—my patient editor—and her top-notch team at Arcadia Publishing as well as the professionals at the City of Savannah Municipal Archives for their assistance and permission to research the history of Daffin and Parkside.

INTRODUCTION

As a young child growing up on the fringes of Ardsley Park, I remember being plopped down in the wire basket connected to the handlebars of one of my older sisters' bicycles. We bounced along Waters Avenue to nearby Daffin Park, where my sisters played tennis and I watched from the sidelines. It was those same tennis courts—albeit spruced up—where my father, as a teenager in 1930, won the Savannah junior boys' tennis doubles championship. A few years after those afternoons at the courts with my sisters, I would accompany my parents to the AMBUCS Stadium in Daffin to watch my brother play Pony League baseball games. When I was 15, Daffin Park was where my mother or father took me to practice driving the Buick LeSabre in anticipation of acquiring my driver's license.

For many years, I was familiar with Daffin, but I really didn't know the history of that great green space in midtown Savannah. In 2006, I was asked to serve on the Daffin Park Centennial Committee in anticipation of Daffin's 100th birthday in 2007. It wasn't until then that I discovered the fascinating background of the park that I thought I knew so well.

During that time, I also learned more about what is officially known as the Parkside Place neighborhood, which is bordered by Washington Avenue to the north, Fifty-First Street Lane (on the Fifty-Second Street side) to the south, Waters Avenue to the west, and Bee Road to the east. Growing up, I attended elementary school and church with several children who lived in Parkside, which was only a few blocks from my stomping grounds. My friends and I also frequented businesses along the Waters Avenue corridor just across the street from Parkside. These places included the Victory Soda Shoppe, This 'n That Variety Store, Madeleine T. Walker's School of Ballet, 49th Street Pharmacy, Lariscy's Service Station, and others. Longtime Parkside residents also may remember Orsini's Market, Kleeman's Market, Manuel's, Niemeyer's Delicatessen, and the DuCharme Beauty Parlor.

The development of Parkside was closely associated with the completion of Daffin Park in 1907. By 1914, the streets and lots south of Daffin had been laid out in the neighborhood, with development continuing through the 1940s.

Thanks to the hard work and diligence of several individuals, but especially the late John DeLorme, a lifelong neighborhood resident, Daffin Park–Parkside Place was listed in the National Register of Historic Places in 1999.

Daffin Park was designed in 1907 by noted landscape architect and city planner John Nolen of Massachusetts, who envisioned 80 acres of open spaces, tree-lined promenades, fountains, and recreational areas. Nolen was paid $500 by the City of Savannah to design the area that initially was named Daffin Athletic Field. Previously, it was a low-lying area with a pond on the south side and part of the DeRenne Canal in the northwest section. A park keeper's home on the west side was built with part of the press stand from the great Savannah automobile races of 1910 and 1911. Many of the more than 150 oak trees that are in the park today were planted in 1908, with more oaks and palmetto trees added later. In those days, the park was managed by Philip "P.D." Daffin, chairman of the Savannah Park and Tree Commission, for whom the park was named.

Many "firsts" took place in Daffin, with one of the earlier moments occurring in 1911 in the pioneering days of aviation. A pilot circled the field and dropped a mail sack that was picked up by a postal worker who delivered the mail to the post office. In 1919, the Savannah Park and Tree Commission granted permission to the government to use the southern side of Daffin Park as a temporary airfield for mail service. In addition to planes flying in and out of the park, southbound tourists traveling to Florida from all parts of the nation camped at Daffin Park.

In the 1920s, a lake was installed along the north side of the park. The tranquil spot was designed by William Henry Robertson, superintendent of the Savannah Park and Tree Commission, and was divided into two parts: one for swimming and the other for boating and fishing.

As the years progressed, other areas in the park began taking shape. In 1926, a municipal stadium was built near what is now Bee Road. In 1935, a grove of pine trees was planted between the stadium and Bee Road and named for chemist Charles Herty, who played a key role in the southern forest industry. Municipal Stadium was the focal point of Savannah's observance of Georgia's bicentennial in 1933, when Pres. Franklin D. Roosevelt spoke to adoring crowds at the stadium.

In 1940, a hurricane destroyed the wooden section of Municipal Stadium. By the following year, the stadium was razed, and work began on a replacement that was named for Gen. William L. Grayson, who chaired the building committee. He was a veteran of the Spanish-American War, clerk of the Superior Court, and a city alderman. Grayson Stadium has been renovated several times and is considered a fine example of a post–World War II stadium.

Six tennis courts were built in Daffin Park in 1927, with nine more added in 1949. Since then, additional courts have been built. A new pool opened in 1954 after the health department determined that the lake was unsanitary for swimming. Additionally, a therapy pool was built for children who suffered from polio. In 1973, the city spent $60,000 on park improvements, including the construction of a new pavilion on the island in the middle of the lake. In 1998 and 2002, more improvements were made to Daffin, including additional space for soccer and football, improved lighting and parking, and new sidewalks.

Daffin Park and Parkside have come a long way since I first visited as a child, but both remain a constant reminder of the beauty and history that Savannahians are fortunate to have experienced for more than a century.

DAFFIN PARK

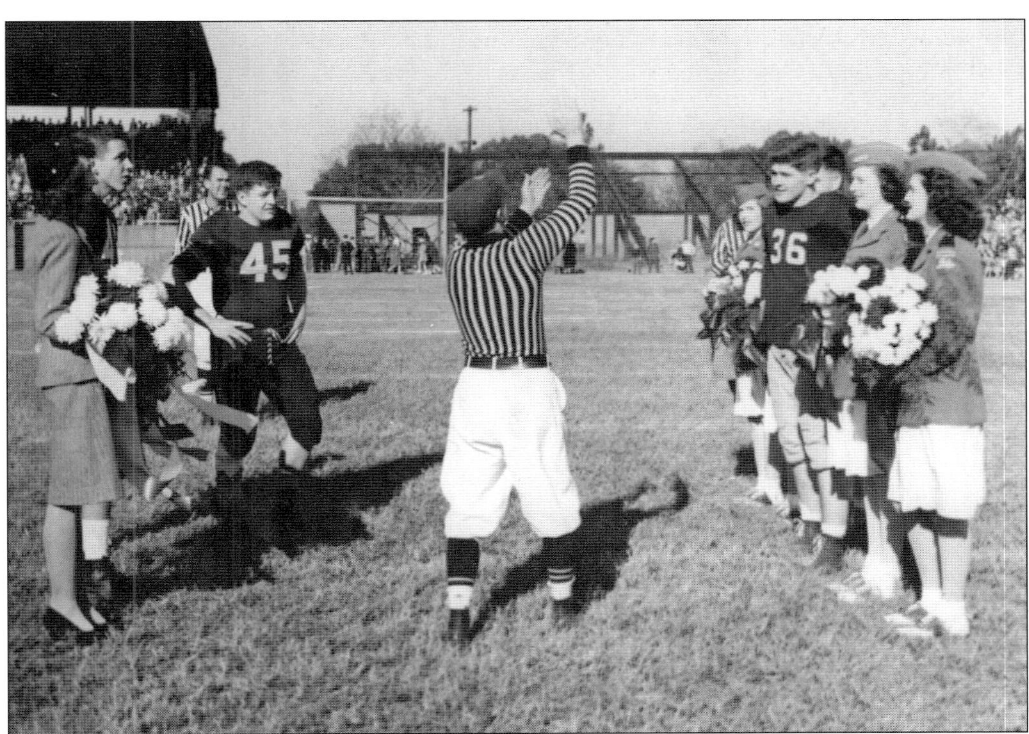

Prior to 1960, local high school football games were played at Daffin Park's Grayson Stadium. Although this referee at a 1940s high school matchup at Grayson looks as if he may have been conducting a double wedding, he was lining up players and their homecoming sponsors during halftime. The girls wore their Sunday best for the occasion. (Courtesy of the Logan family.)

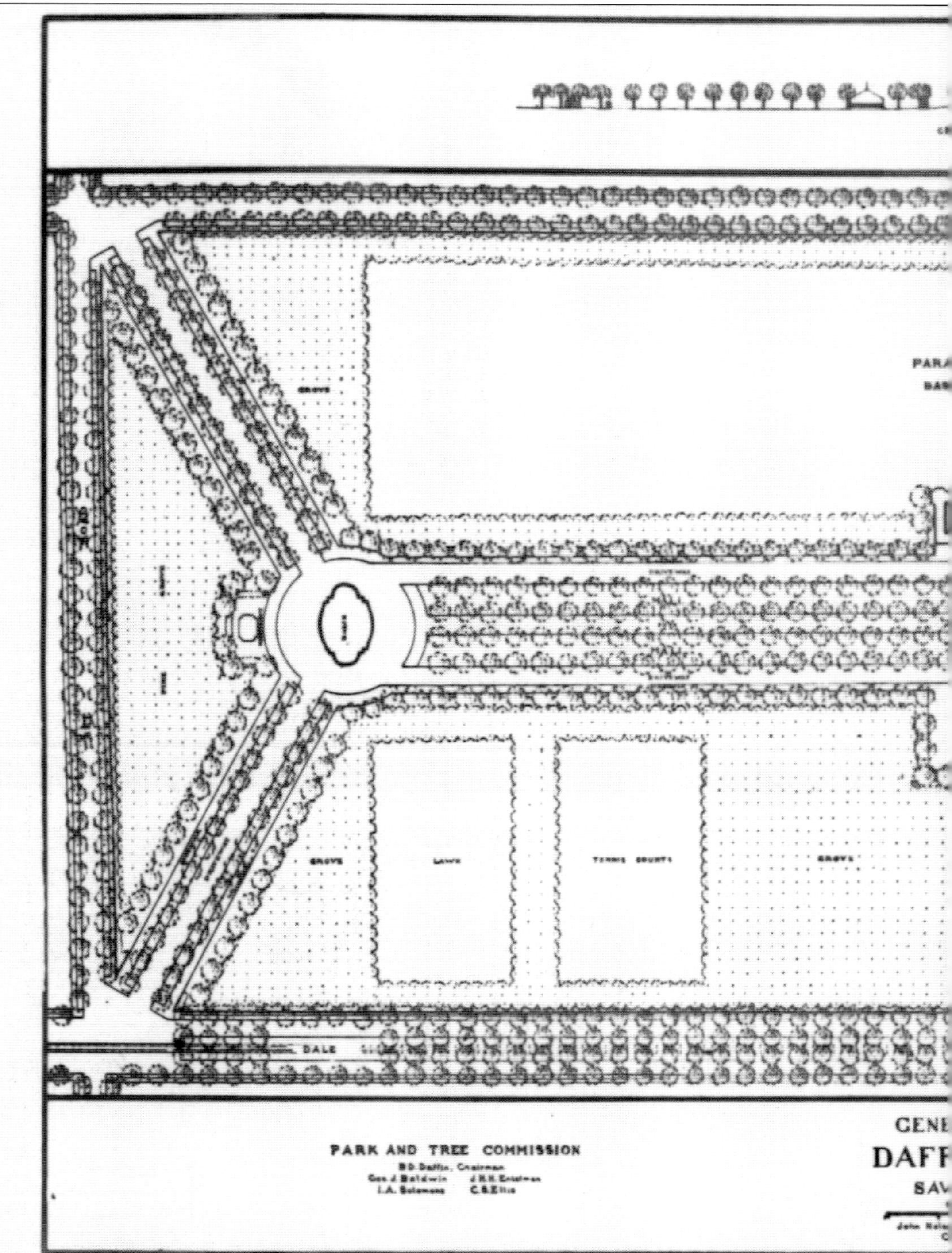

Noted landscape architect John Nolen was hired in 1905 by the City of Savannah to transform 80 acres of low-lying land on what was then the city's southern edge into a lush green recreational area. He was a graduate of Harvard's School of Landscape Architecture and was paid $500 for his Daffin Park design. His vision of the park was completed in 1907. Later, his firm worked on

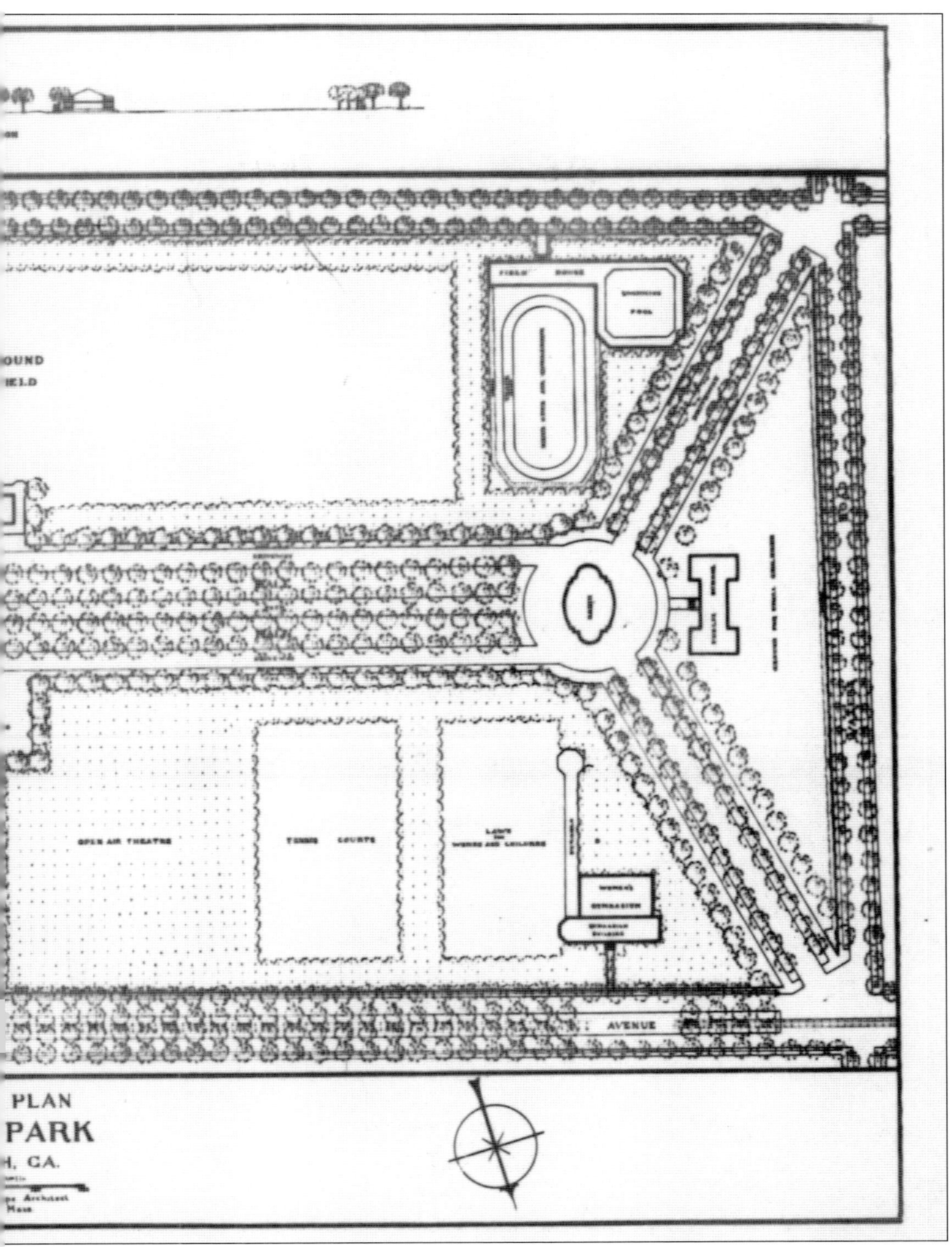

more than 400 projects throughout the United States, including plans for several Florida cities, the University of Wisconsin, and the Wisconsin state park system. (Courtesy of the City of Savannah's Municipal Archives.)

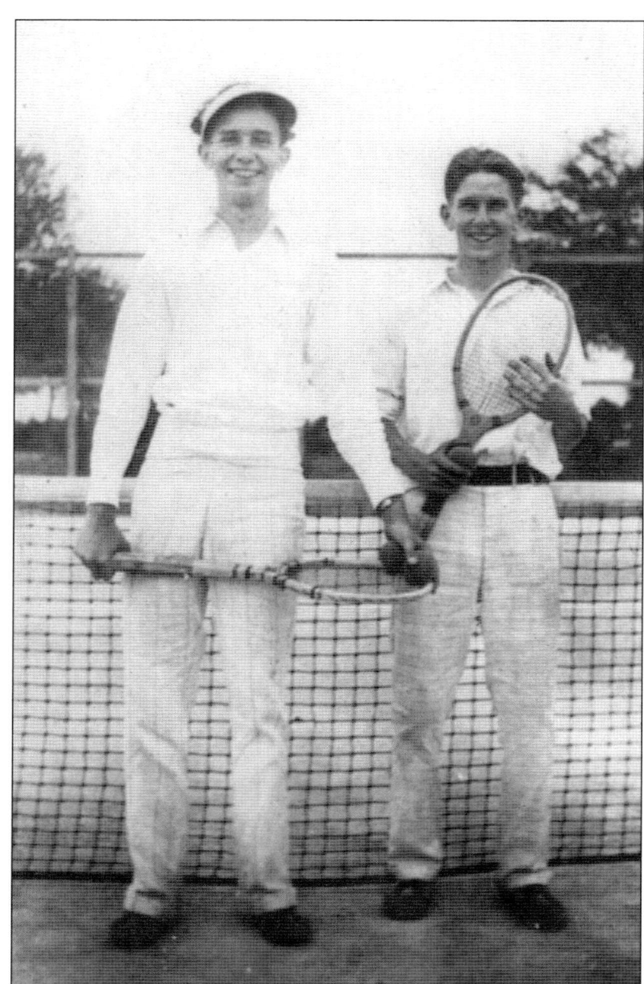

A half-dozen tennis courts were first added to Daffin Park in the late 1920s. A few years later, Waldo Sowell and Leander Powers, both of Guyton, traveled 22 miles to Savannah by train to play tennis on those courts. In 1930, Sowell (left) and Powers won the Savannah junior boys' doubles championship at Daffin. (Author's collection.)

Through the years, the Daffin tennis complex has grown to include more than a dozen courts. In 1991, a new tennis clubhouse was dedicated to William Washington "B" Gordon IV, who was known as Savannah's grand old man of tennis and was a frequent player on the Daffin courts. Gordon was a relative of Girl Scout founder Juliette Gordon Low of Savannah. (Courtesy of the DeLorme family.)

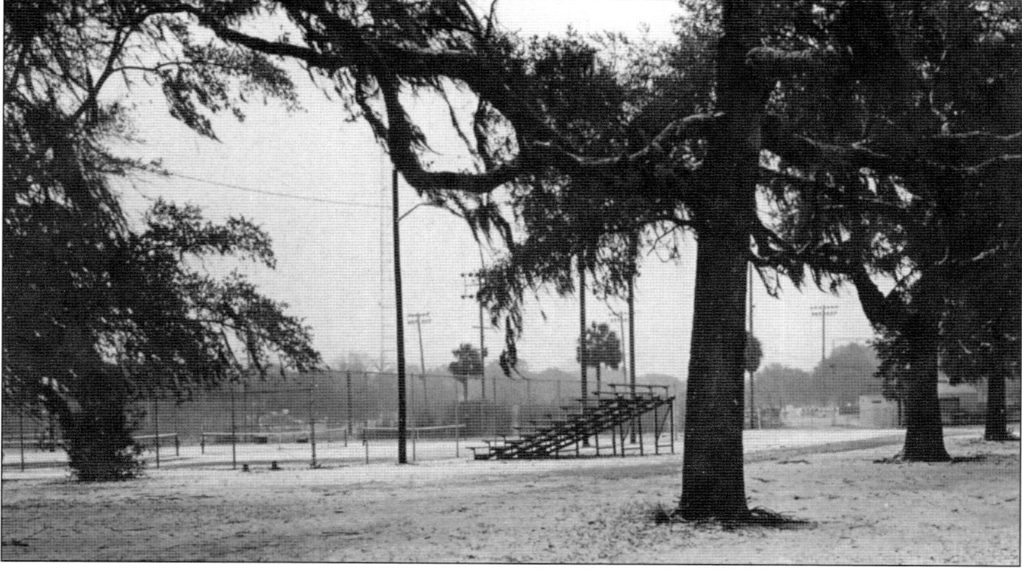

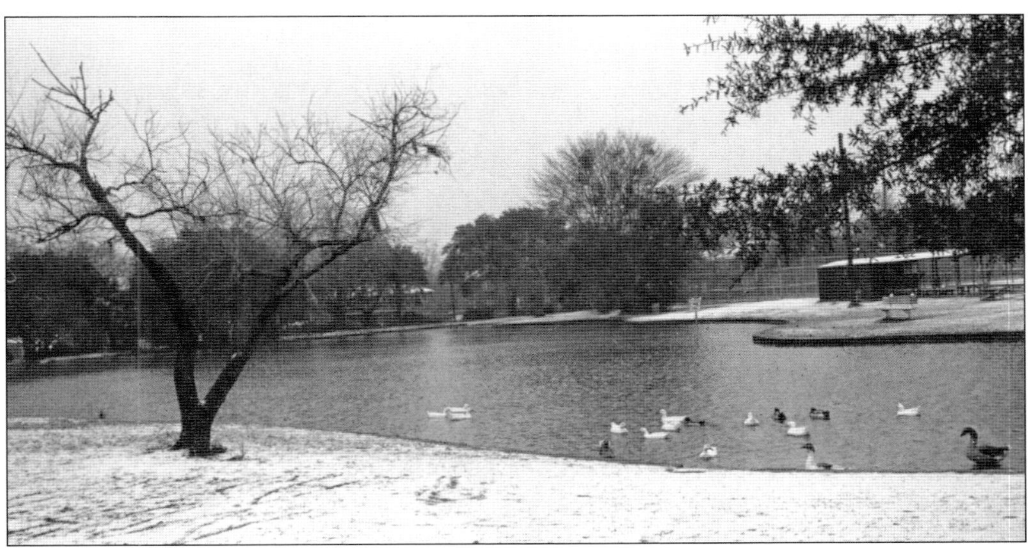

The Daffin Lake, or pond, as some people refer to it, was designed in the shape of the United States with the Canadian border running along Victory Drive and divided into an area for swimming and one for boating and fishing. This picture of the lake was taken on a snowy day in the early 1970s. (Courtesy of the DeLorme family.)

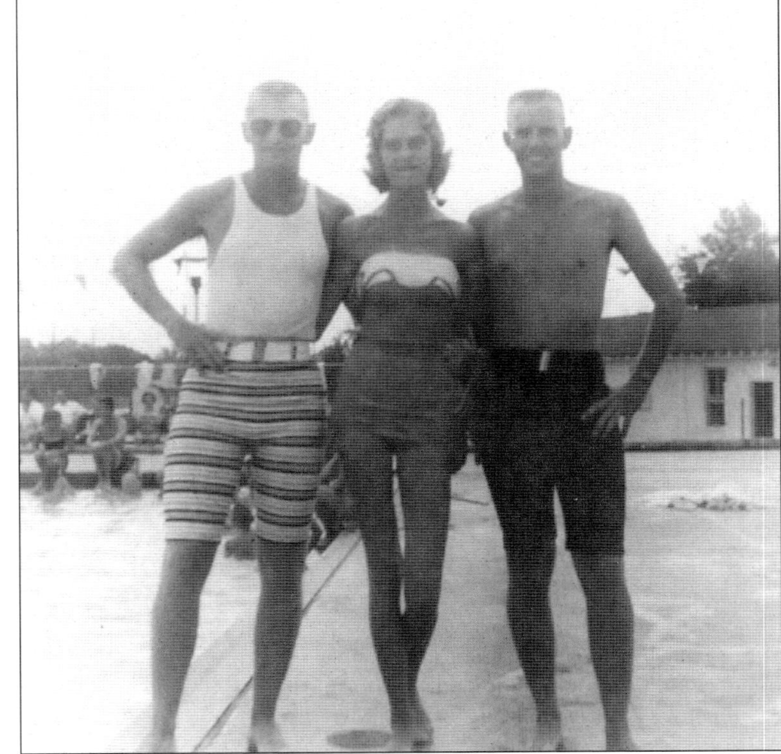

During the 1950s, Pat Little worked as a lifeguard at the newly opened Daffin Park Swimming Pool. In this photograph, he is the one wearing striped swimming trunks and posing with two swimmers. The pool opened in 1954 after the health department determined that the lake was no longer suitable for swimming. (Courtesy of the Belford family.)

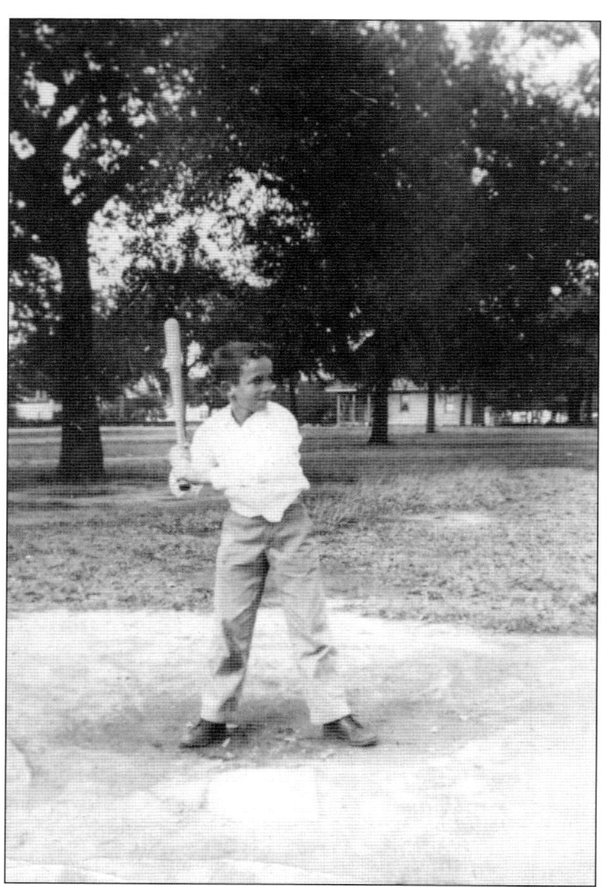

In the 1950s, Daffin Park was a great spot for Bobby Morrissey to fine-tune his baseball skills. The Morrissey family lived just across Washington Avenue from the park in a grand, two-story Craftsman-style house that was built in 1916. The house was one of the first to be constructed in the Parkside Place neighborhood. (Courtesy of the Morrissey family.)

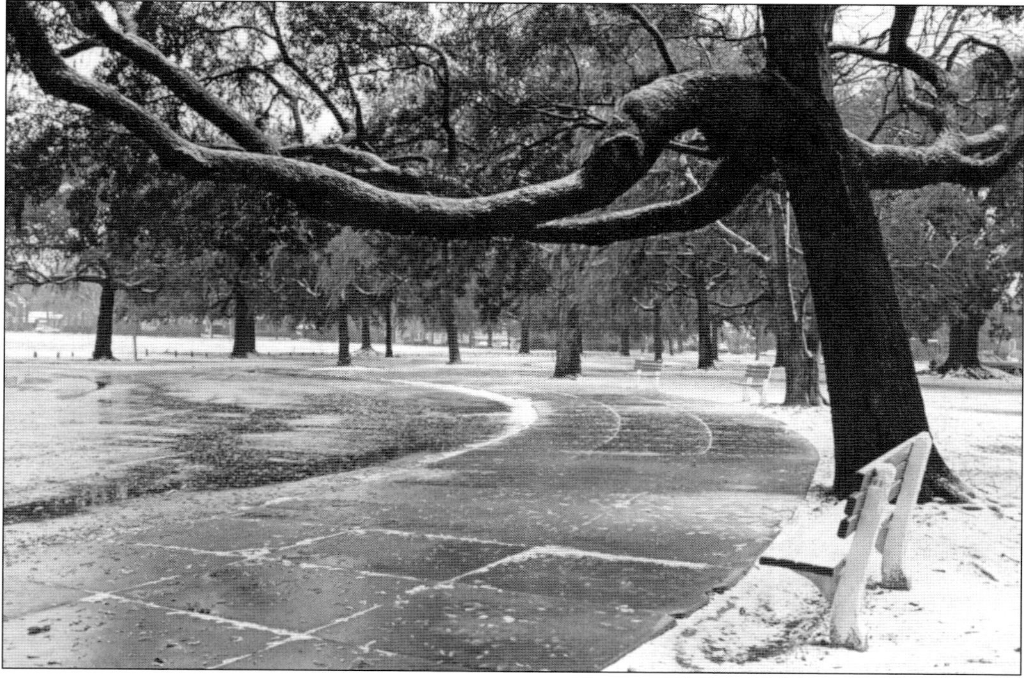

John Nolen's design for Daffin Park included elements of the early 20th century's City Beautiful Movement, a philosophy that promoted harmony and symmetry. Originally, cars could enter the park from four diagonal roads (two at each corner), but through the years, the northernmost streets leading to and from Grayson Stadium have been re-routed. (Courtesy of the DeLorme family.)

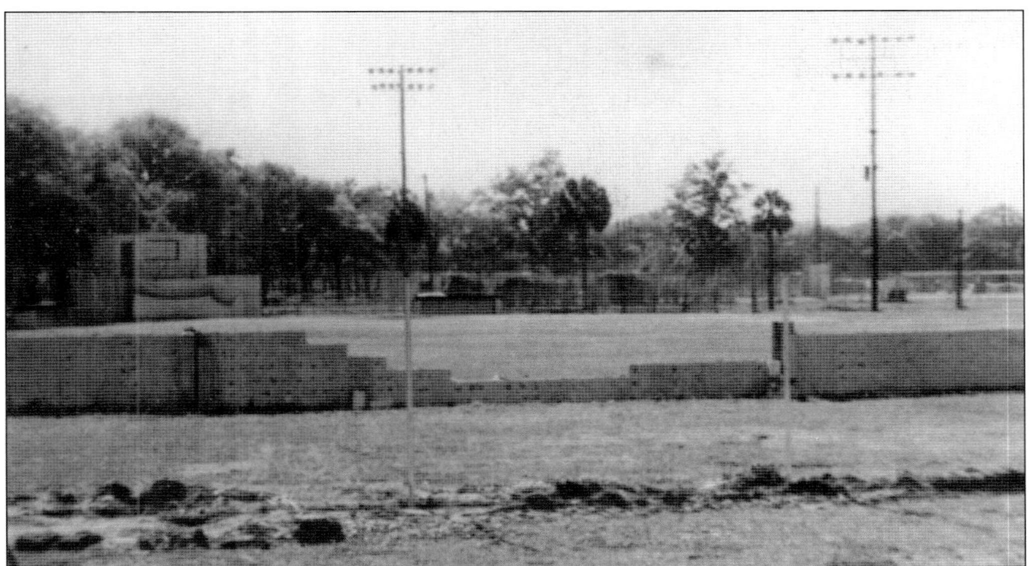

In 1959, the finishing touches were put on a new, small stadium in Daffin Park. The stadium was built with funds raised by the Savannah chapter of the American Business Club (AMBUCS). The field was welcomed by Pony League baseball teams that had previously played at Coke Field, an area prone to flooding. (Courtesy of Wallace Moye and the Savannah AMBUCS.)

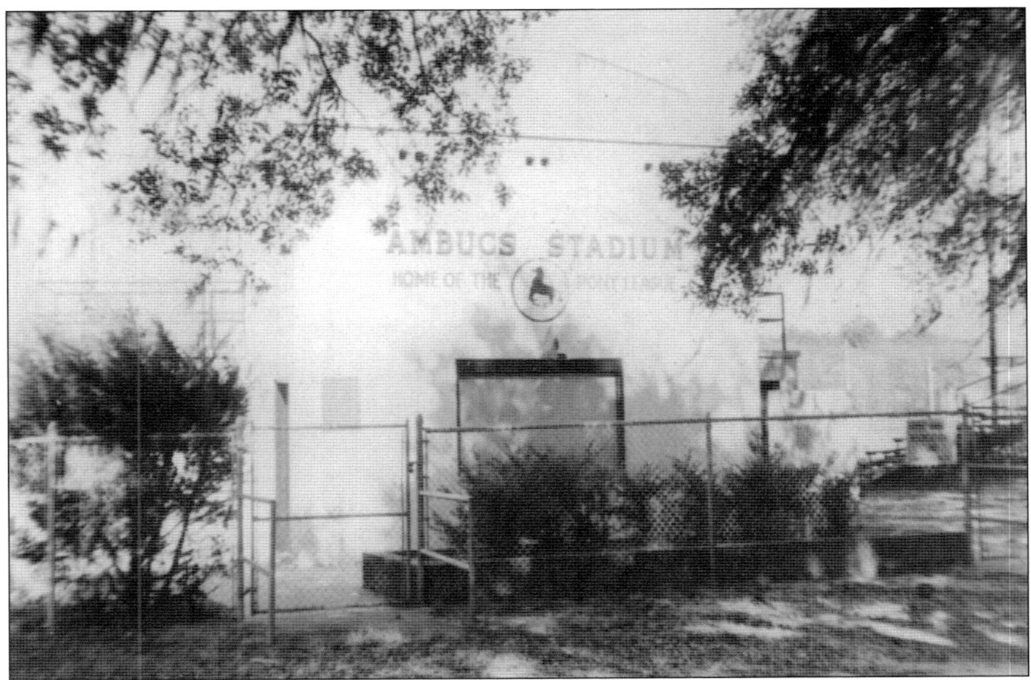

The entrance to AMBUCS Stadium in Daffin Park was across the street from the tennis courts. The stadium was demolished in the late 1990s after new fields were built on Savannah's south side. (Courtesy of Wallace Moye and the Savannah AMBUCS.)

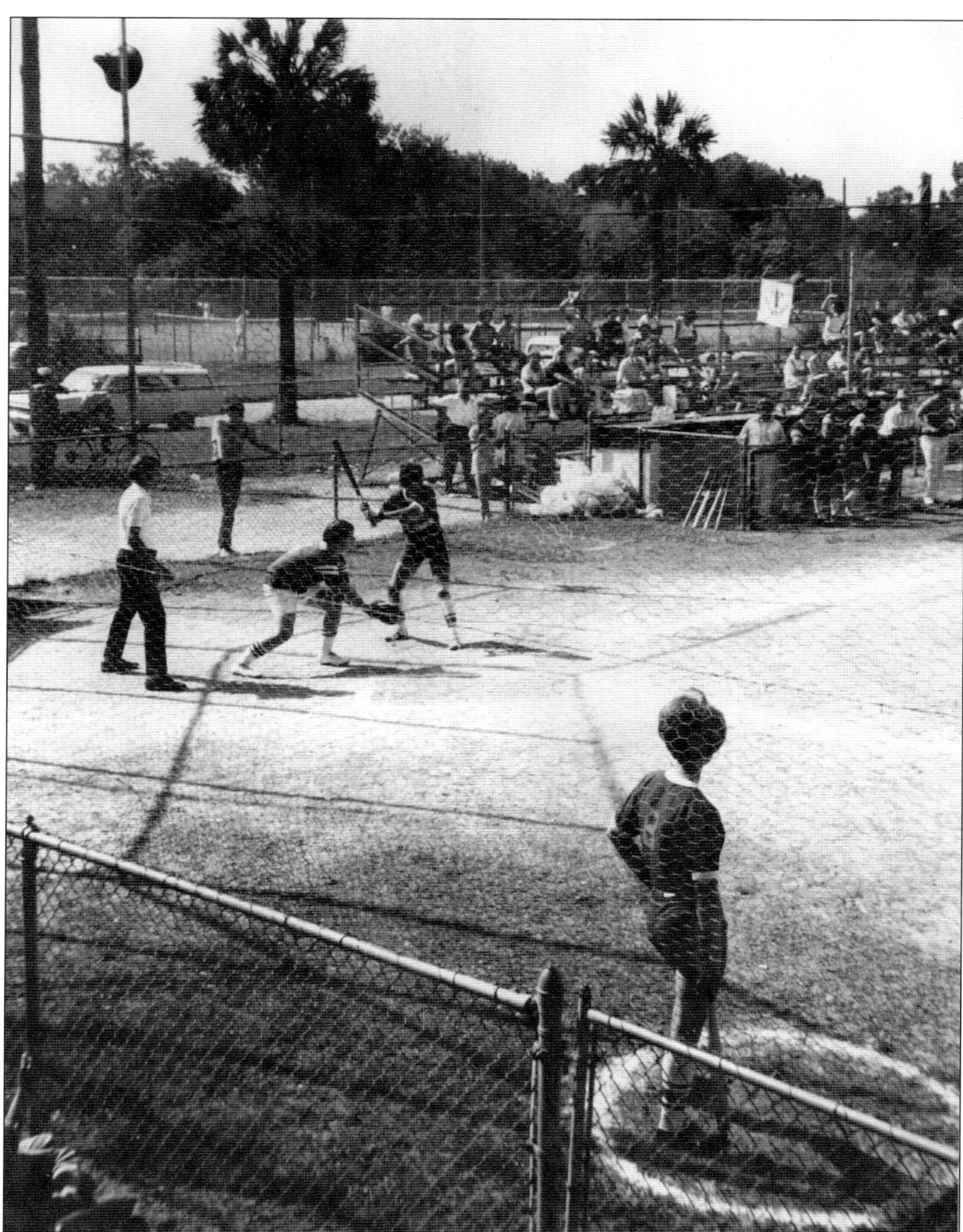

AMBUS Stadium in Daffin Park was a convenient spot for local baseball and softball teams, whose members remember it fondly as an outstanding facility for its time. The stadium offered visitor and home team bleachers, a scoreboard, a concession stand, and a concrete block wall in the outfield to keep balls from being hit into Victory Drive. This c. 1959 picture shows a bit of the action from the first annual women's invitational AMBUCS softball tournament at the stadium. (Courtesy of Wallace Moye and the Savannah AMBUCS.)

An excited David Eason shows off the game ball that was presented to him during a game at AMBUCS Stadium in the 1960s. The bleachers most always were full when games were played here. (Courtesy of Wallace Moye and the Savannah AMBUCS.)

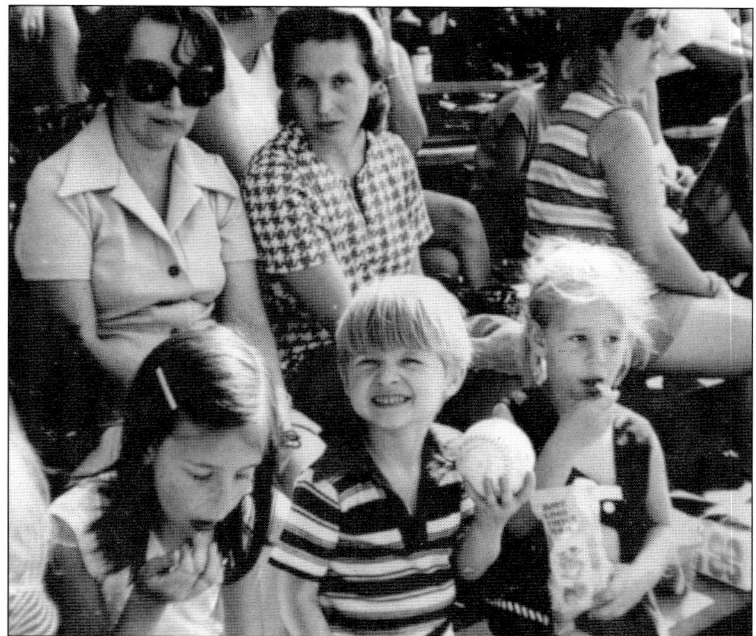

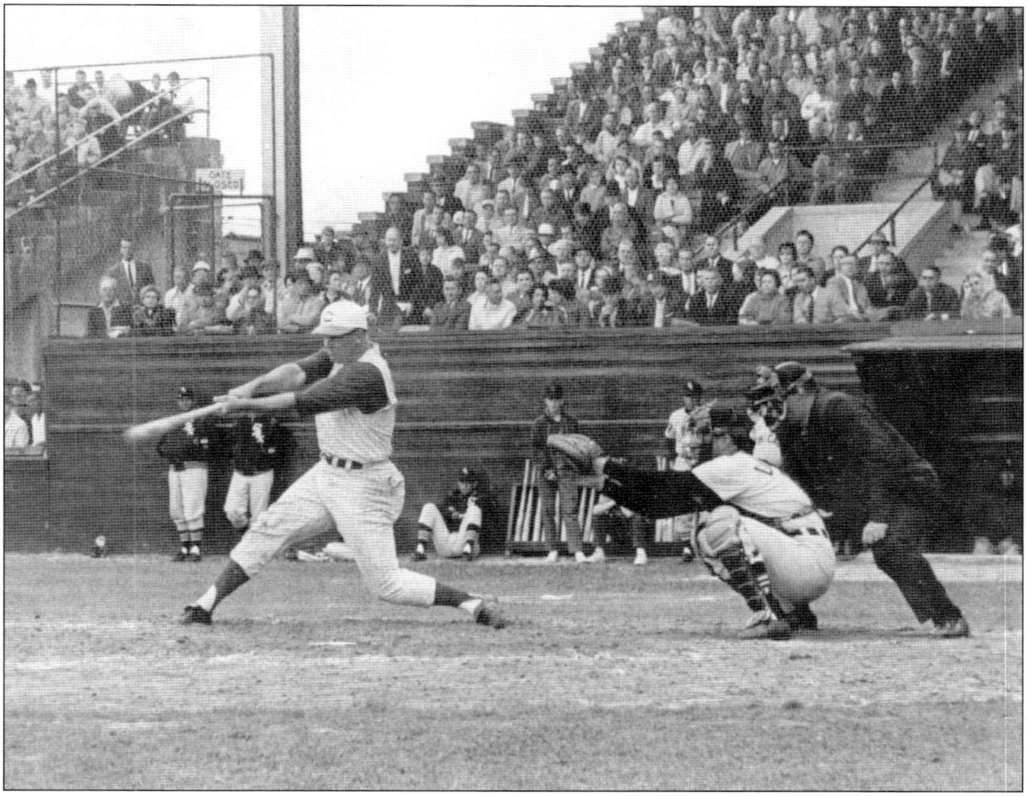

In the early 1960s, several Major League Baseball exhibition games were played at Grayson Stadium while the teams were on their way to spring training in Florida. Among other matchups, the Chicago White Sox took on the Cincinnati Reds, as seen here. The batter is Don Blasingame, second baseman for Cincinnati, and the catcher is Sherm Lollar. (Courtesy of Buz Ellis.)

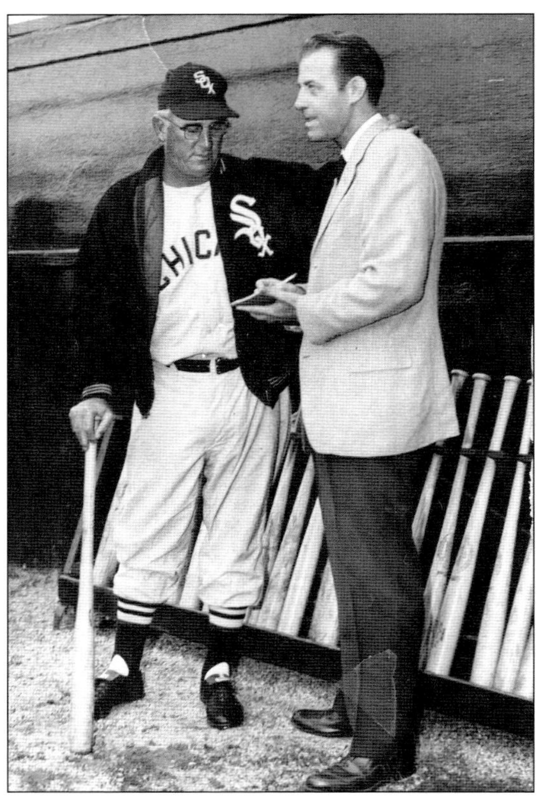

Savannah Morning News sports editor Neal Ellis is interviewing Al Lopez of the Chicago White Sox after his team played the Cincinnati Reds at Grayson. Through the years, Grayson has been the home field for various Savannah minor league baseball teams including the Indians, Braves, Cardinals, and Sand Gnats. In 2016, the city welcomed the Savannah Bananas of the Coastal Plain League. (Courtesy of Buz Ellis.)

Many standout Major League players showed off their talents during exhibition games in Savannah in the early 1960s. Those who went on to successful careers included Frank Robinson, Donn Clendenon, Don Buford, and Dave DeBusschere, among others. (Courtesy of Buz Ellis.)

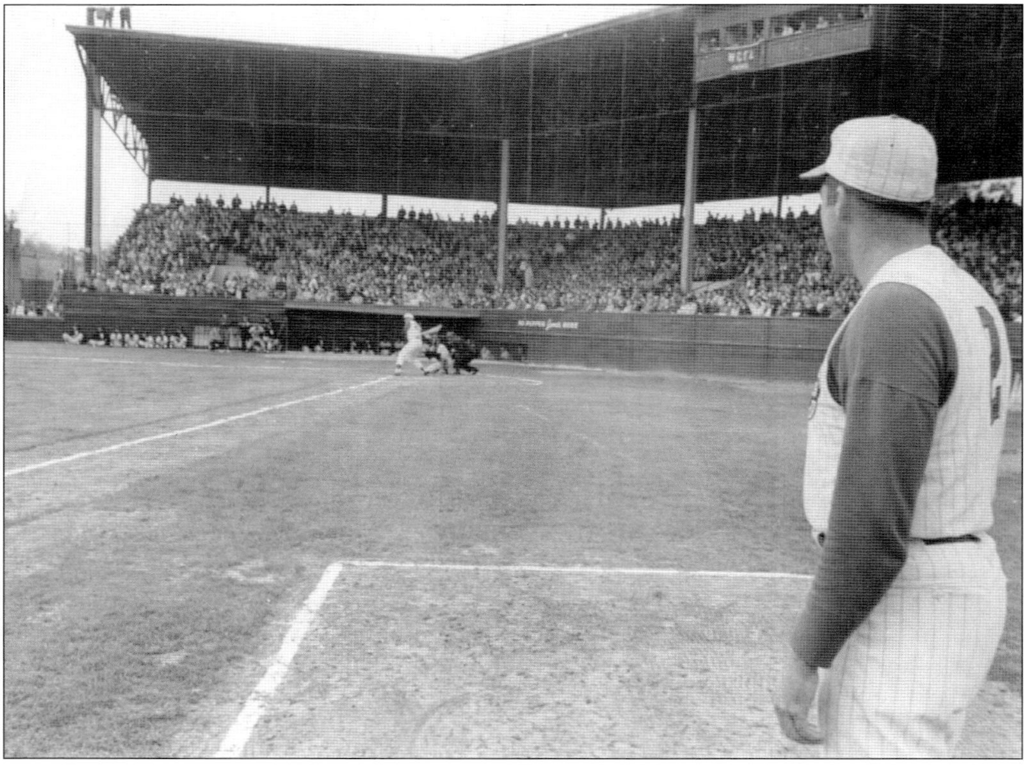

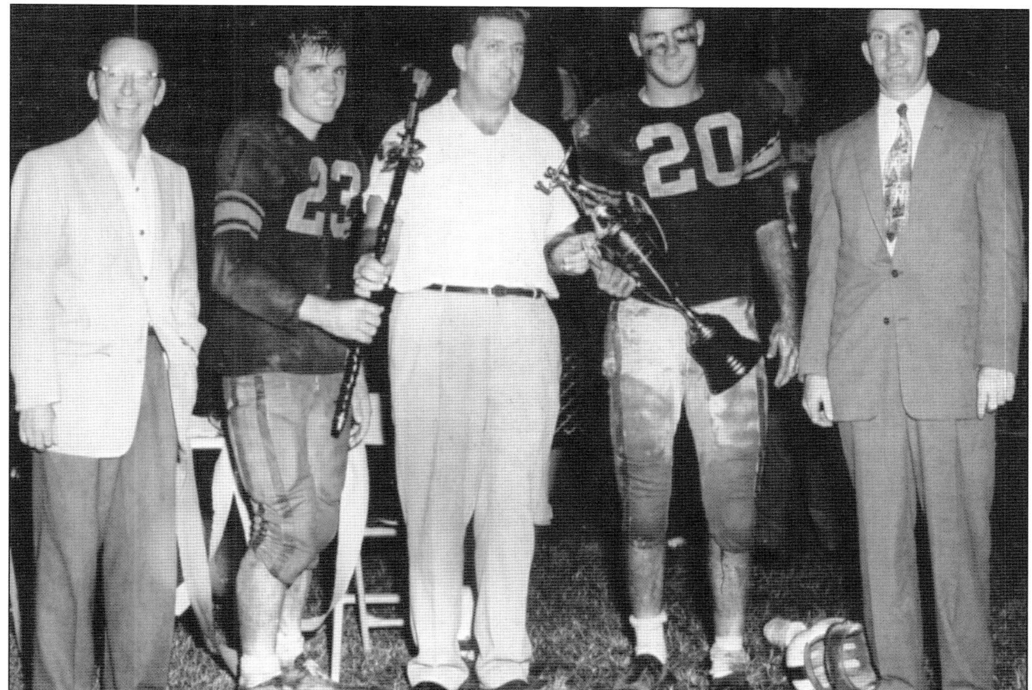

In 1956, Benedictine Military School played Boys Catholic High School of Augusta in the Shamrock Bowl. From left to right are coach Denny Leonard of Boys Catholic, John Reckling, longtime Benedictine coach Vic Mell, Tom Brown, and unidentified. The year after this picture was taken, Boys Catholic merged with Mt. St. Joseph Academy to become Aquinas High School. (Courtesy of the Reckling family.)

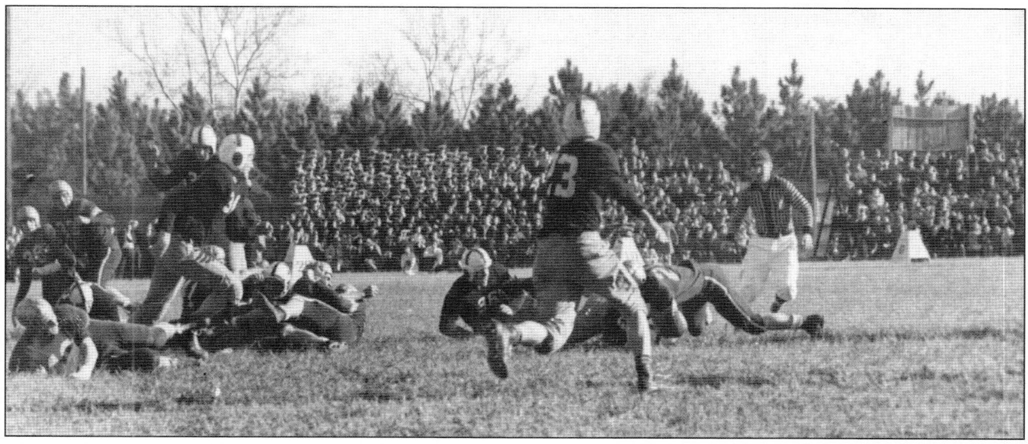

This referee was really getting into the action during a 1940s high school football game at Grayson Stadium. The pine trees that can be seen over the bleachers in the background were planted in a park named for Chares Herty, a pioneer in the southern forest industry. Herty Park is on the Bee Road side of Daffin and now boasts a public dog park. (Courtesy of the Logan family.)

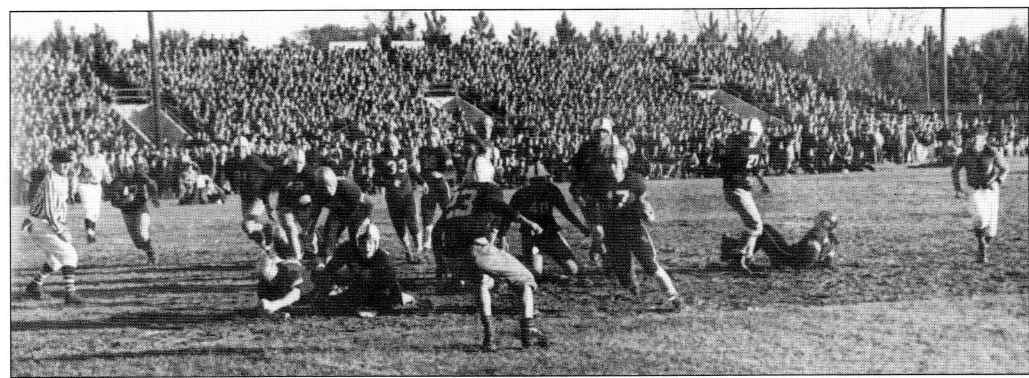

High school football games at Daffin Park's Grayson Stadium usually were standing room only, especially when the match was between Savannah High and Benedictine. This picture shows the stadium bleachers jam packed at a game in the mid-1940s. (Courtesy of the Logan family.)

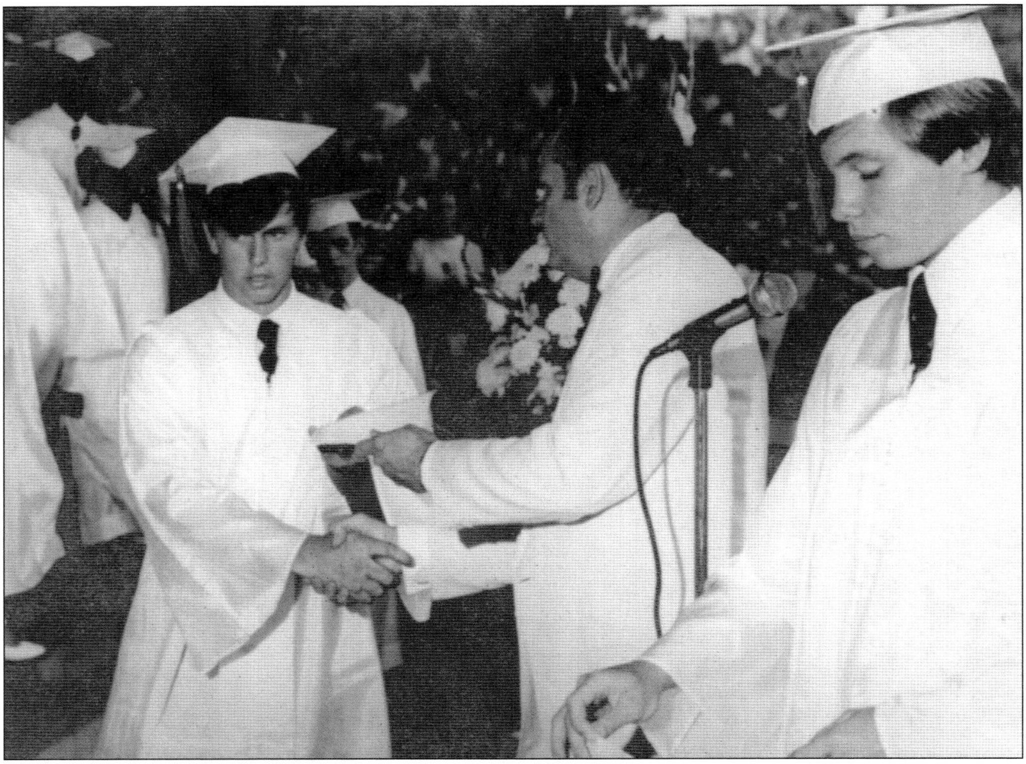

Grayson Stadium was the venue for high school football games until 1960 and for high school graduations until the early 1970s, when the Savannah Civic Center was built. Here, Ricky Smith (left) receives his Savannah High School diploma in 1970 during graduation ceremonies at Grayson Stadium. At right is Jim Gardner, president of the student council. (Courtesy of the Smith family.)

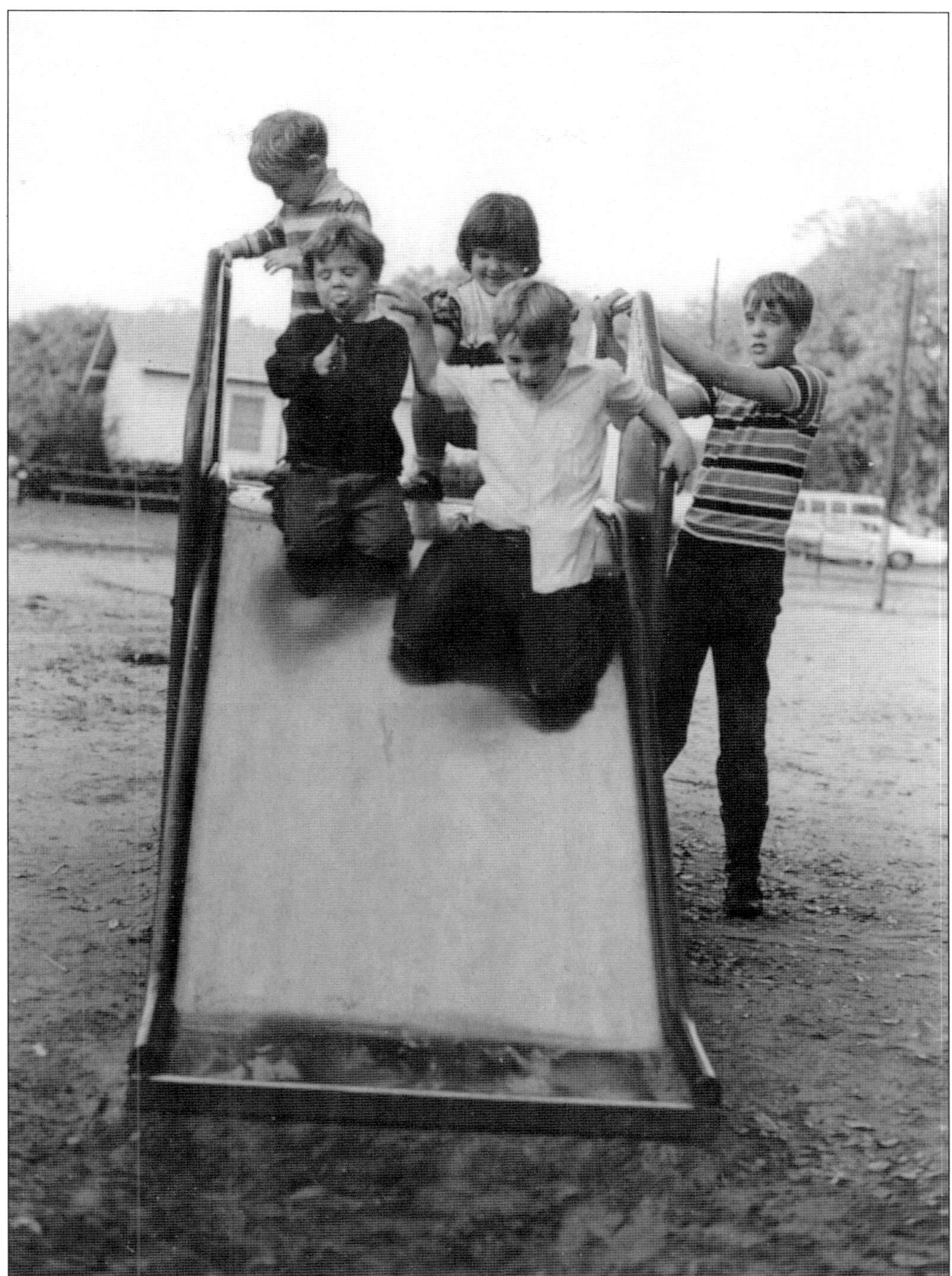

Children have always loved the Daffin Park playground. In the 1970s, these fun-seekers were photographed on the sliding board. Paul DeLorme is first going down the slide, his sister Leonie is behind him, and their brother Joe is at the top left holding onto the railing. The other two boys are unidentified. In the 1980s, the city installed a barrier-free playground at Daffin and named it for Ashley Dearing Jr., who contracted polio in the 1940s. When dedicated, it was the second barrier-free playground in the country. (Courtesy of the DeLorme family.)

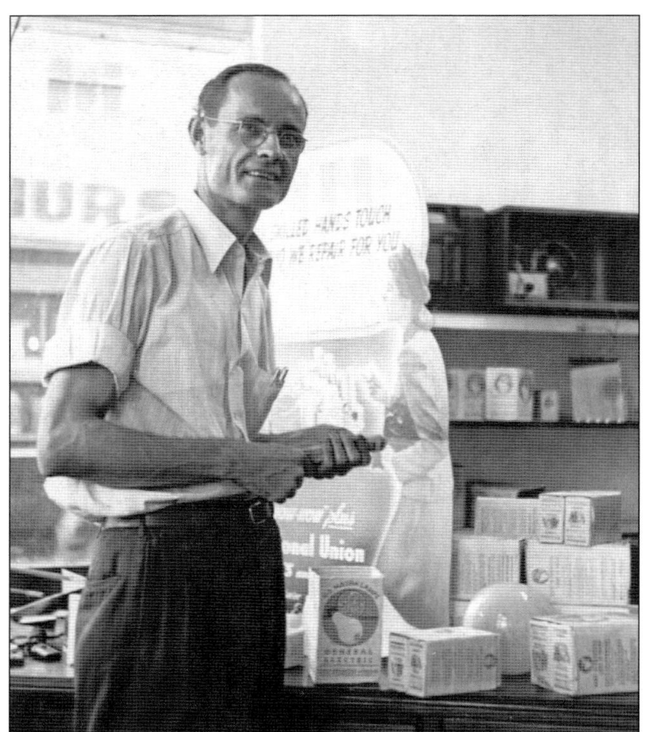

Growing up in Savannah, David Floyd excelled in baseball. He played professional ball for the Boston Red Sox and later became a scout for several major league teams, including the Cincinnati Reds in the 1950s, when they participated in an exhibition game against the New York Yankees at Grayson Stadium. Floyd also was assistant superintendent for the City of Savannah's recreation department and has been described as establishing "park baseball" at Daffin. His daughter said that during the years he worked for the city, he was in charge of the Daffin swimming pool and Grayson Stadium. (Courtesy of Ann Floyd Webster.)

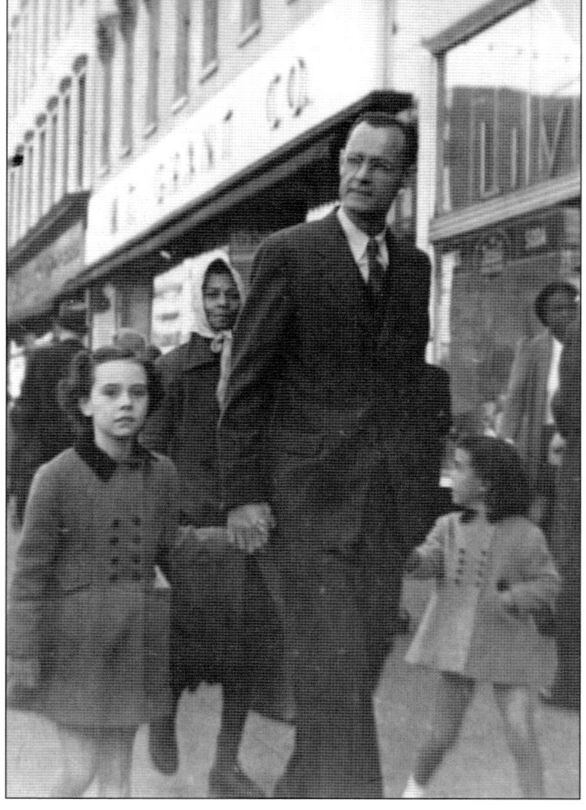

David Floyd was a scout for several Major League teams, including the Detroit Tigers and Pittsburgh Pirates. He is shown here with daughters Ann (left) and Gail. When the Pirates won the 1960 World Series, Ann said he was given a set of drinking glasses etched with the names of the players. (Courtesy of Ann Floyd Webster.)

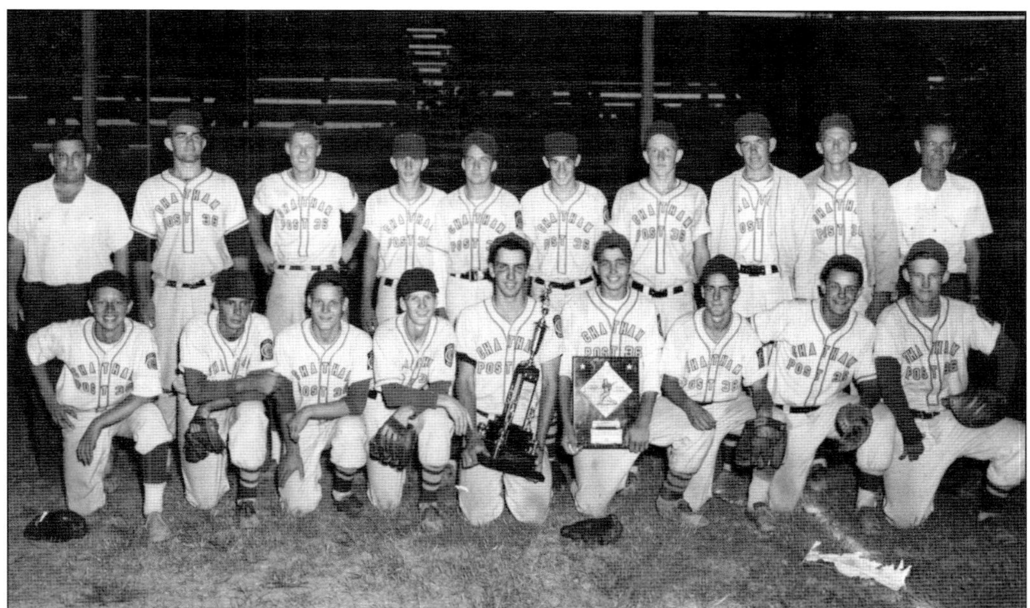

David Floyd was nicknamed Skipper by the American Legion baseball players he managed. This 1950 team from Chatham Post 36 became state champs. From left to right are (first row) Elmer Lott (batboy), Paul Hammock, Aubry Sekon, Bobby Anderson, Joe Herpin, Will Madison, Alex Cann, Fred Hart, and Frank Ciucevich; (second row) coach Joe Mell, John Campbell, Bill Frain, Allen Jones, Layton Sheppard, Hugh McDougald, Billy Giles, Bernard Cleary, Ed Johnson, and Floyd (the manager). (Courtesy of Ann Floyd Webster.)

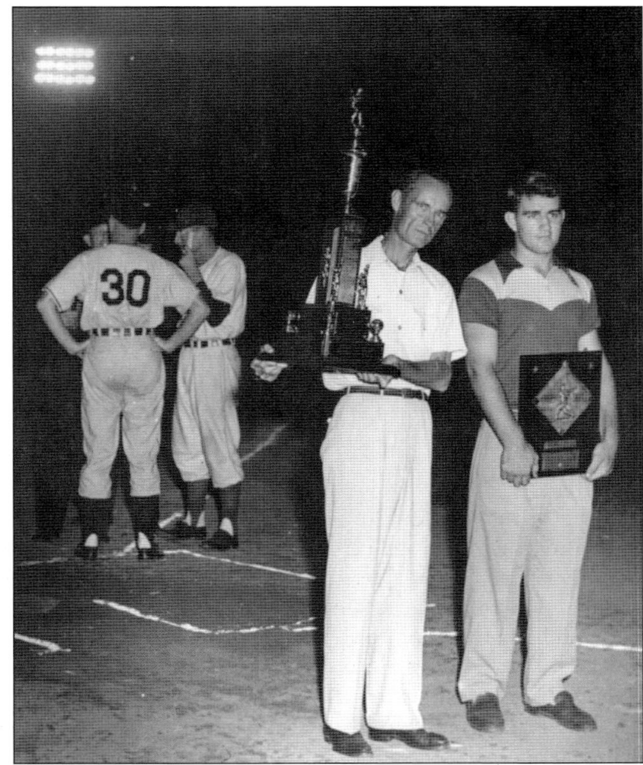

David Floyd and one of his coaches from the American Legion Chatham Post 36 team pose with the state championship trophy in 1950. For his contributions to local sports, Floyd was posthumously inducted into the Greater Savannah Athletic Hall of Fame in 2010. (Courtesy of Ann Floyd Webster.)

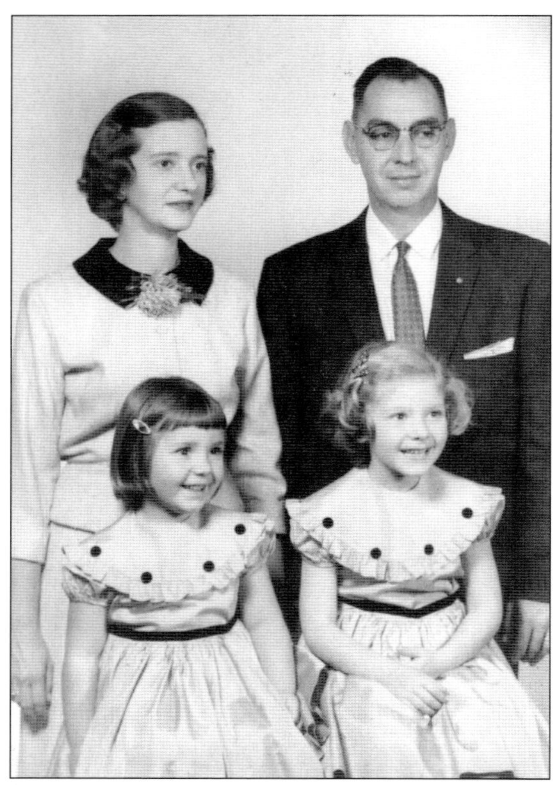

Penn Nixon was an outstanding amateur tennis player who was on the tennis team at Duke University in the 1930s. After moving to Savannah, his home court became Daffin. He is shown here with his wife, Louise, and daughters Margy (left) and Barbara, who remembers her father stringing racquets at the kitchen table. Sadly, Nixon suffered a fatal heart attack in 1962 while playing tennis at Daffin. His contemporaries included avid tennis enthusiasts like Abe Eisenman and Drs. Darnell Brawner and John Angell. (Courtesy of the Nixon family.)

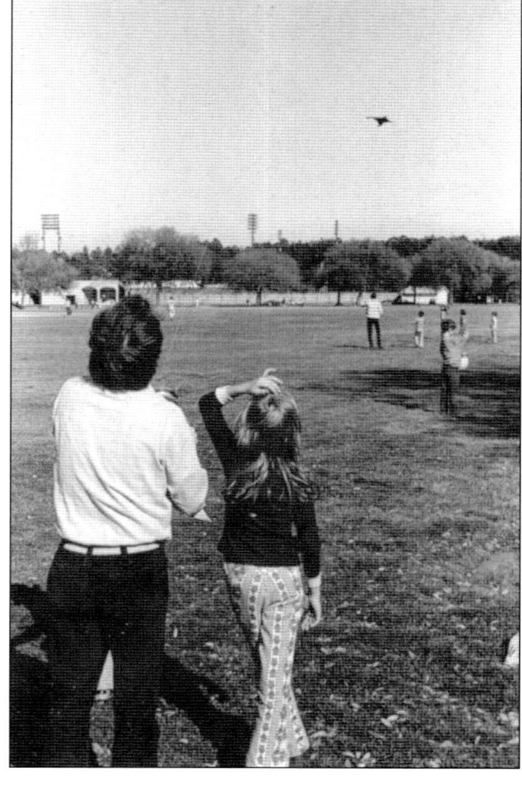

Open green spaces in Daffin Park were part of John Nolen's 1907 design. The Daffin lawn between the promenade of oaks in the center of the park and Washington Avenue continues to provide a venue for all sorts of sports, as well as kite flying. (Courtesy of the DeLorme family.)

Two

PARKSIDE PLACE

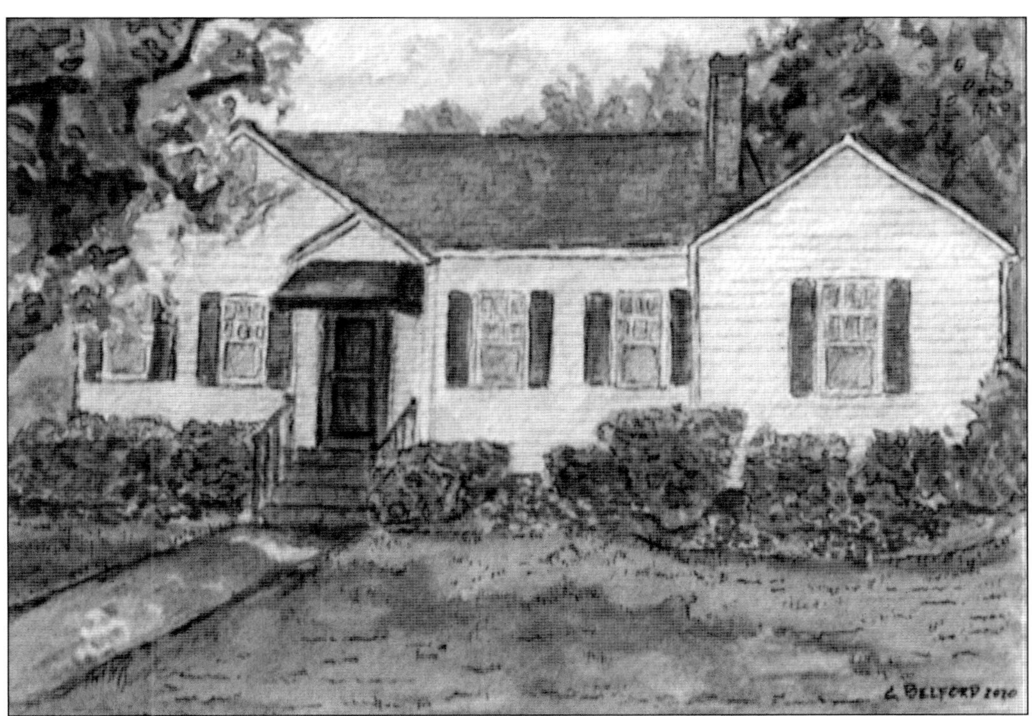

Cathy Belford sketched this charming Parkside bungalow for Natalie Walker Deriso, who grew up in the house, which her parents bought in the late 1940s. The address is 1501 East Fiftieth Street at the corner of Hickory Street. All the north-south streets in Parkside are named for trees, such as Hickory, Cedar, Ash, and Live Oak. (Courtesy of Natalie Walker Deriso.)

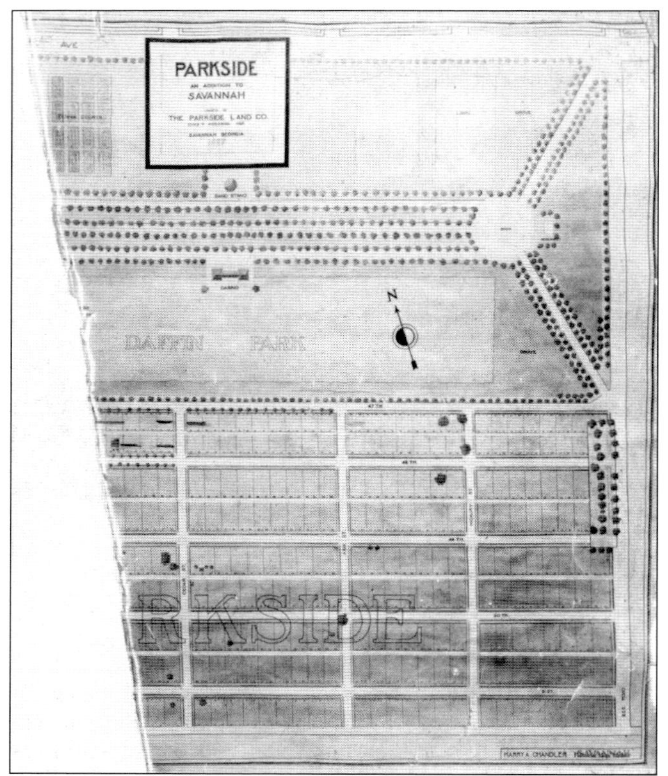

This partial layout of the Parkside Place neighborhood shows its proximity to Daffin Park. The development of Parkside began a few years after the park was completed in 1907. The construction of homes in Parkside, as it became known, continued until the 1940s. (Courtesy of the City of Savannah Municipal Archives.)

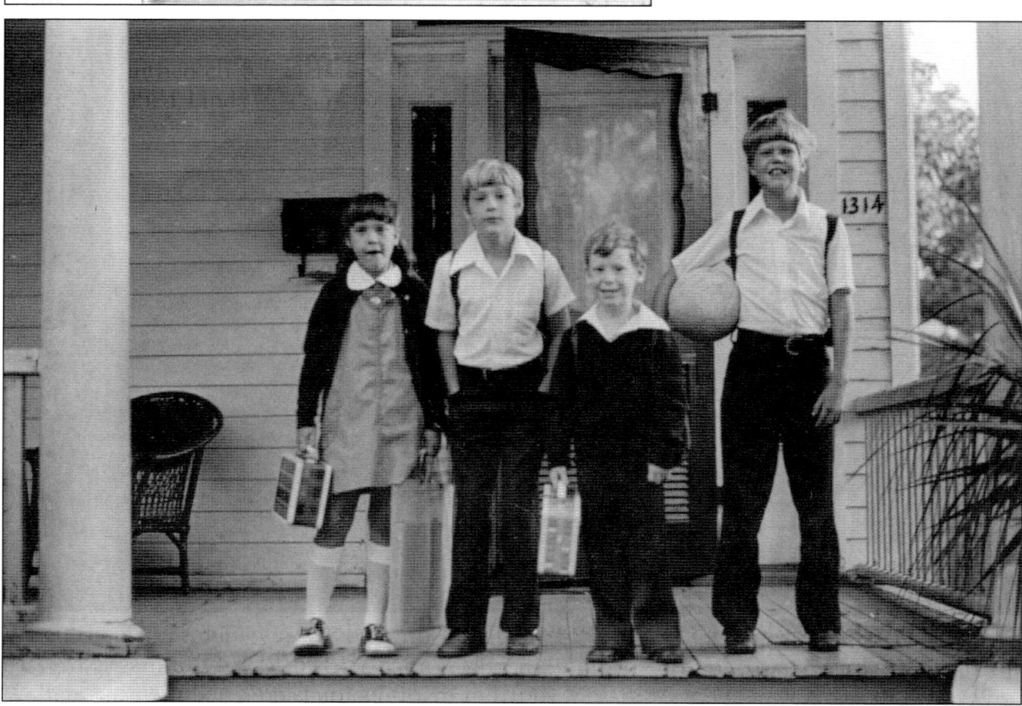

In the early 1970s, the DeLorme children (from left to right) Leonie, Paul, and Joe, with neighbor Pat Parker holding the ball, stand in front of the DeLorme home on East Forty-Ninth Street. They were headed to school at Blessed Sacrament. (Courtesy of the DeLorme family.)

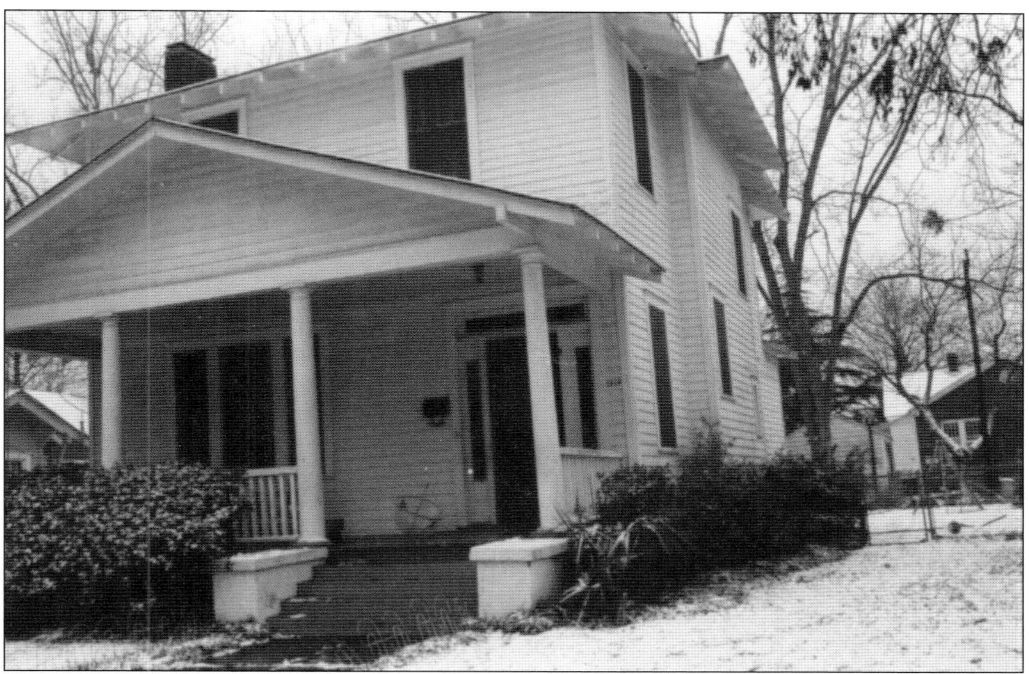

Harry and Rita DeLorme moved into this two-story house at 1314 East Forty-Ninth Street in Parkside in the early 1960s. Harry was a letter carrier for the US Postal Service for 38 years. He also loved gardening and was a talented photographer. Rita, an accomplished writer, still lives in the home where she and her husband raised their family. (Courtesy of the DeLorme family.)

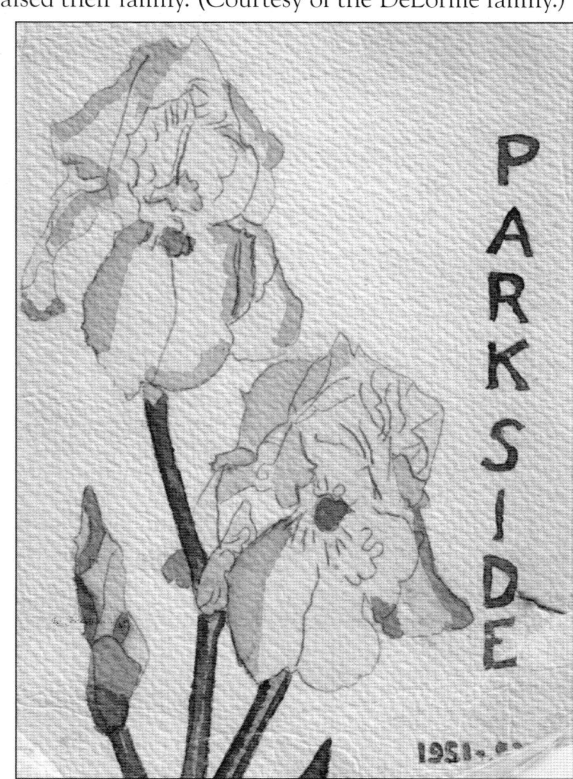

The Parkside Garden Club was organized in 1949, and this directory from 1951 features a hand-painted iris, the club flower, on the cover. The organization's civic project was Cohen's Old Men's Retreat. The hostesses for the October 18, 1951, meeting were Frances Kuhlke, Letha Harmon, and Mrs. K.V. Anderson. Gardening tips shared that day included "Plan and plant your iris bed . . . save your leaves to mulch your flower beds and hide that garbage can with an evergreen." (Courtesy of the Kuhlke family.)

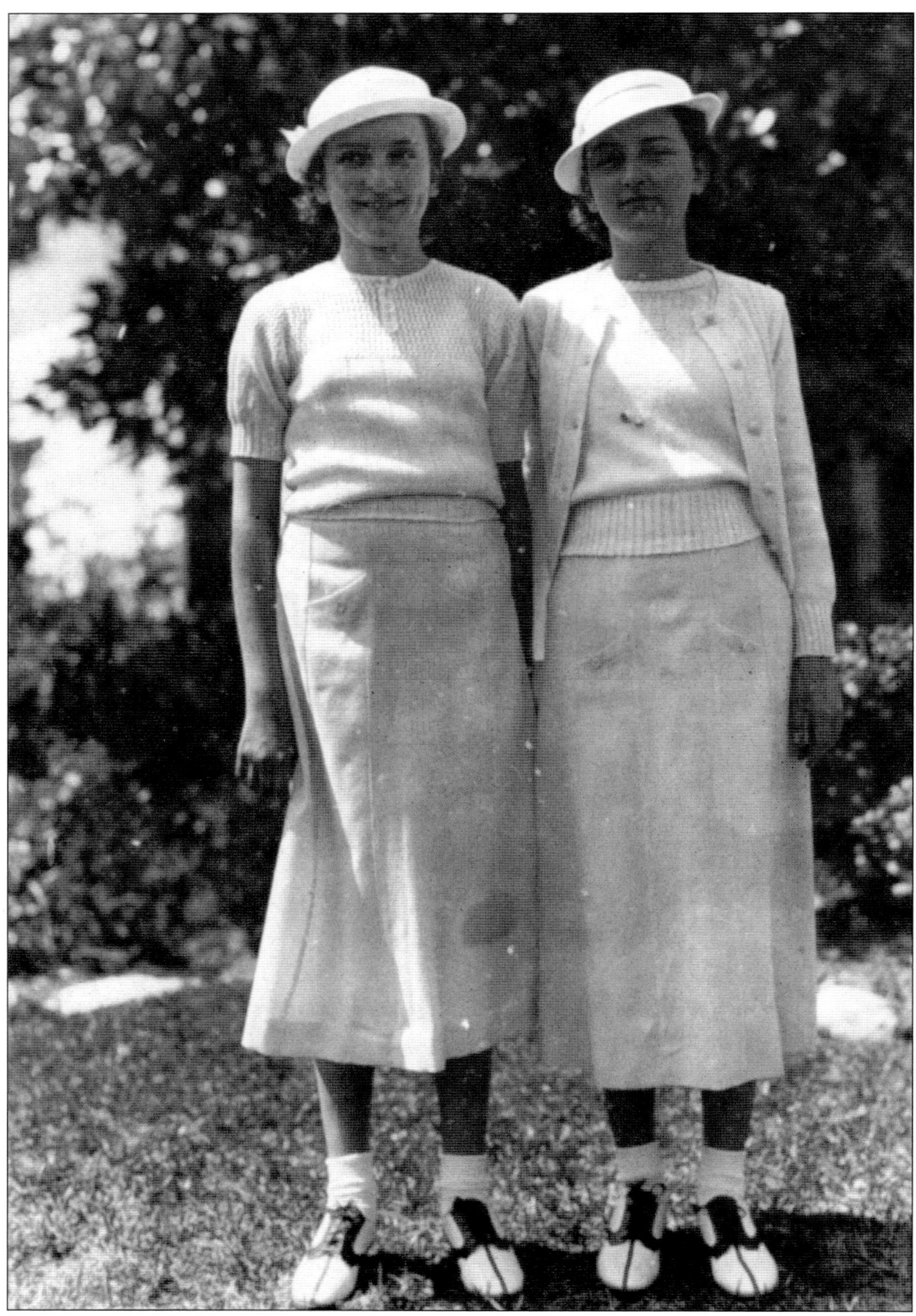

Even as teenagers, sisters Virginia and Caroline Bumann both were talented seamstresses. In this picture, probably taken during the late 1930s, they decided to dress alike, complete with matching hats and shoes. (Courtesy of the Wilson/Smith family.)

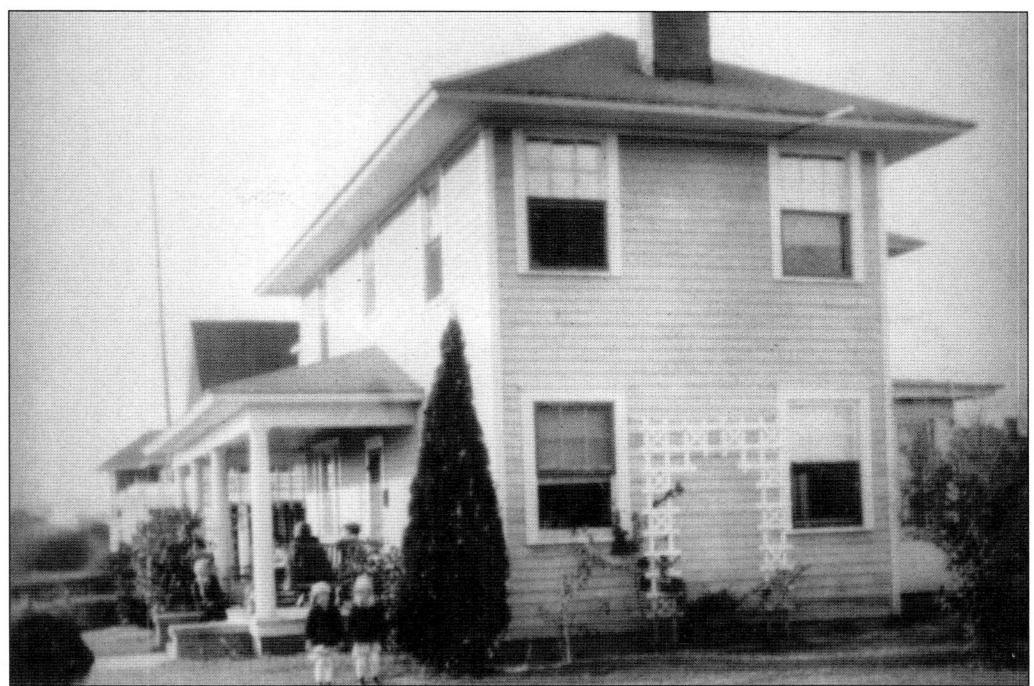

In 1925, Harry and Sydney Bumann became the second owners of this house at 1120 East Fiftieth Street. The couple's daughters, Virginia and Caroline, became longtime, well-respected teachers in the Savannah public school system. Eventually, Caroline B. Hamilton and her family bought a home right around the corner from her parents. (Courtesy of the Wilson/Smith family.)

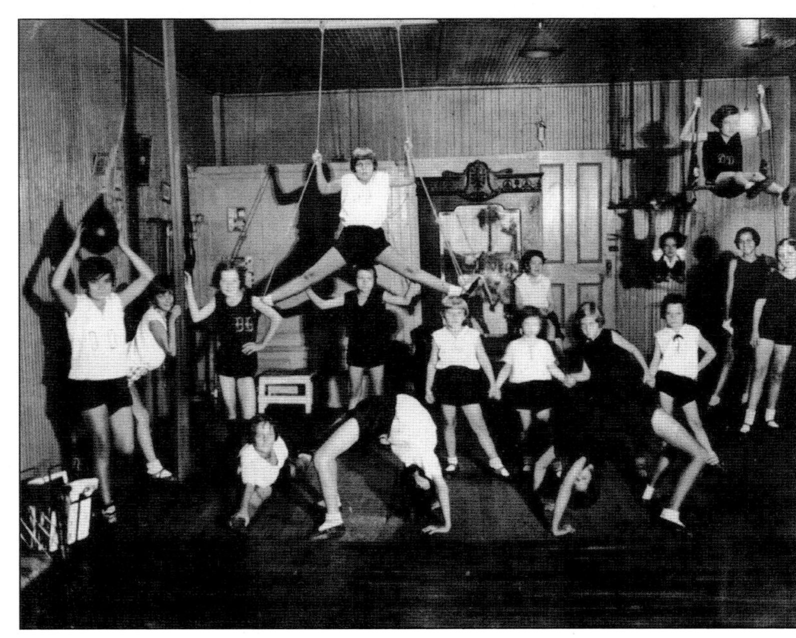

Among other talents, Virginia Bumann could sew, cook, and perform acrobatics, as shown in this picture. She is the one doing the split at bottom left. (Courtesy of the Wilson/Smith family.)

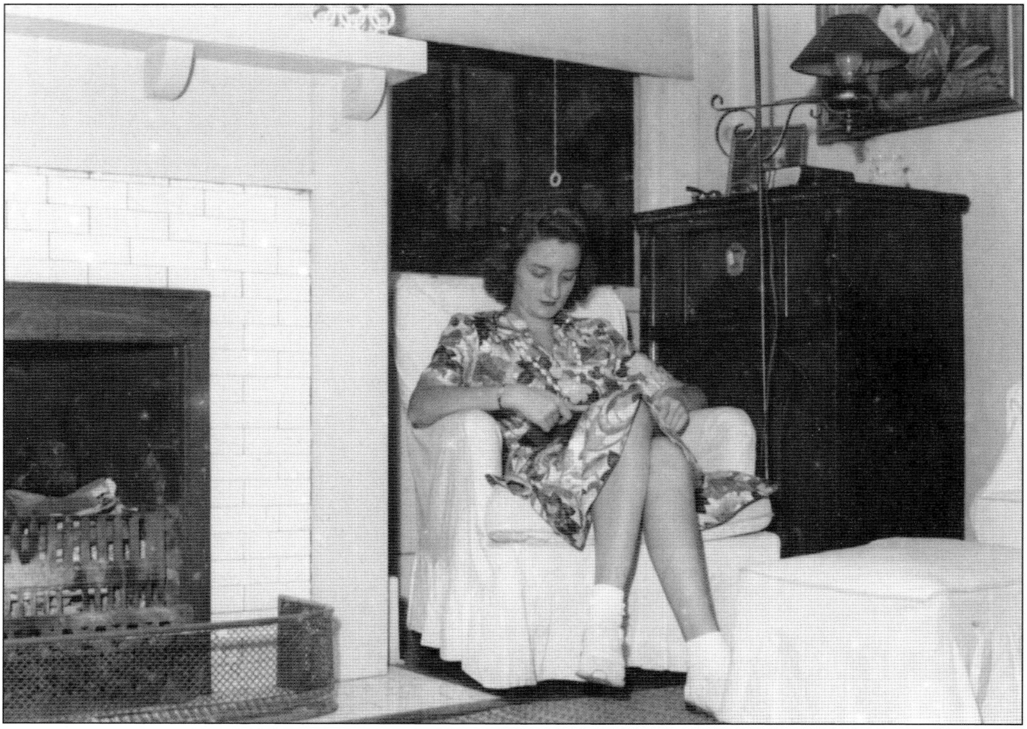

Caroline Bumann is relaxing in the living room of the family home at 1120 East Fiftieth Street. Her father, Harry, was a civil engineer who came south when road jobs opened up in the area. After arriving here, he met his bride-to-be, Sydney, who was from McIntosh County. The Bumanns' granddaughter Frances Wilson Smith and her husband, Scott, now own the Parkside home. (Courtesy of the Wilson/Smith family.)

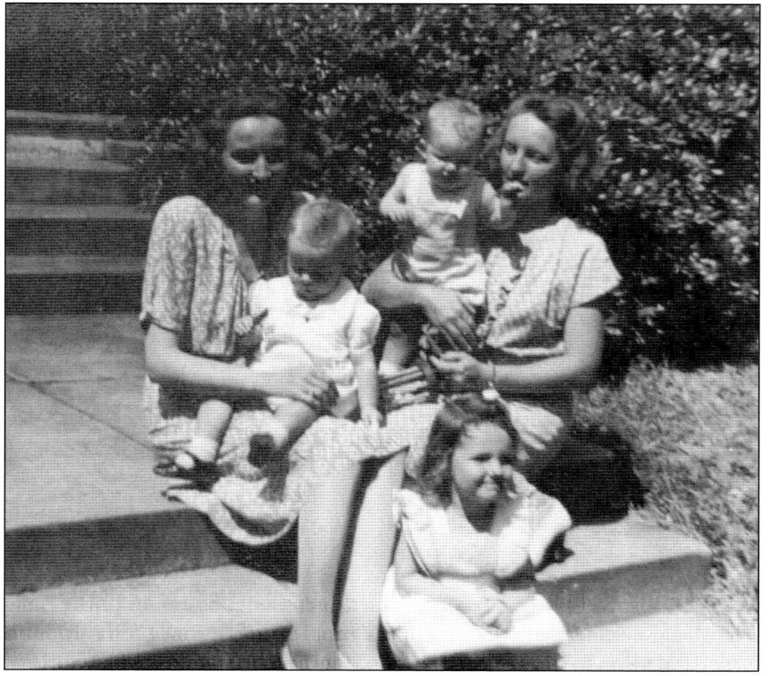

Caroline B. Hamilton (left) and Virginia B. Wilson sit on the steps in front of their parents' house at 1120 East Fiftieth Street. Caroline is holding her daughter, Susan, and Virginia is cradling daughter Judy while big sister Ellen Wilson sits on the bottom step. (Courtesy of the Wilson/Smith family.)

This 1948 plat of lots 493 and 494 on East Fiftieth Street in Parkside shows the Calhoun home at 1105 East Fiftieth. The brick bungalow was the second residence east of Waters Avenue on the south side of the street. The house was built on two lots in the city's Pierpont Ward. (Courtesy of Linda Calhoun Lynes.)

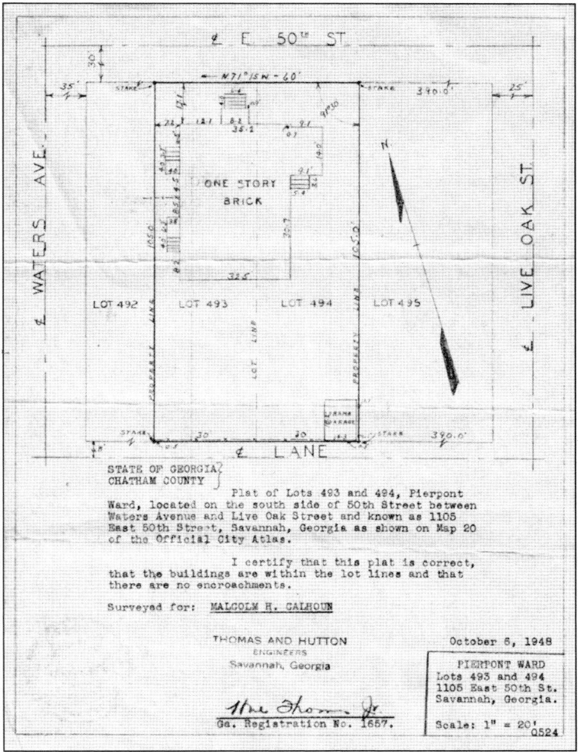

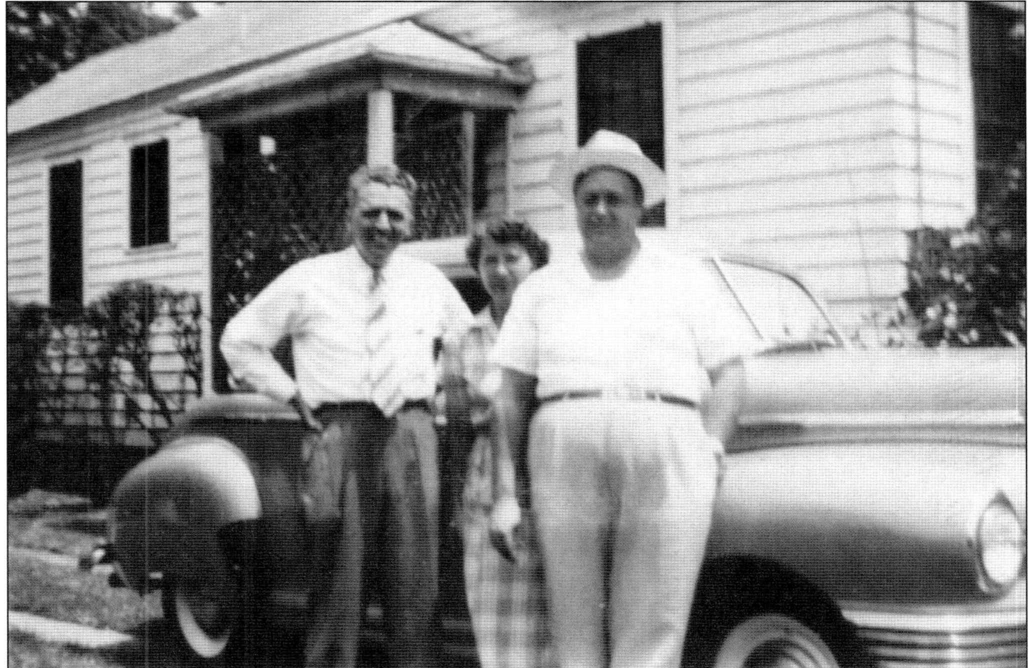

Malcolm "Mac" and Clarice Calhoun were best friends with Natalie and Arlie Fields. In the 1940s, when the Calhouns bought their Fiftieth Street home, the Fieldses moved in with them and stayed until Linda was born. Shown here from left to right are Mac, Natalie, and Arlie. Later, Clarice and Natalie taught at Charles Ellis School. (Courtesy of Linda Calhoun Lynes.)

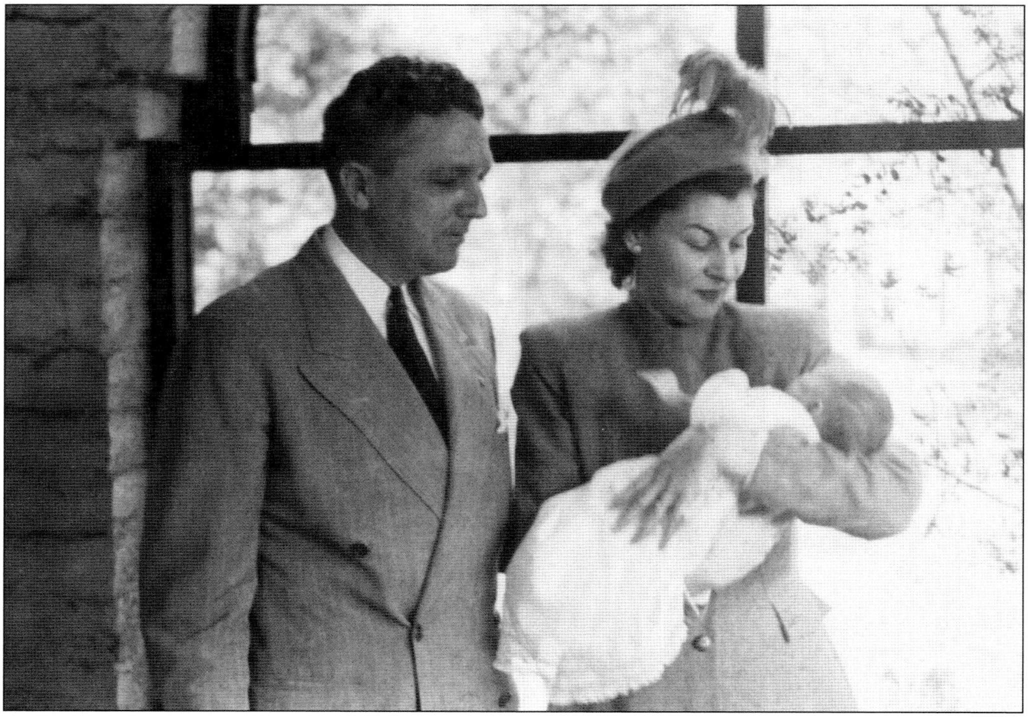

Proud parents Mac and Clarice Calhoun brought baby Mary Linda home from the hospital in 1948. This memorable picture was taken on the sun porch of the family's Fiftieth Street home. Like many Parkside residents, Linda said her whole life revolved around Parkside, nearby churches, and Waters Avenue businesses. When she was in high school, she worked at a store called the Oddity Shop in the 3400 block of Waters. (Courtesy of Linda Calhoun Lynes.)

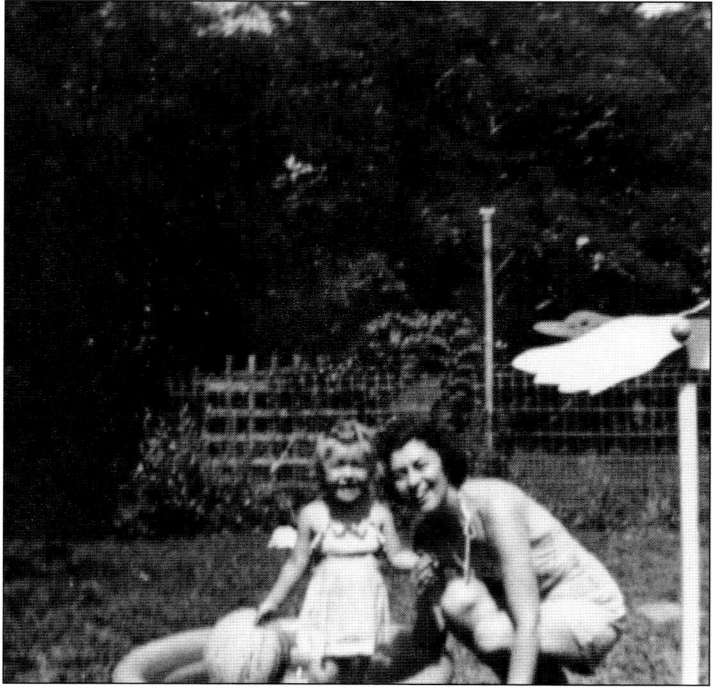

As a three-year-old, Linda Calhoun splashed around in this little pool in the backyard of her Parkside home. During the 1950s, children were advised to steer clear of public swimming pools because of the polio scare. They also were encouraged to get plenty of rest by taking midday naps so they would not contract the disease. (Courtesy of Linda Calhoun Lynes.)

Mac Calhoun worked in the yard constantly and knew all the neighbors, recalled daughter Linda, who is shown here with her father in the 1950s. "A born salesman, he was super friendly, and all the neighborhood children called him Uncle Mac," she added. (Courtesy of Linda Calhoun Lynes.)

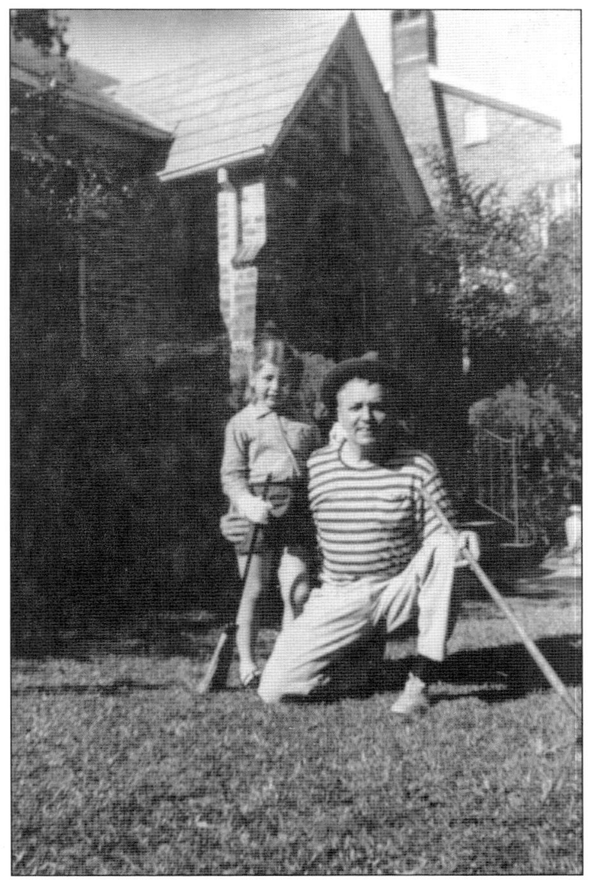

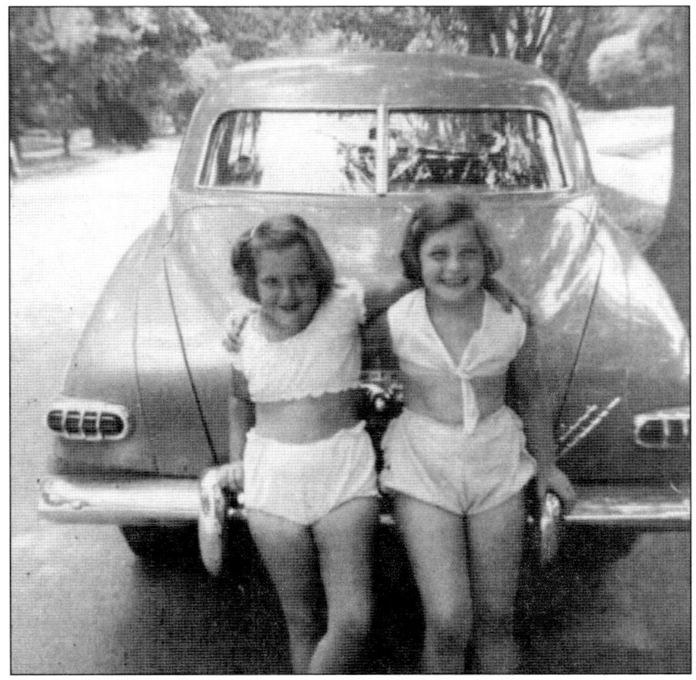

Both Linda Calhoun and Nancy Causey were only children and were "joined at the hip," Linda said. The Causeys lived in the 1100 block of East Fifty-First Street, almost directly behind the Calhouns' house. Loyal Causey was Nancy's father and worked at Lesser's Men's Quality Shop for many years. Her mother, Louise Causey, was employed at Desbouillion's on Broughton Street and later at Medical Arts. (Courtesy of Linda Calhoun Lynes.)

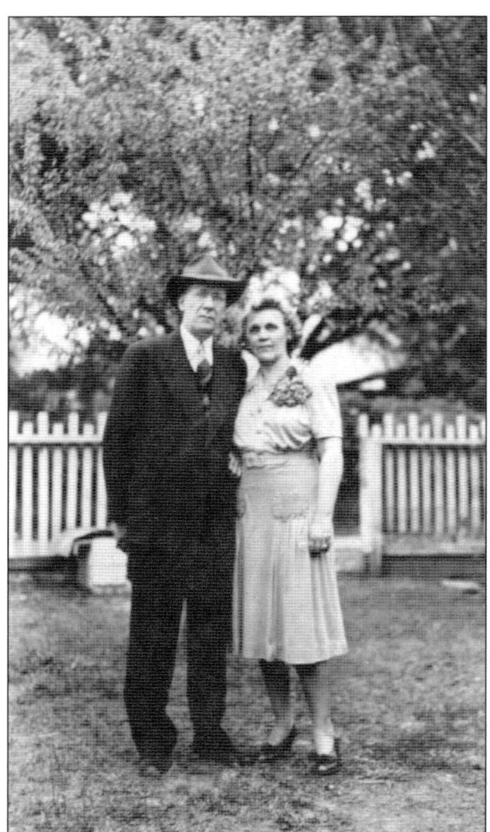

B.F. Kuhkle and his wife, Frances, bought the home at 1321 East Fiftieth Street in the late 1930s. B.F. was a claims adjustor for the Central of Georgia Railroad for more than 50 years. The bungalow was constructed in 1927 and was the place where the Kuhlkes raised their six children. (Courtesy of the Kuhlke family.)

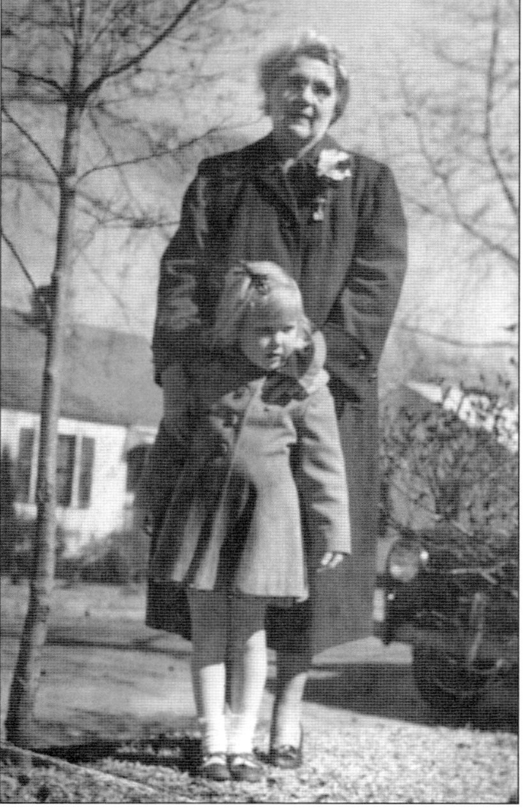

Around 1950, Frances Kuhlke, wearing what looks like a camellia corsage on her coat, stands with her granddaughter Jan Anderson in front of the Kuhlke home in the 1300 block of East Fiftieth Street. Jan was one of 10 Kuhlke grandchildren. The homes in the background are across the street from the Kuhlke home. (Courtesy of the Kuhlke family.)

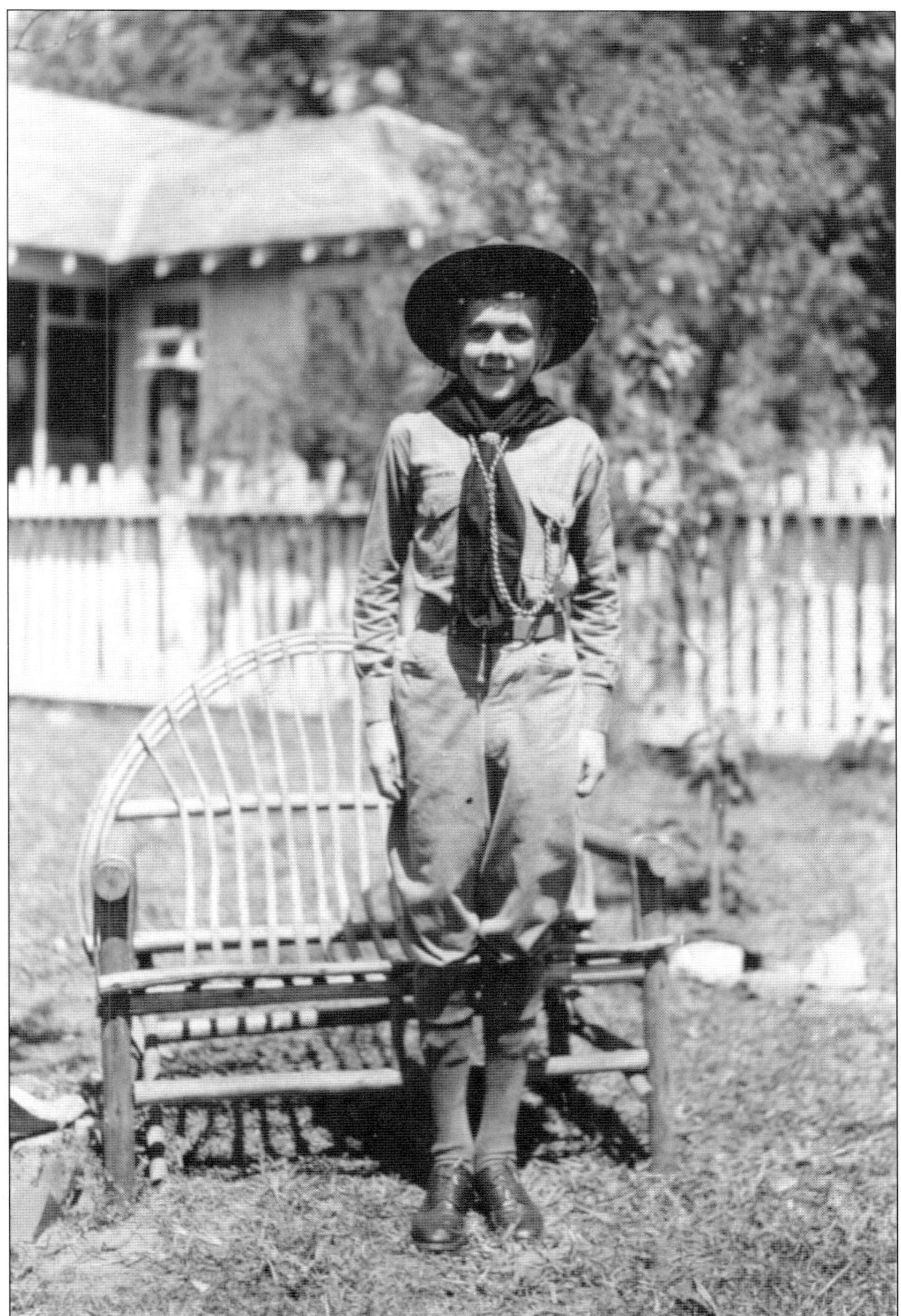

Bud Kuhlke was a dedicated Boy Scout and eventually earned the rank of Eagle. He lived with his parents, brother, and sisters at 1321 East Fiftieth Street. This picture of the proud Boy Scout was taken in 1942 in the family's backyard, which was the backdrop for many of the family's treasured photographs. During the blackout drills of World War II, Bud was a proud assistant block captain. (Courtesy of the Kuhlke family.)

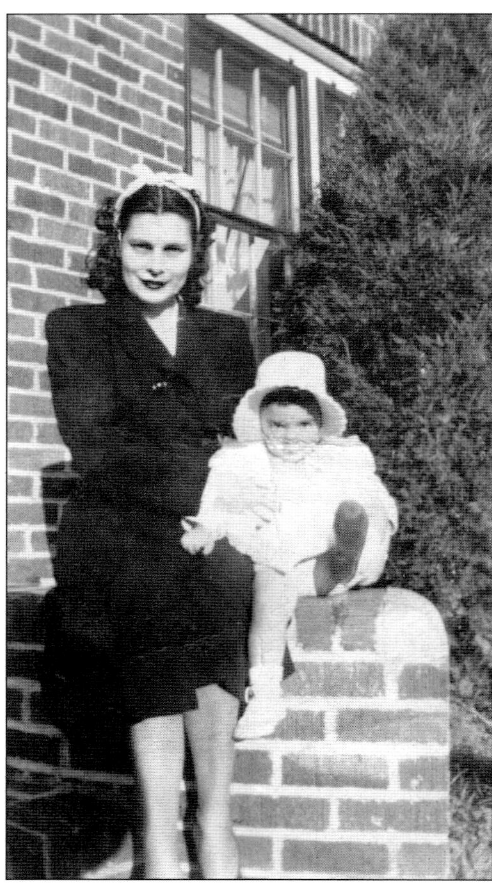

Al Orsini built a brick home at 1528 East Fiftieth Street in the late 1940s. Shown in front of the house are his wife, Concetta, and baby daughter Mary, who today owns her childhood home. From the beginning, many families like the Orsinis were charmed by Parkside. According to the book *George Woodruff, A Life of Quiet Achievement*, shortly after their 1918 marriage, the Woodruffs rented the bungalow at 1209 East Forty-Ninth Street for $47 a month and described it as a "country home." (Courtesy of the Orsini family.)

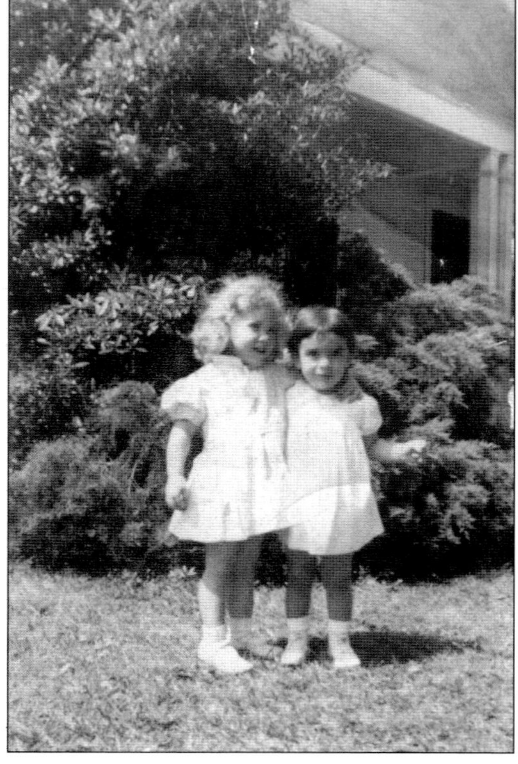

In the late 1940s or early 1950s, playmates Mary Orsini and Ann Wessels were photographed in front of the Wessels home on East Fiftieth Street. In later years, the family moved, and eventually the house was torn down. Two homes were built on what had been the Wessels lot. (Courtesy of the Orsini family.)

The Fred Wessels family lived across from the Orsini home on East Fiftieth Street. Shown here are lifelong friends Mary Orsini (left) and Ann Wessels. "[Ann's] mother drove my mother to the hospital when I was born," Mary said. (Courtesy of the Orsini family.)

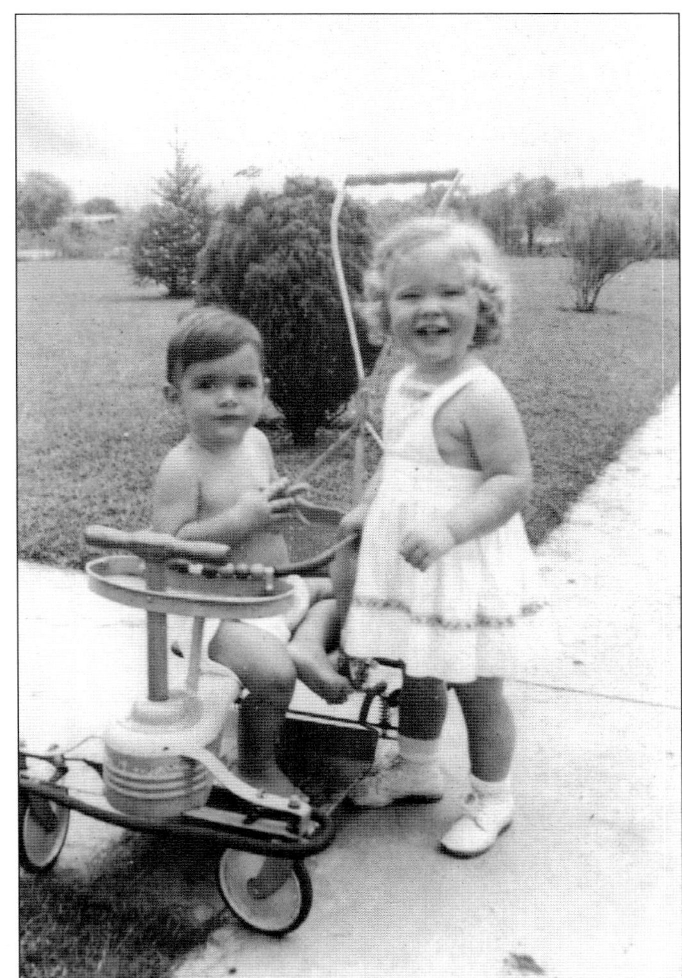

Mary Orsini (right) and Jan Joyce were classmates at St. Vincent's Academy when this picture was taken in front of the Orsinis' Parkside home. They graduated from Savannah High School in 1964. (Courtesy of the Orsini family.)

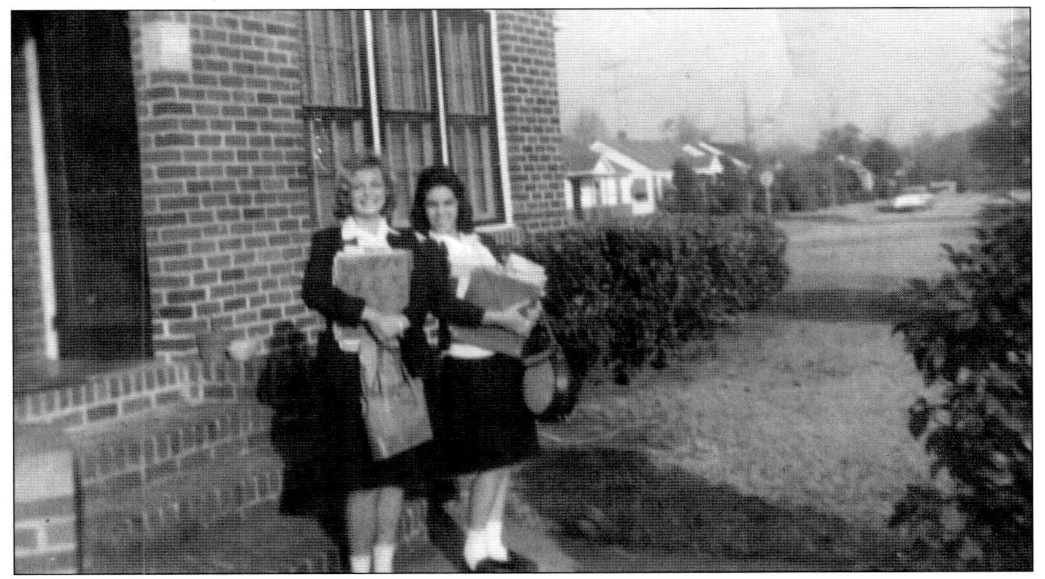

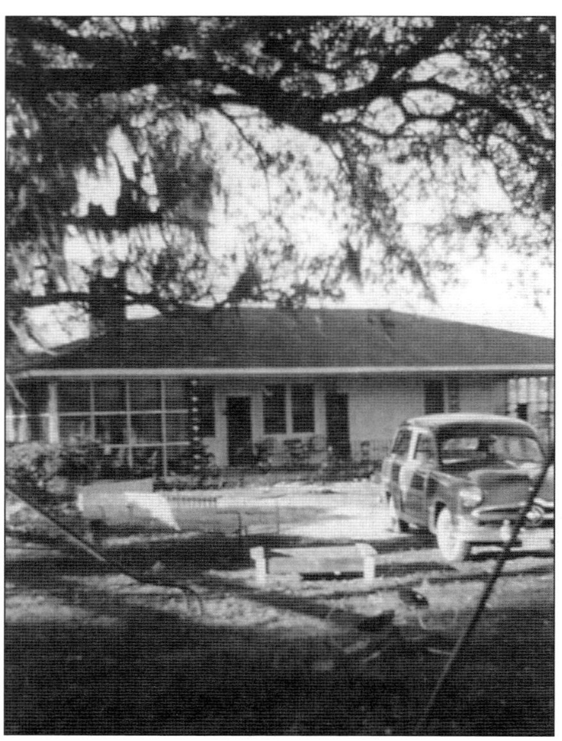

The Richard Belford family lived at 3114 Bee Road from 1950 until 1962. The property stretched from what is now Kerry Street on the north side to the Sunshine Kindergarten on the south, which was next to the Primitive Baptist Church. (Courtesy of the Belford family.)

Pony rides were part of the fun-filled days at the Belford home on Bee Road. In this photograph, Beauty the pony is hitched up to a wagon carrying four passengers. Pat and Barbie Little are in front, with Lee (left) and Rick Belford wearing hats in back. (Courtesy of the Belford family.)

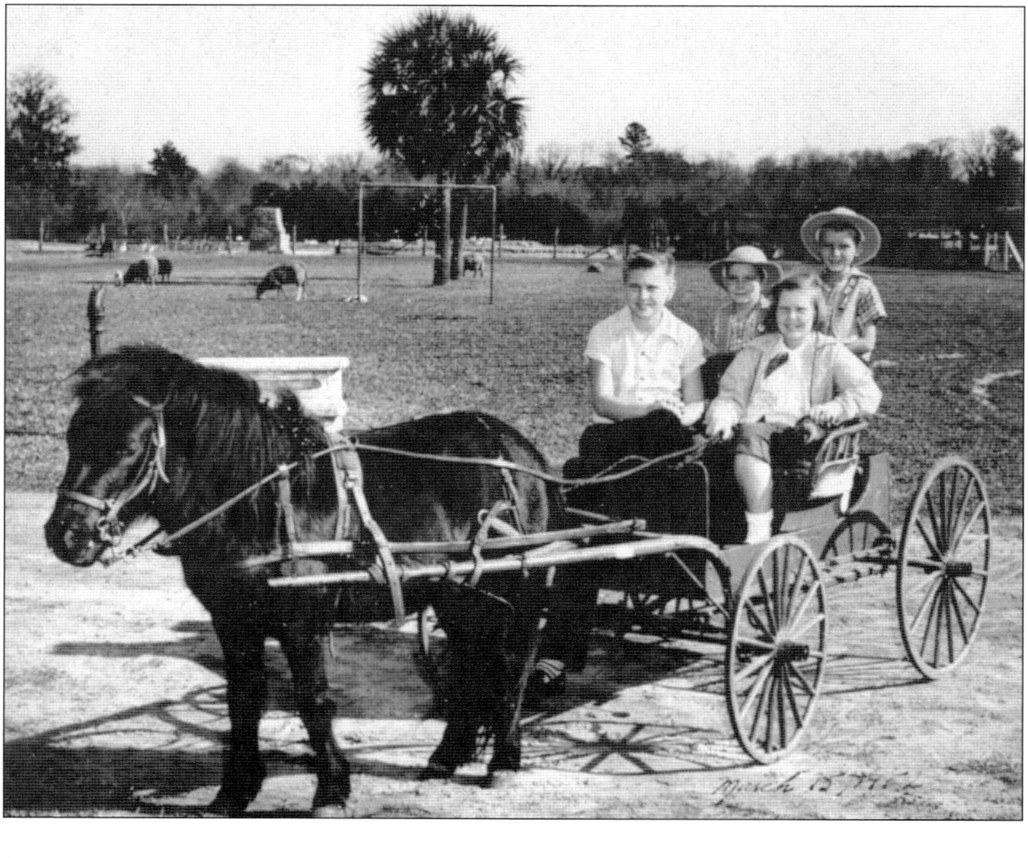

The Belfords' Bee Road compound consisted of 18 acres that extended from Bee Road on the west to the Casey Canal on the east. Although not officially part of Parkside, the property was just across the street from the neighborhood and most everybody, it seems, was familiar with the "zoo" as some called it, because of the family's collection of exotic animals. Among other favorite spots on the property was a man-made pond with a small island in the middle. Rick Belford described the Bee Road property as "the greatest place in the world." (Courtesy of the Belford family.)

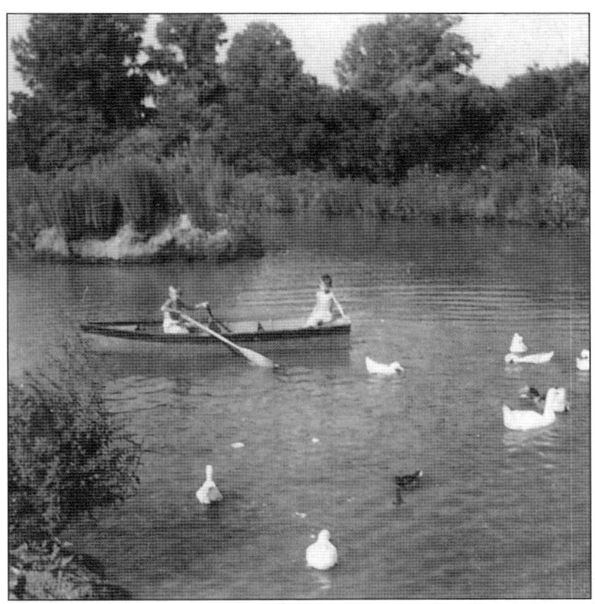

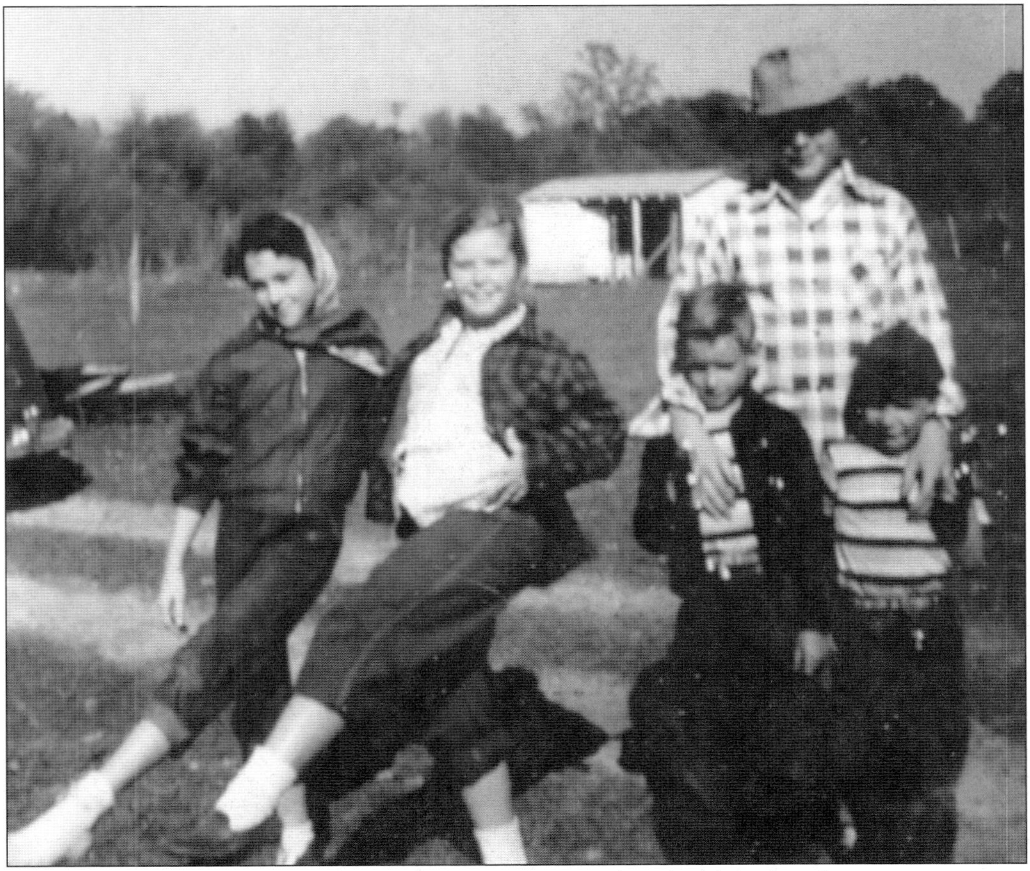

In the 1950s, Barbie Little (second from left) and an unidentified friend perform an impromptu can-can for the camera. Richard Belford is at right with sons Rick (left) and Lee. (Courtesy of the Belford family.)

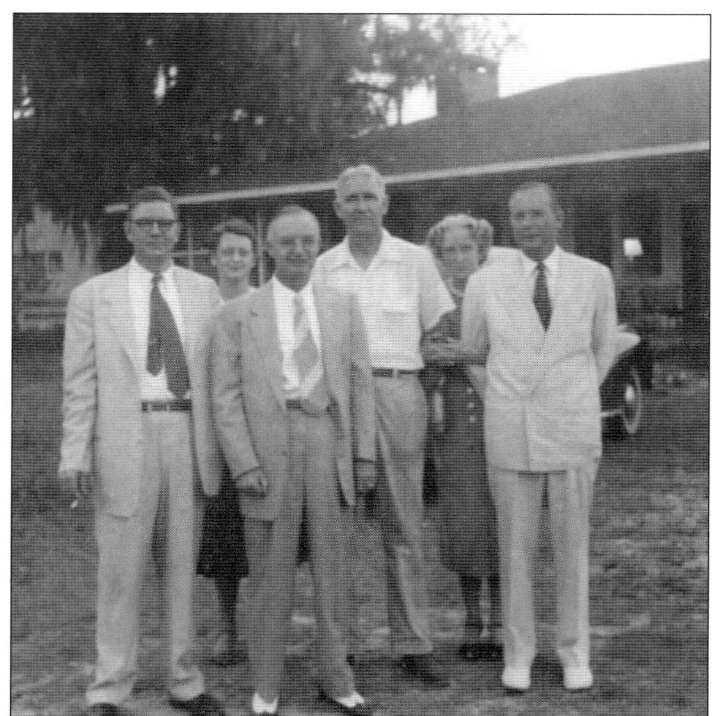

During the 1950s, Richard and Martha Belford gathered with Richard's siblings for a family picture at their Bee Road home. From left to right are Lee Belford, Frances Belford, W.T. "Doc" Belford, Richard, Martha, and Toby Belford. Lee Belford was an Episcopal priest who lived in New York and became John F. Kennedy's religious advisor, according to his nephew Rick Belford. Lee also was friends with Dodgers baseball great Jackie Robinson and, beginning in 1961, participated in the Freedom Rides in the segregated South. (Courtesy of the Belford family.)

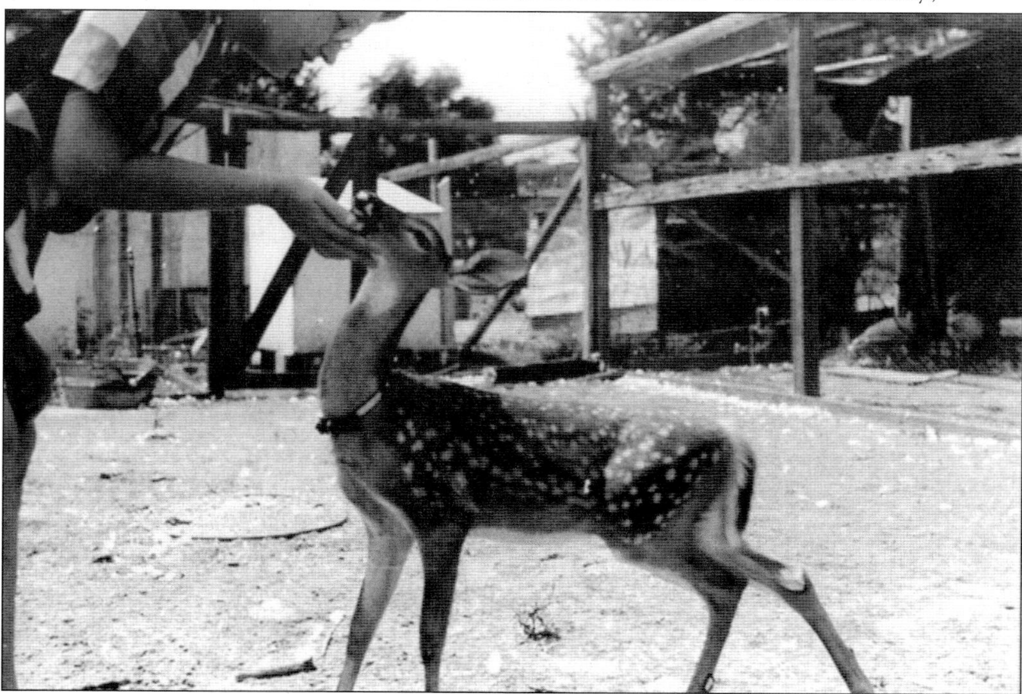

Rick Belford remembers how, during the 1950s, people in cars would ride slowly along Bee Road hoping to see the family's animals put on a show. He said it was entertaining to watch the monkeys hitch rides on the backs of the dogs, goats, or ponies, who would take off running. The Belfords' menagerie also included sheep, ducks, peacocks, a fox named Rennie, and a deer named Bambi. (Courtesy of the Belford family.)

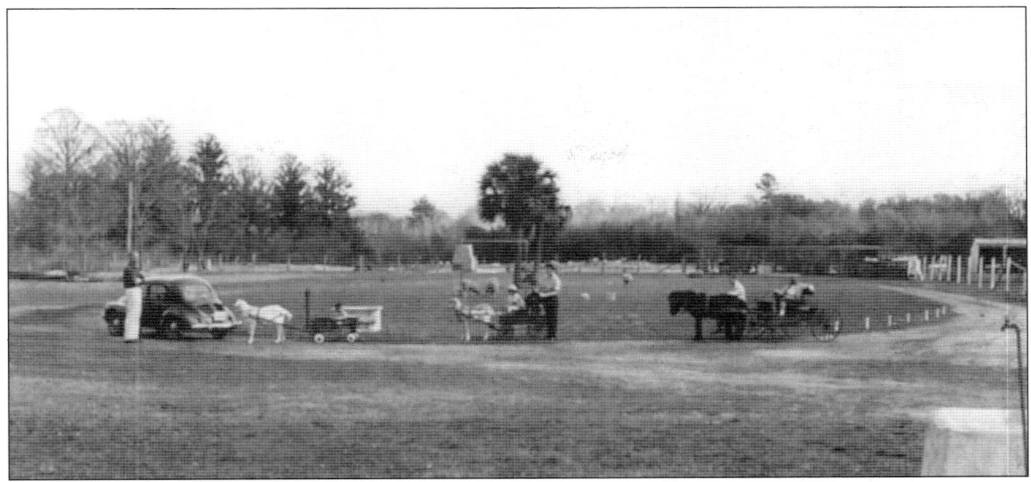

The Belford property included a round dirt track where the family and their friends rode ponies or were pulled in wagons led by ponies or goats. The little car on the left was the one Martha Belford used to learn how to drive. Son Rick said his mother did not know how to drive until the family moved to Bee Road. (Courtesy of the Belford family.)

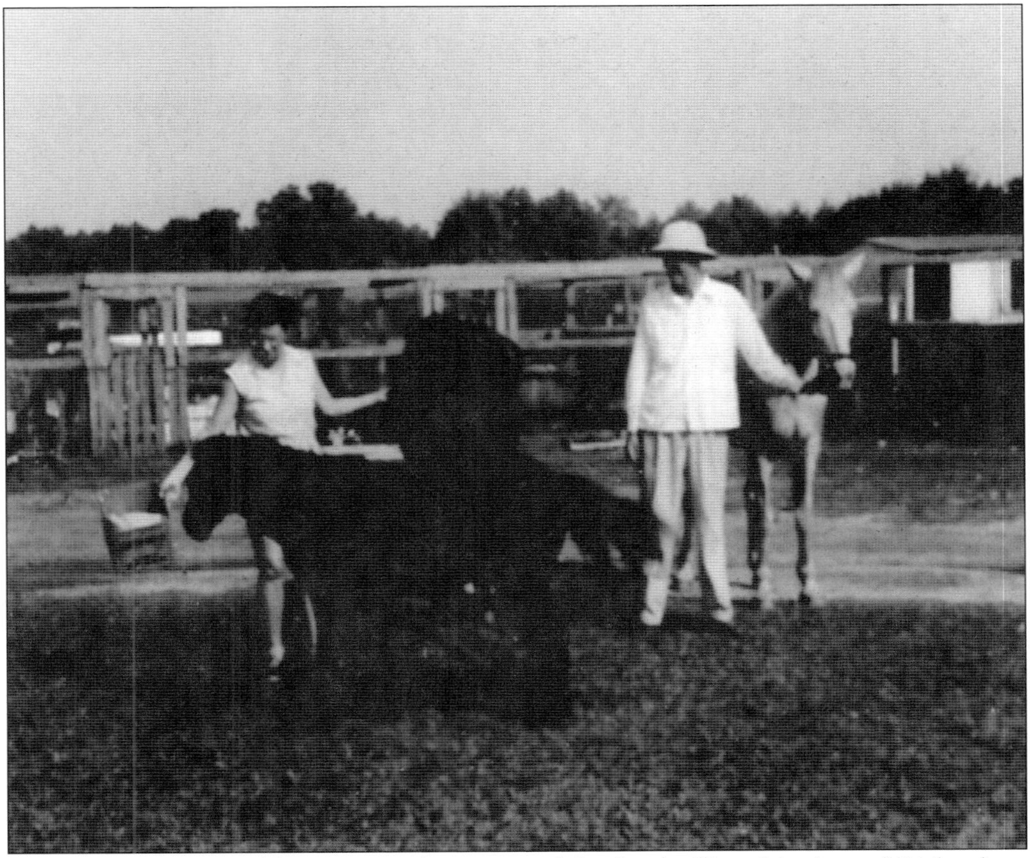

The Belford ponies and horses were almost part of the family. Here, Martha and Richard are pictured with Beauty, a rescue pony, and Flash, who was Rick's horse and was named for his speed. (Courtesy of the Belford family.)

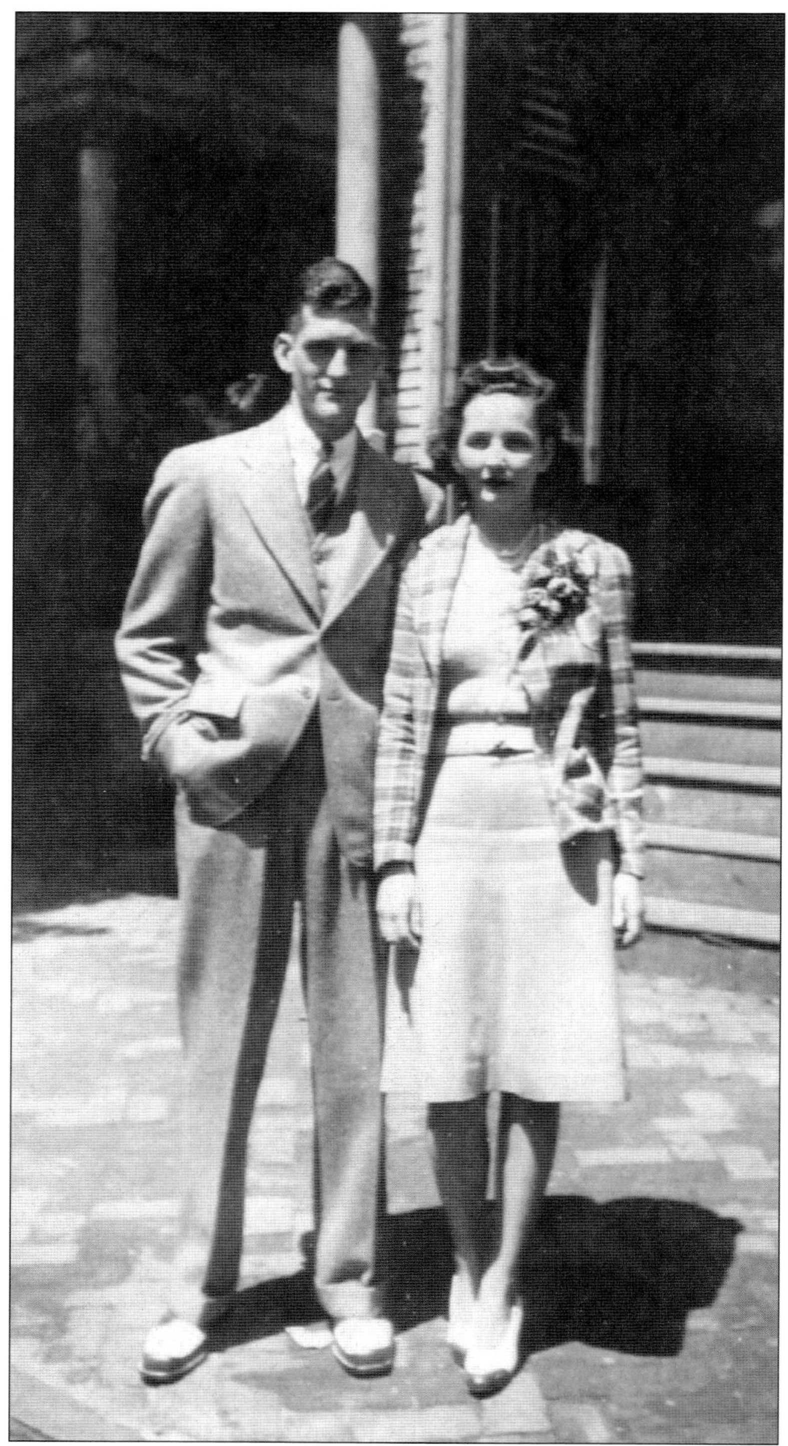

George Wilmot "Willie" Adams and Florence Counihan were married in the early 1940s and moved into a bungalow at 1426 East Forty-Eighth Street in early 1947. Their son Billy Adams still owns the home. In 1993, Willie was elected grand marshal of Savannah's St. Patrick's Day Parade. (Courtesy of the Adams family.)

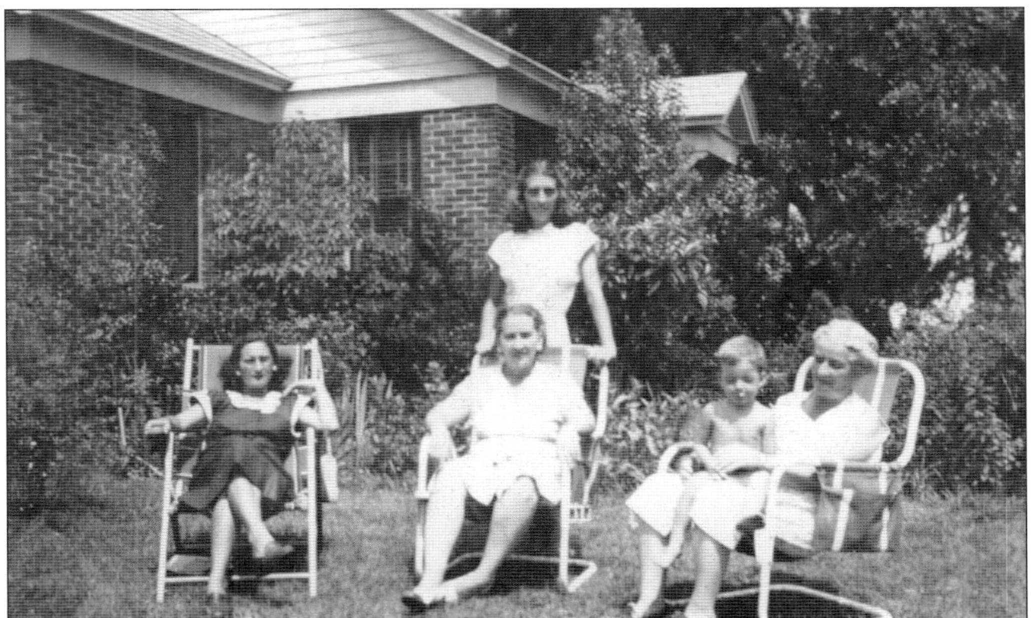

In Parkside, family members and friends often sat outside to socialize and watch the goings-on in the neighborhood. On a Forty-Eighth Street lawn during the late 1940s are, from left to right, Mary Handiboe, Elizabeth Hunter, Julia Lingenfelser (standing), and Catherine Walls holding Billy Adams. (Courtesy of the Adams family.)

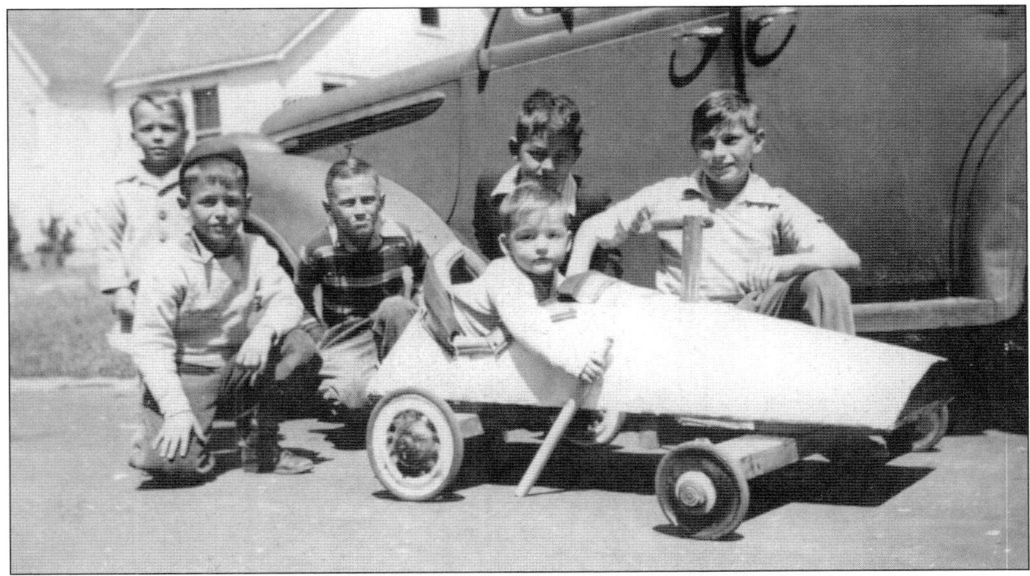

Boys will be boys, especially when it comes to cars. Playing with this toy vehicle around 1950 in the 1400 block of East Forty-Eighth Street are, from left to right, Richard Tuttle, Charlie Tuttle (kneeling), Walton Bazemore, Jimmy Meyers, Billy Adams (driving), and Teddy Rovolis. (Courtesy of the Adams family.)

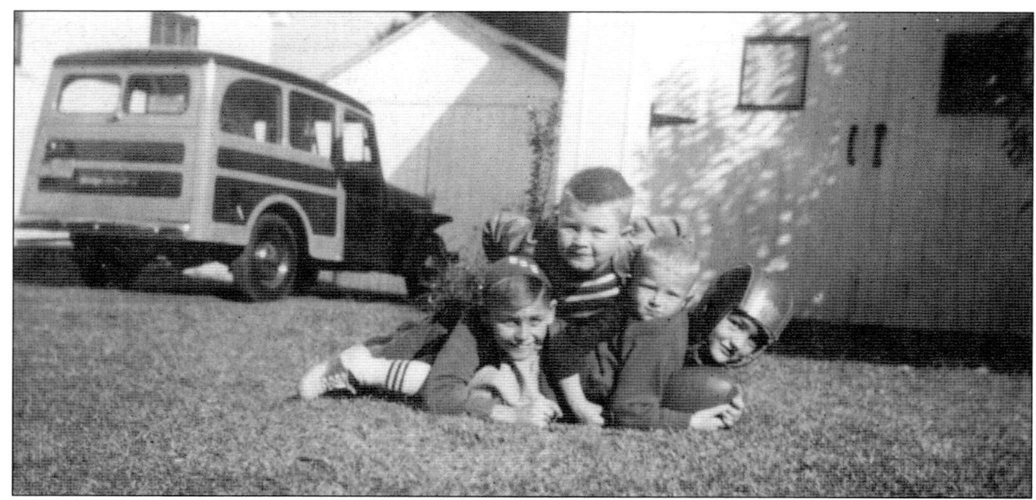

Even the littlest boys in the Parkside neighborhood loved playing football, both at Daffin Park and in their own yards. In the 1950s, these buddies gathered in the 1400 block of Forty-Eighth Street. From left to right are Charlie Tuttle wearing the beanie, Jimmy and Johnny Dunn, and Billy Adams with the ball. (Courtesy of the Adams family.)

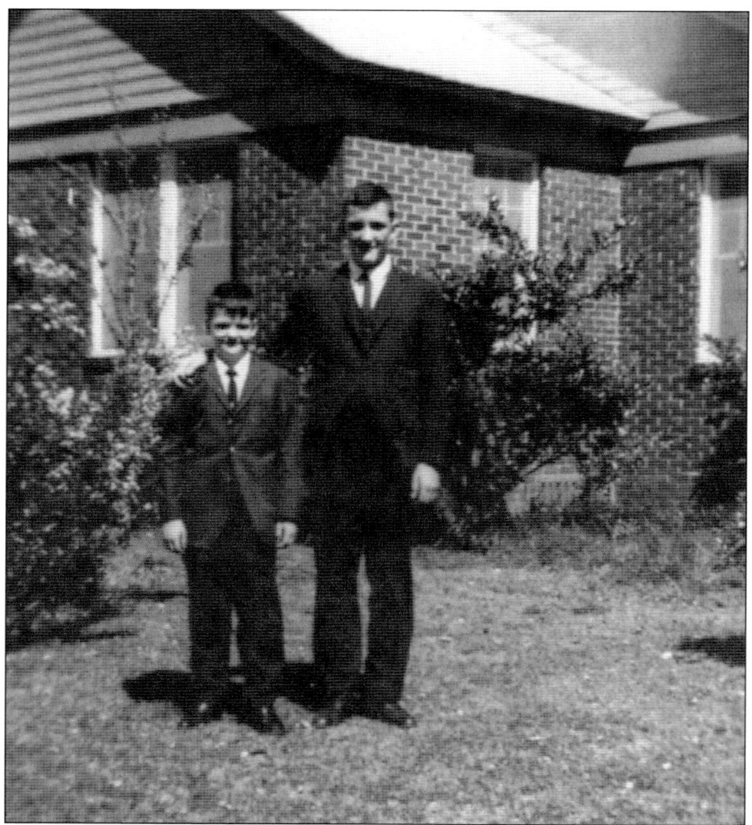

Billy Adams (right) stands with his younger brother Bobby on the lawn in front of the Adams home in the 1400 block of East Forty-Eighth Street. The Adamses were one of many Catholic families that lived in Parkside. Former residents of the 1500 block included the Tuttles, the Mulligans, and the Counihans. Around the corner were the Hennesseys and the Parkers, among others. (Courtesy of the Adams family.)

The Craftsman-style home at 1109
East Forty-Ninth Street was owned by
the Powers family from around 1930 to
the late 1950s. Thomas Edward Powers
was a widower and lived there with
his two sisters, who helped care for his
four children who were under five. The
eldest was Thomas E. Powers Jr., who
served in England during World War
II. (Courtesy of the Powers family.)

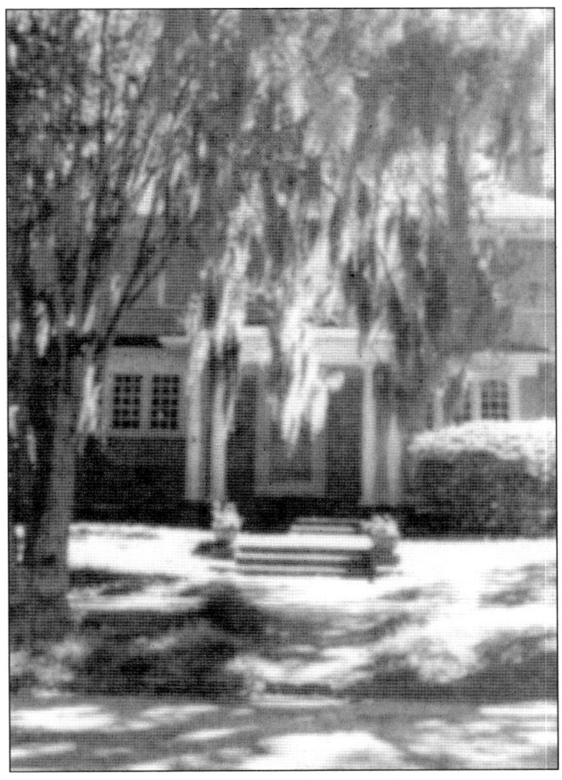

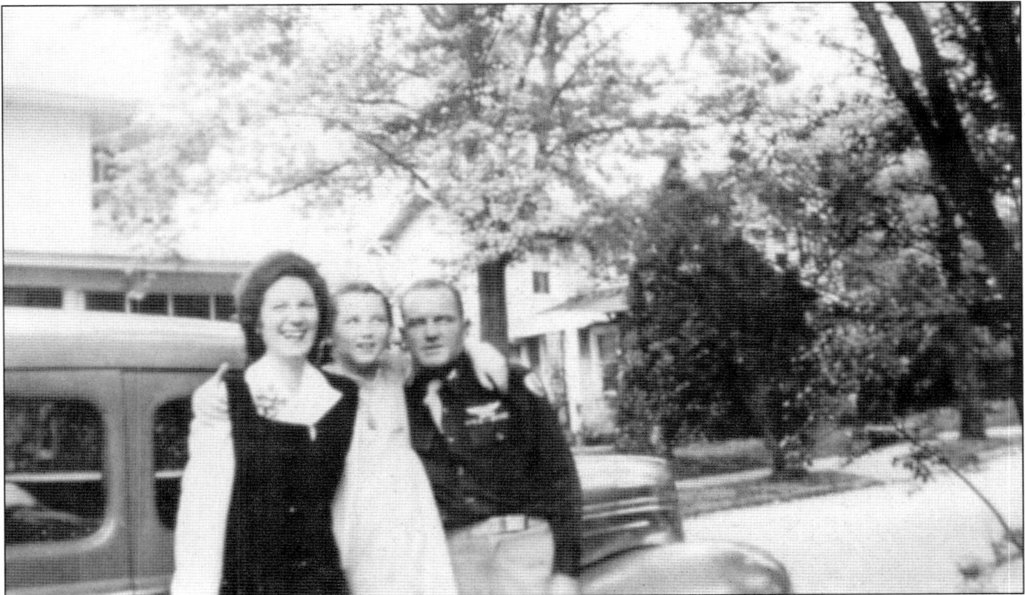

Thomas E. Powers Jr. of Savannah married Margaret Ann Lambert of England in London during
World War II. As the war was winding down, he returned to Savannah without his bride, who
came later via ocean liner like all war brides. The newly married couple moved in with his family
on East Forty-Ninth Street, where his relatives had transformed the front parlor into a honeymoon
suite. The newlyweds are pictured here in 1944 with Thomas's cousin Mary McCracken (center).
(Courtesy of the Powers family.)

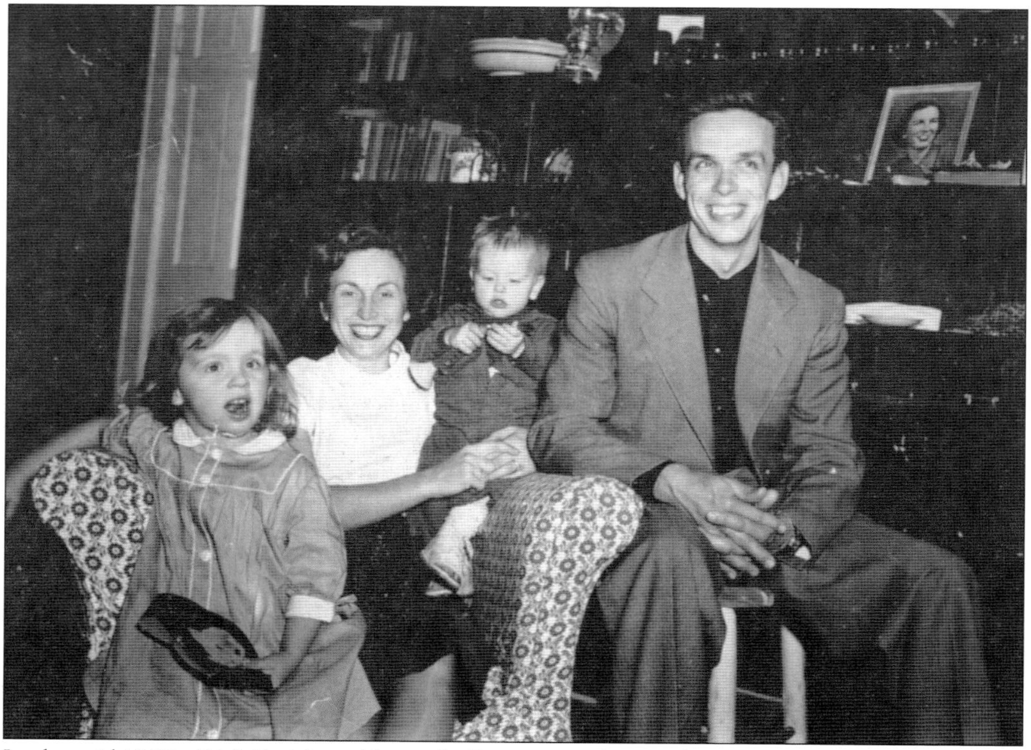

In the mid-1940s, Dick Smith and his wife, Patty, moved into a house at 1207 East Forty-Eighth Street and soon started a family. Shown here in the 1950s from left to right are daughter Laura, Patty (holding baby Ricky), and Dick. The youngest child, Johnny, did not come along until a couple of years later. (Courtesy of the Smith family.)

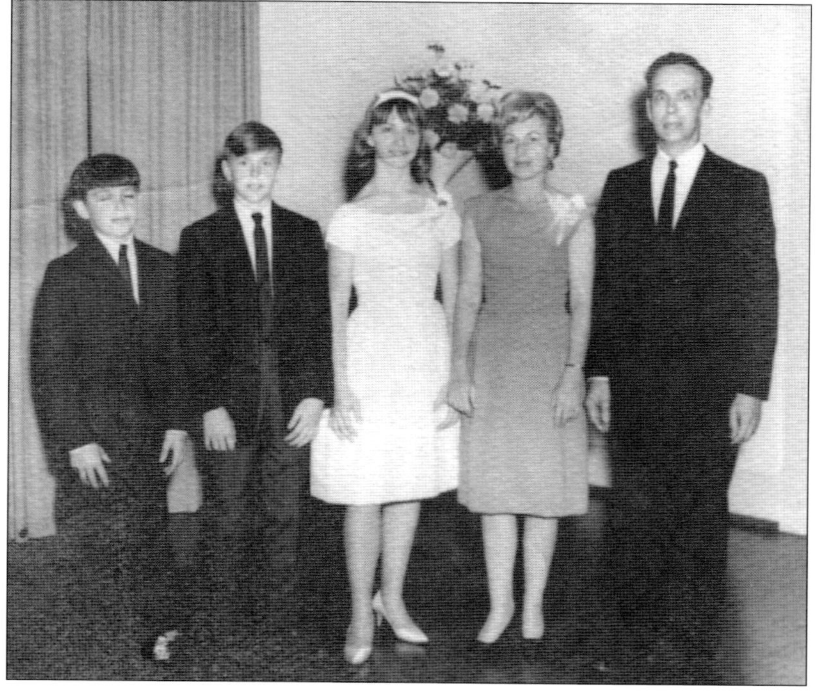

The Dick Smith family gathers for a photograph in the early 1970s. From left to right are Johnny, Ricky, Laura, Patty, and Dick. The family owned their Forty-Eighth Street home for more than 40 years. (Courtesy of the Smith family.)

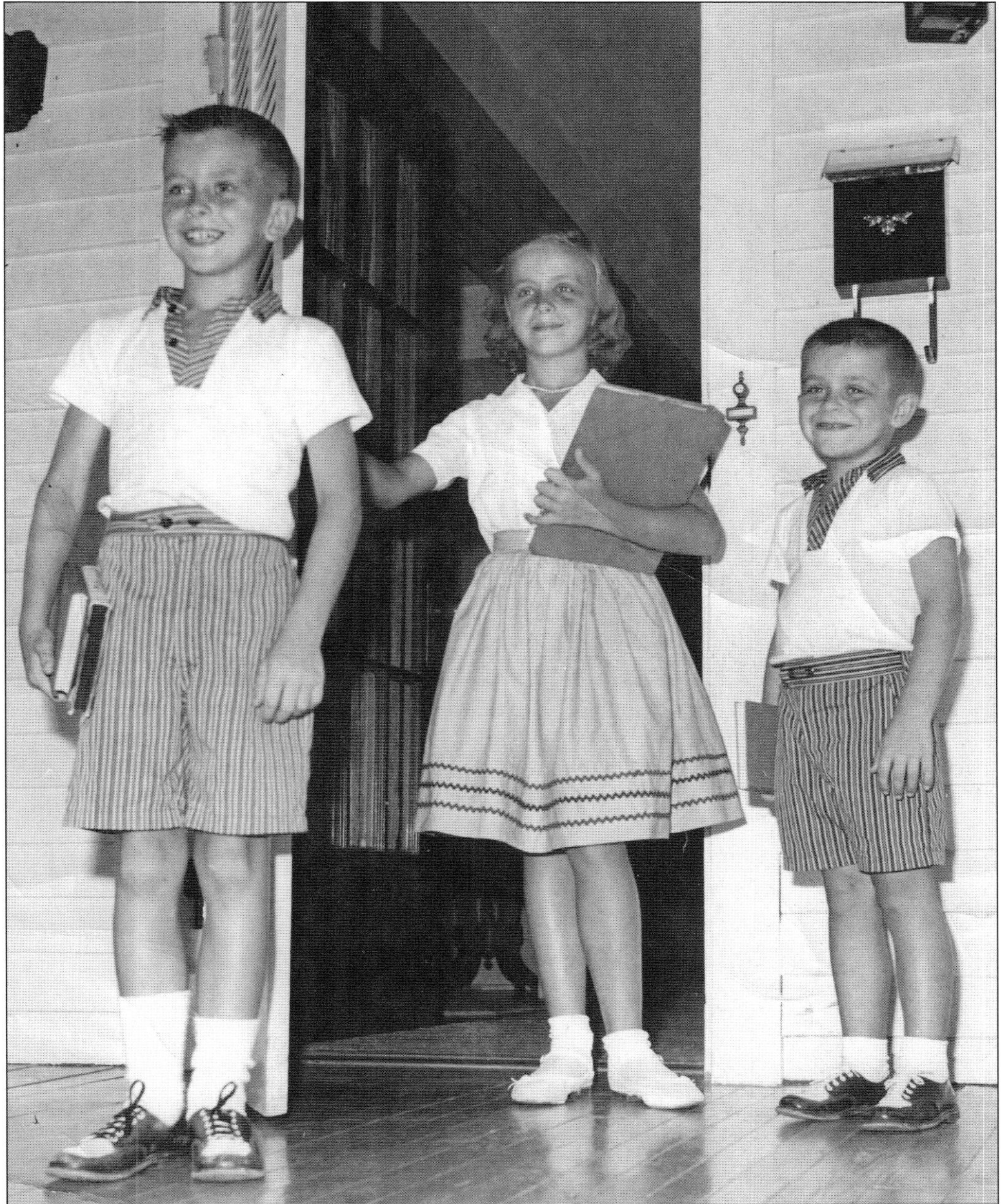

Ricky, Laura, and Johnny Smith look mighty spiffy and ready for school in this photograph from the early 1960s. Ermine Clemens lived next door to the Smiths on East Forty-Ninth Street and was a longtime employee of the *Savannah Morning News*. Ricky said Ermine often would call upon the Smith children to be in newspaper photographs. (Courtesy of the Smith family.)

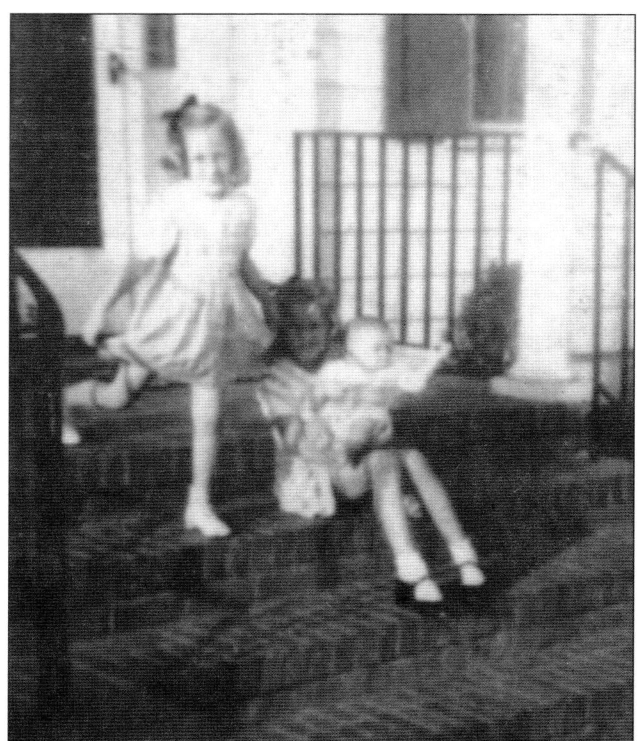

George and Helen Summerell Sr. bought a home at 1530 East Fifty-First Street on the corner of Fifty-First and Bee Road in 1942, two years after it was built. This 1948 picture shows part of the front porch with Pat Summerell and her sister Lynne, who is holding brother George. (Courtesy of the Summerell family.)

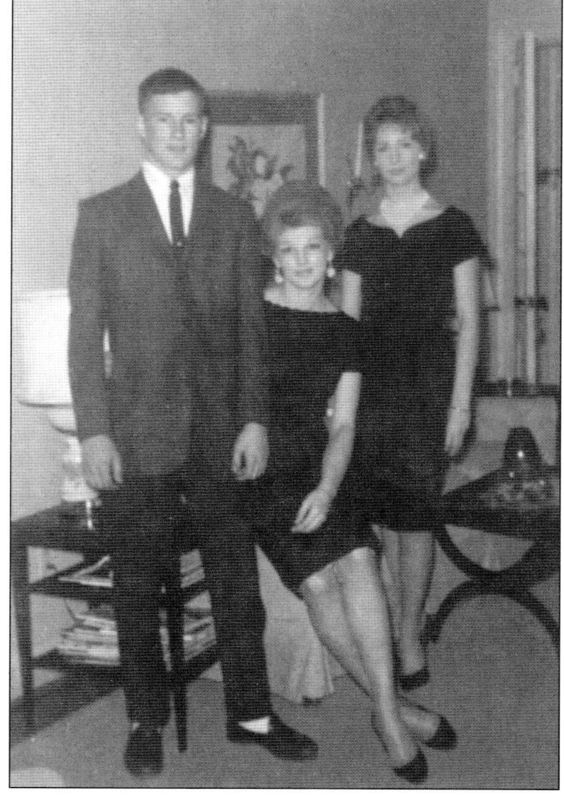

In 1960, the Summerell siblings posed for this photograph. From left to right are George, Lynne, and Pat. The Summerell family owned the Fifty-First Street home until around 2005, when they sold it following Mrs. Summerell's death. George Summerell Sr. died in 2003. (Courtesy of the Summerell family.)

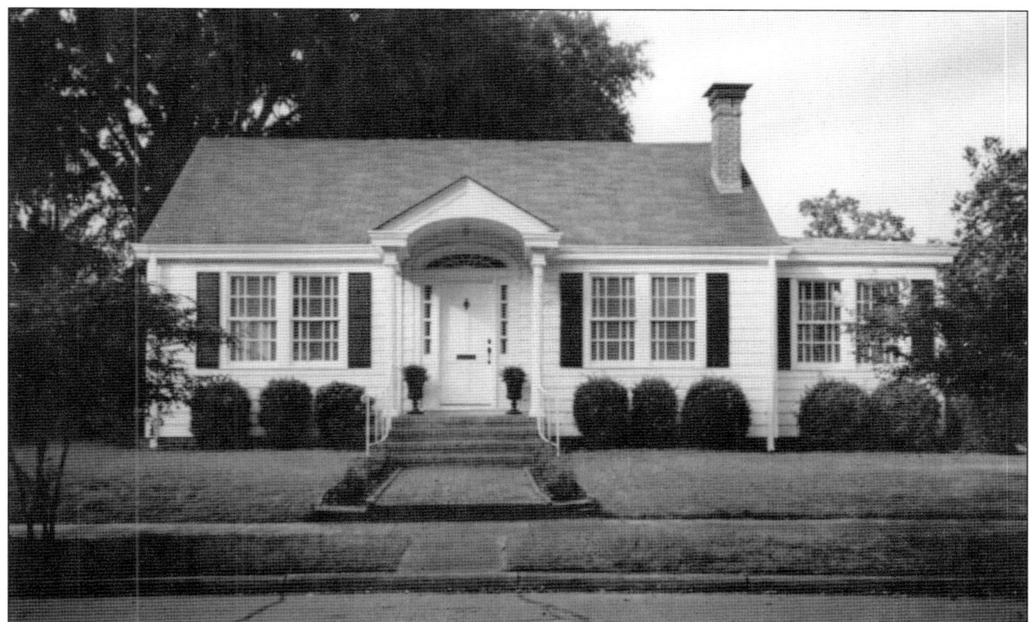

The Summerell home on Fifty-First Street continues to be a bright spot in the Parkside neighborhood. The current owners installed a picket fence along the front and Bee Road sides of the home. The single-car garage faces Bee Road. Some Parkside homes do not have driveways because originally, the neighborhood was considered to be a streetcar suburb of Savannah. (Courtesy of the Summerell family.)

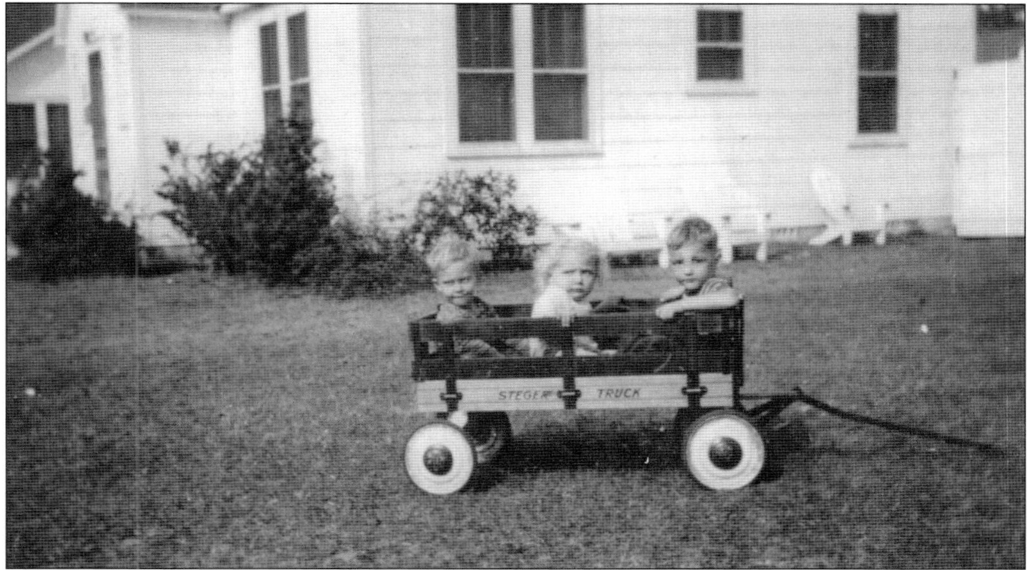

This trio of little Parkside passengers was photographed in the 1400 block of East Forty-Eighth Street during the late 1940s or early 1950s. For many years, the 1500 block of Forty-Eighth was an unpaved, dead-end street, which made it a veritable playground for neighborhood children who played stickball, built castles, and swerved their bicycles in the soft sand. (Courtesy of the Adams family.)

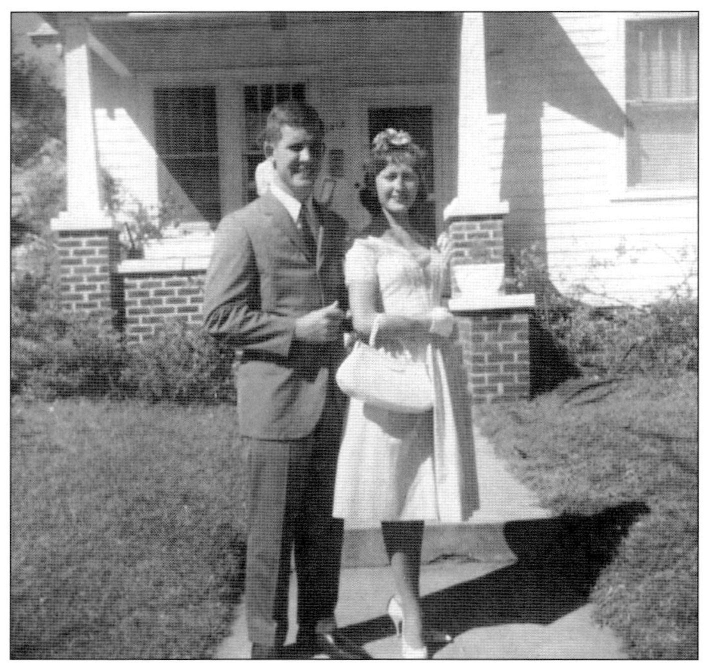

The Toole family lived in this house at 1412 East Fiftieth Street for about four decades, beginning in the 1940s. The family included parents Giles and Mamie, Shirley, Jean, Betty, and Carolyn. Mamie's mother, Rozella Mitchell, lived with the family. Giles was a master carpenter who was especially proud of making the cabinets for the original Ships of the Sea Museum on River Street, according to his daughter Shirley. (Courtesy of Shirley Toole Reckling)

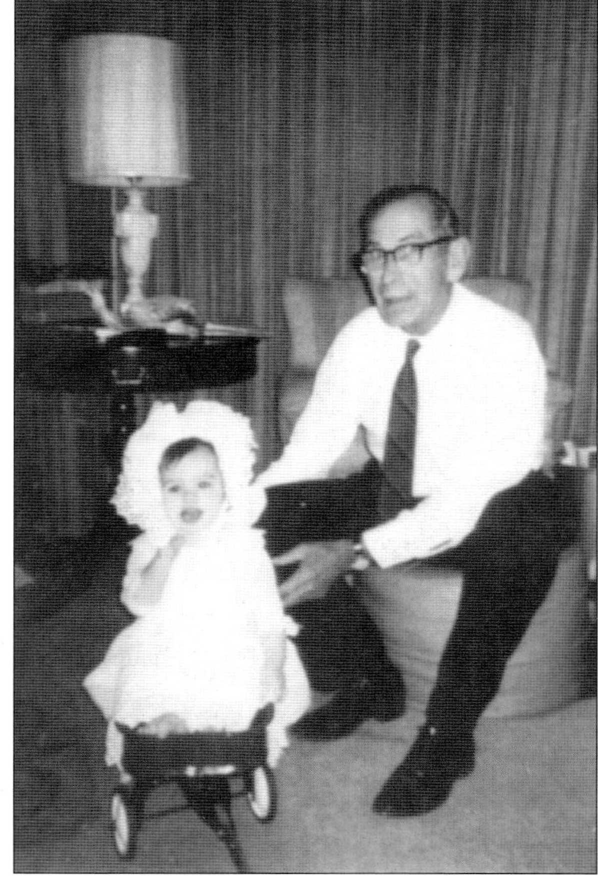

In 1968, Giles Toole was photographed in the living room of the family's Parkside home with grandson Trey Reckling wearing Giles's baby outfit. The Toole children sold the house in 1995 after the death of their mother, Mamie. (Giles had died previously.) The house was built in 1945. (Courtesy of Shirley Toole Reckling.)

Harry and Ola Skinner moved to Forty-Ninth Street in Parkside in the mid-1950s and raised their two sons, John and Charles, in the friendly neighborhood. Here, Harry and Ola pose for a photograph on the sidewalk in front of their home. The background includes a few of the houses across the street in the 1200 block. (Courtesy of the Skinner family.)

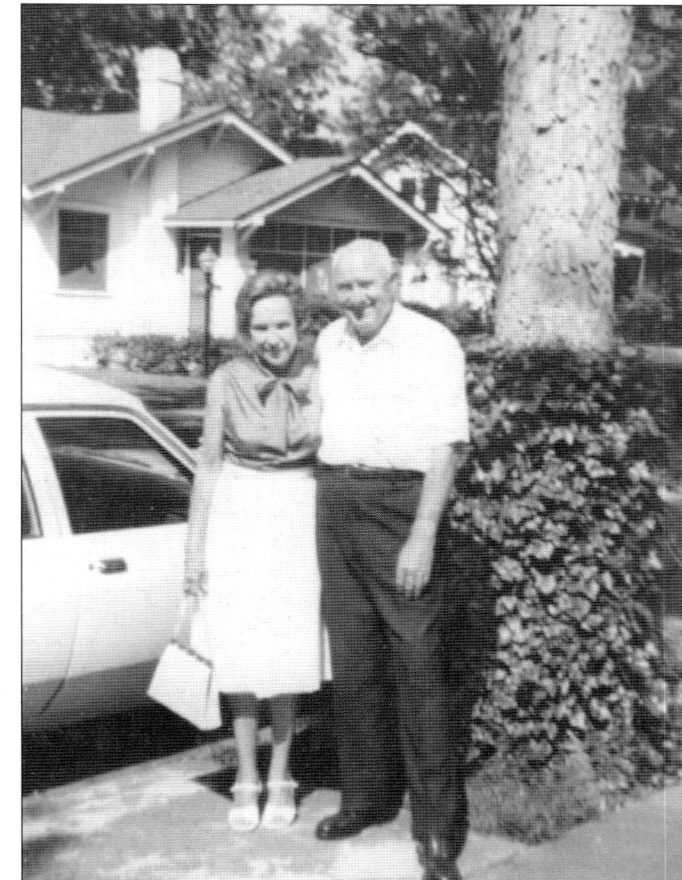

The Skinner family lived in this house at 1207 East Forty-Ninth Street for more than 40 years. The house probably was built in the 1920s and may have been from a Sears Roebuck plan, according to a family member. (Courtesy of the Skinner family.)

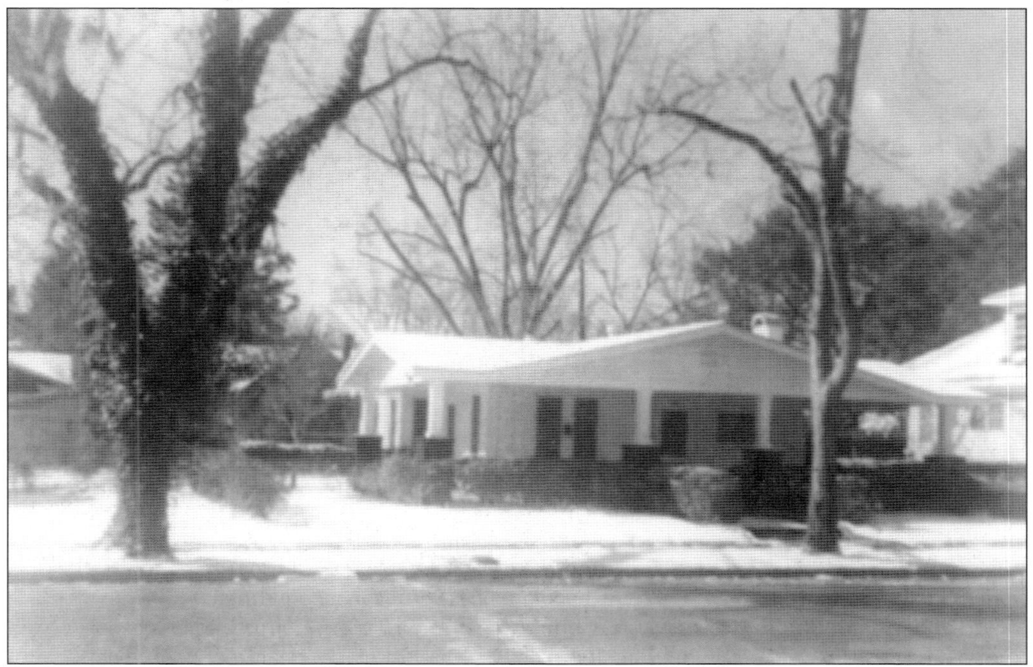

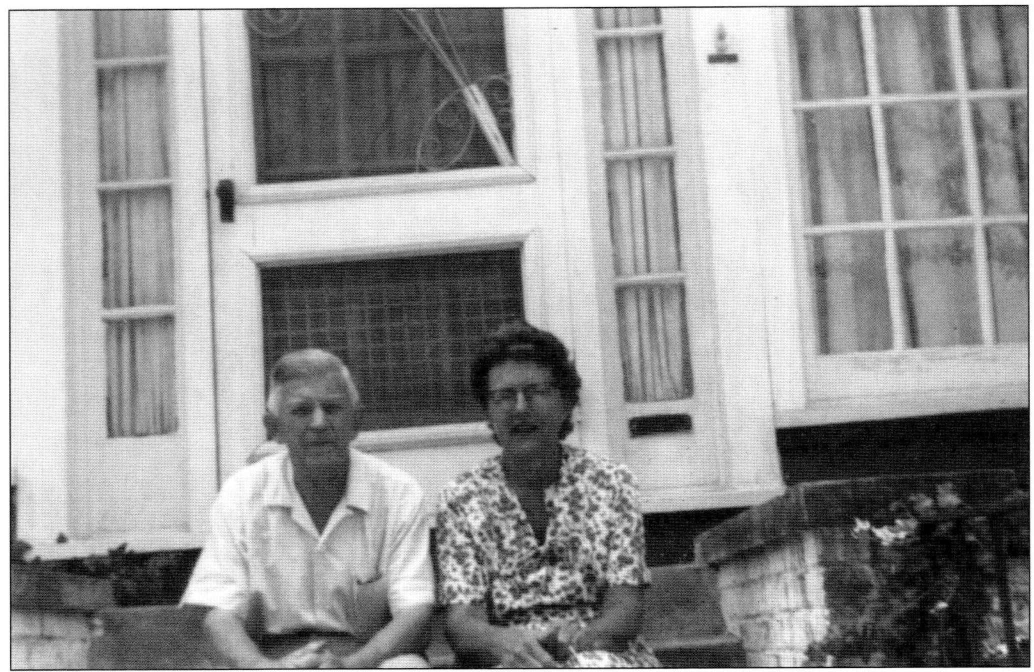

The first homes built in Parkside included a handful on Washington Avenue that faced Daffin Park. Fred and Katherine Garis are shown sitting on the steps of their residence at 1317 Washington Avenue. (Courtesy of the Garis family.)

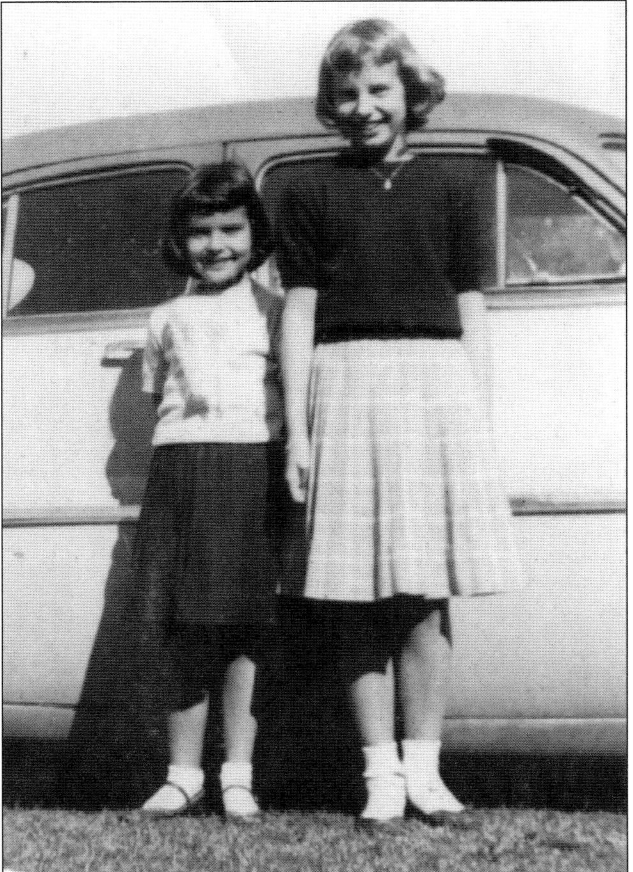

The Walker family moved the house at 1501 East Fiftieth Street (at Hickory Street) in the late 1940s. Here, their daughters Natalie (left) and Madeleine pose by the family car in the 1950s. Many Parkside girls and scores of others took ballet lessons from Madeleine Walker Sr. at her studio on Waters Avenue and Fiftieth Street. (Courtesy of Natalie Walker Deriso.)

Three

THE TIGER CLUB

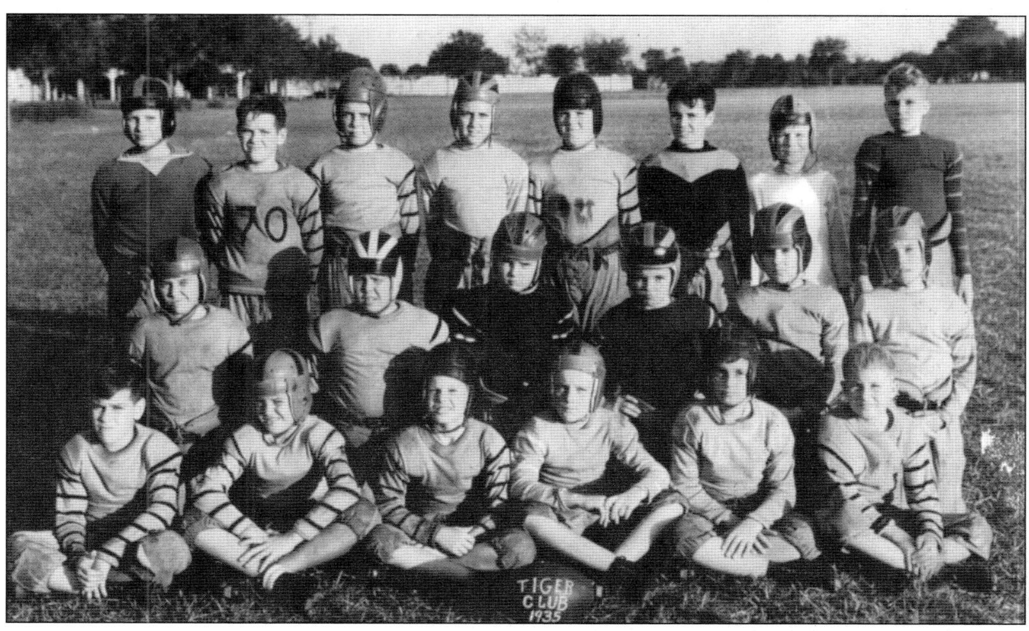

These 1935 Junior Tigers pose on Daffin's green space closest to Washington Avenue. Municipal Stadium (in the background) was the predecessor to Grayson Stadium. (Courtesy of the Garis family.)

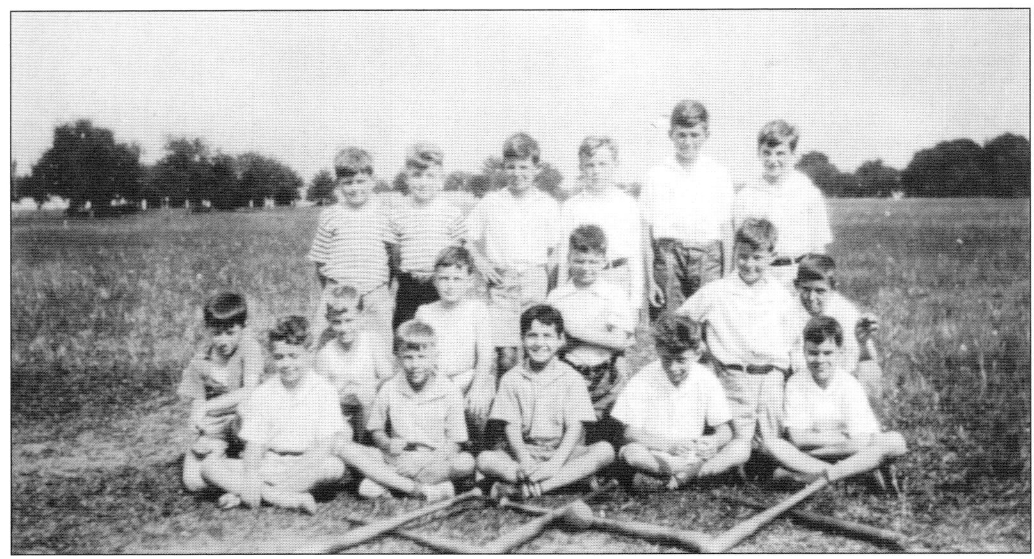

The Tiger Club was organized in 1933 by R.M. Demere with a membership of 30 boys and Fred Garis as director. This is an early softball team posing in Daffin Park, where the boys practiced. Notice how small the oak trees are in the background. Some of the oaks came from Ossabaw Island. (Courtesy of the Garis family.)

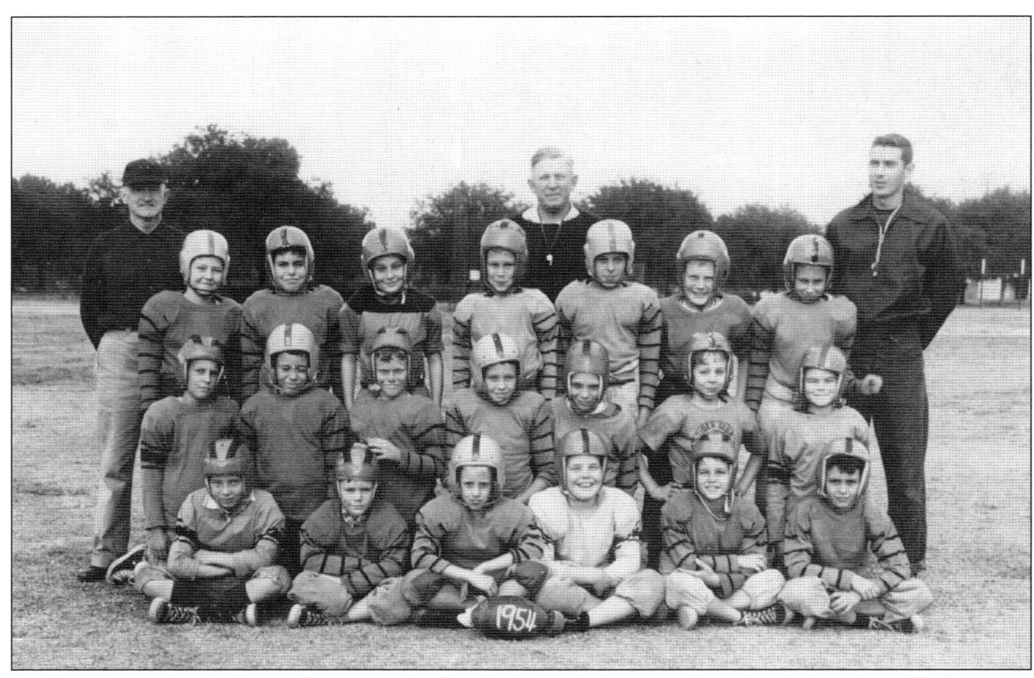

A 1954 Tigers football squad poses in Daffin Park. Fred Garis and his family lived on Washington Avenue, and the location could not have been more perfect for Garis, who only had to walk across the street to watch his Tigers practice. (Courtesy of the Garis family.)

Fred Garis moved to Savannah from Charleston, South Carolina, in the 1920s when he accepted a position with the YMCA on Bull and Charlton Streets. He was a founding member of the Greater Savannah Athletic Hall of Fame and was inducted into the hall in 1969. Former Tigers remember him as a kind man who had a great impact on their lives. (Courtesy of the Garis family.)

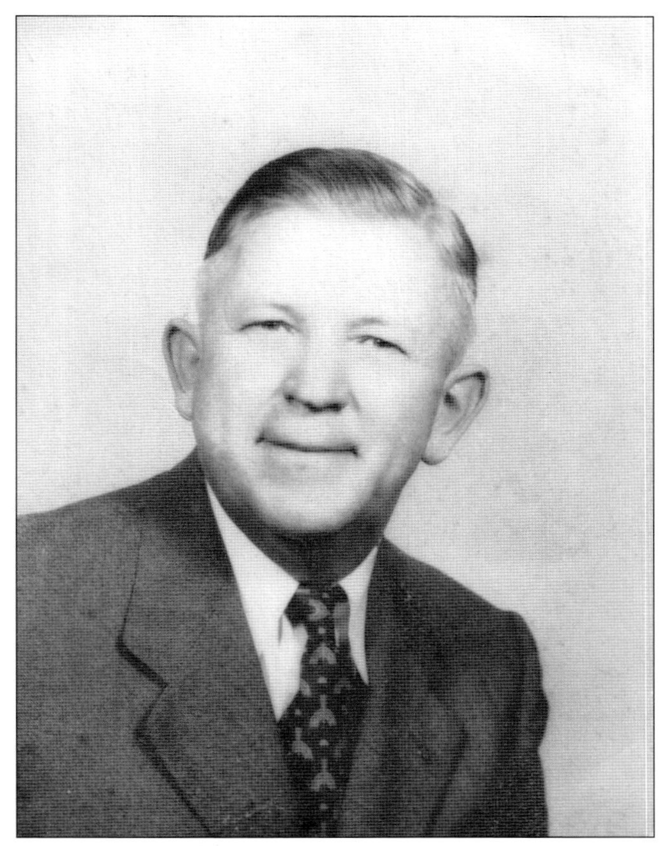

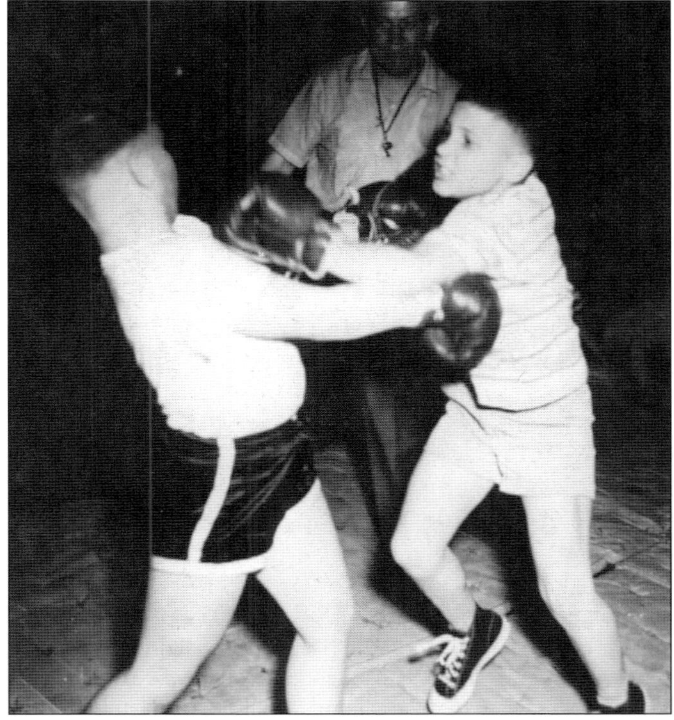

In addition to playing football and tennis, members of the Tiger Club also could try their hands at boxing. This picture was taken during the 1950s, with Fred Garis as referee. (Courtesy of the Garis family.)

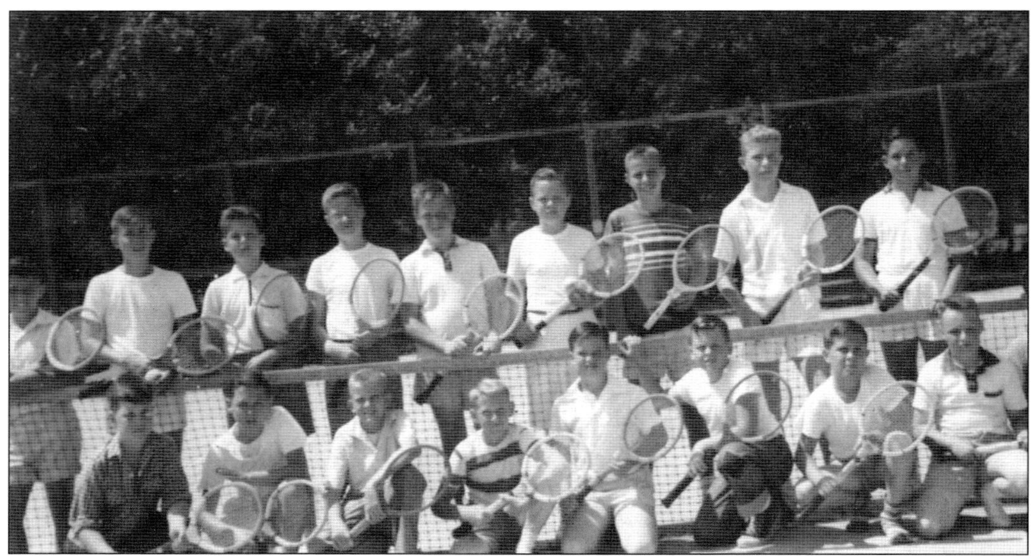

The Tiger Club also encouraged boys to play tennis. This picture shows a few players ready with their rackets. Julian Sipple is at far right in the second row. (Courtesy of the Garis family.)

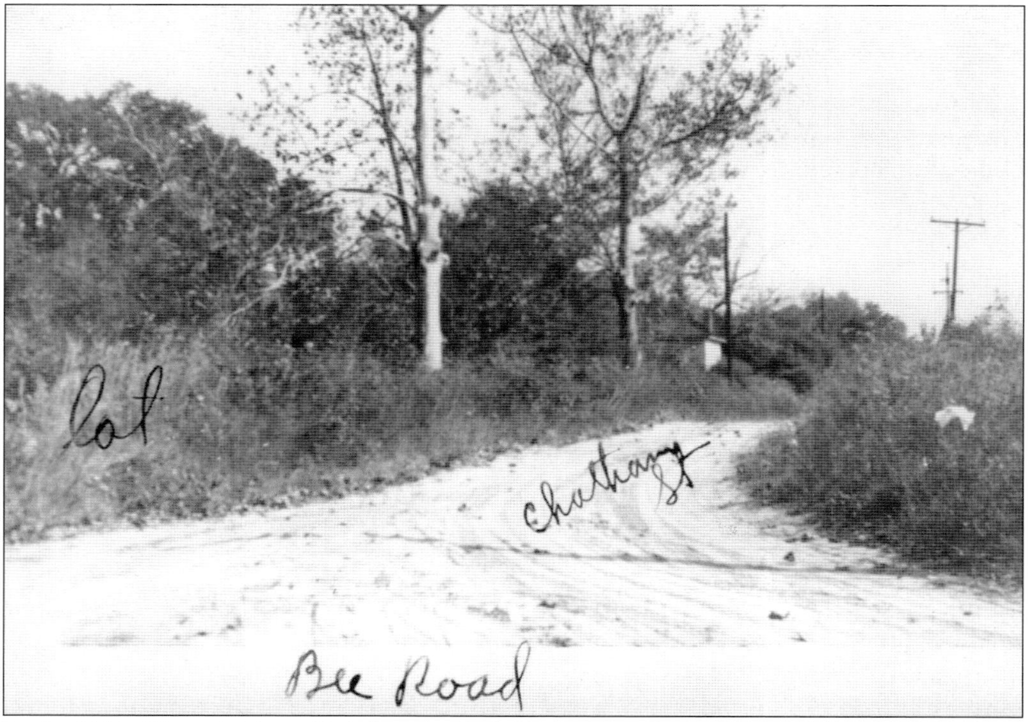

In the 1950s, Tiger Athletic Club founder Fred Garis mapped out what would become the Tiger gym and roller-skating rink on Bee Road across from Herty Park at Daffin Park. His handwriting can be seen on this photograph. (Courtesy of the Garis family.)

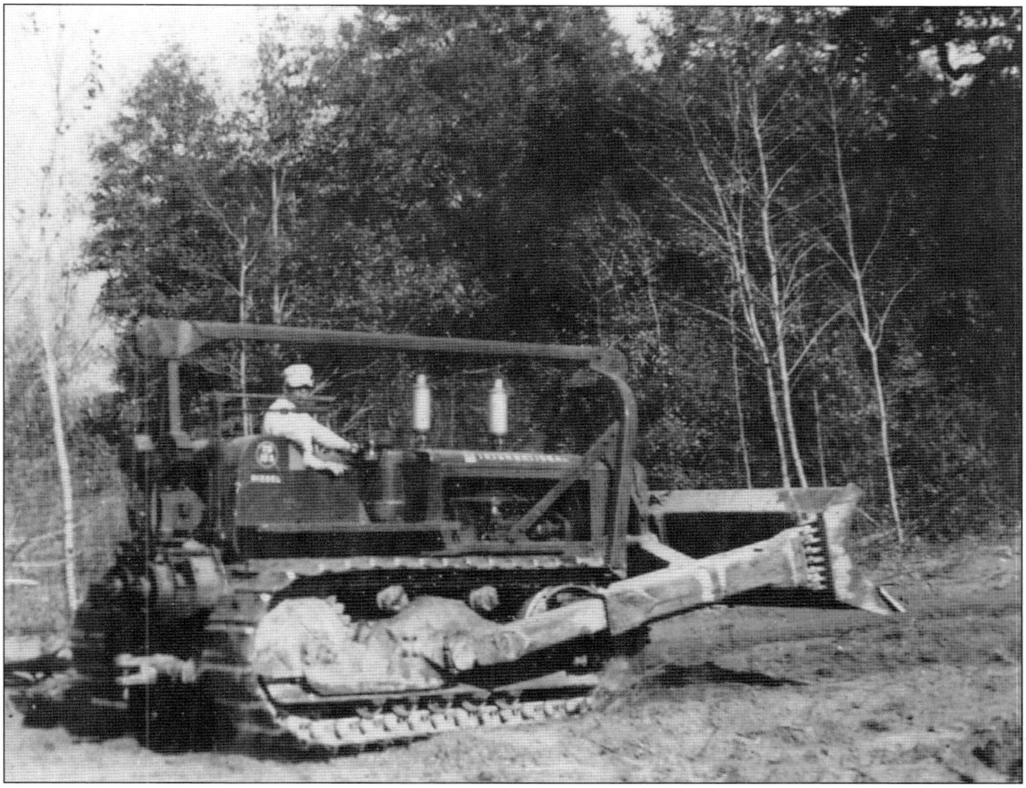

A bulldozer operator clears land on Bee Road near Washington Avenue, where a gym was eventually built for the Tiger Athletic Club. The land was acquired in 1953 by Tiger director Fred Garis, who wore many hats, including that of fundraiser. (Courtesy of the Garis family.)

A 1954 building fund organized by the Tiger Athletic Club was for the purpose of building the Bee Road gym. This flyer explains that "games within the club are a means of teaching sportsmanship, a desire to win and learning to play with others (which is one of the club's biggest contributions to the boys). Acquaintances made in the Tiger Club as boys develop into real, lasting friendships." (Courtesy of the Garis family.)

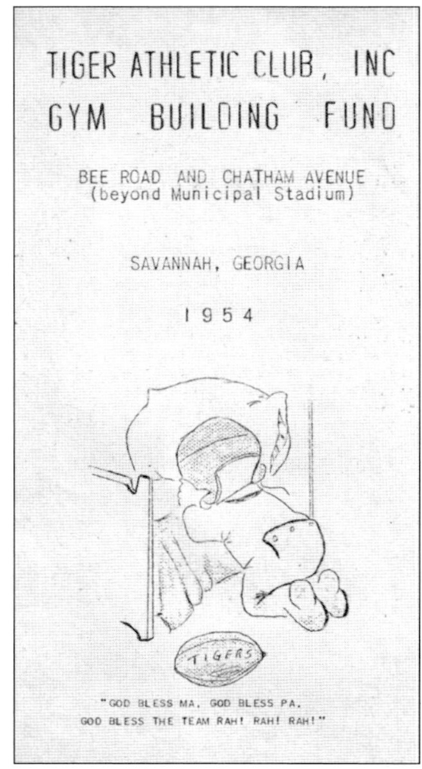

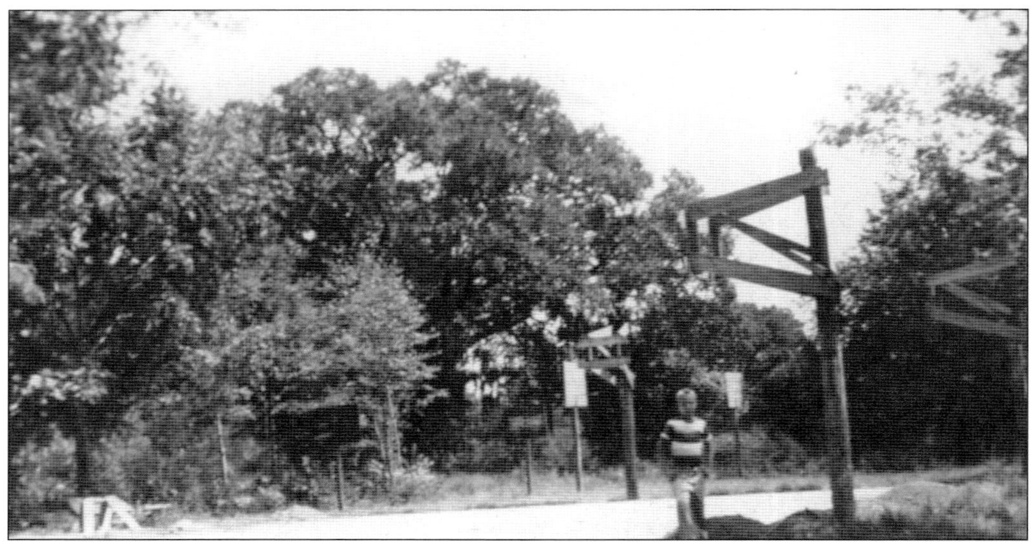

After the Tigers' Bee Road lot was cleared, concrete was poured for outdoor basketball courts, shown here. A photograph in the January 9, 1954, *Savannah Evening Press* showed several boys making full use of the courts, which had wooden goals. The newspaper caption read, "This From a Wilderness." (Courtesy of the Garis family.)

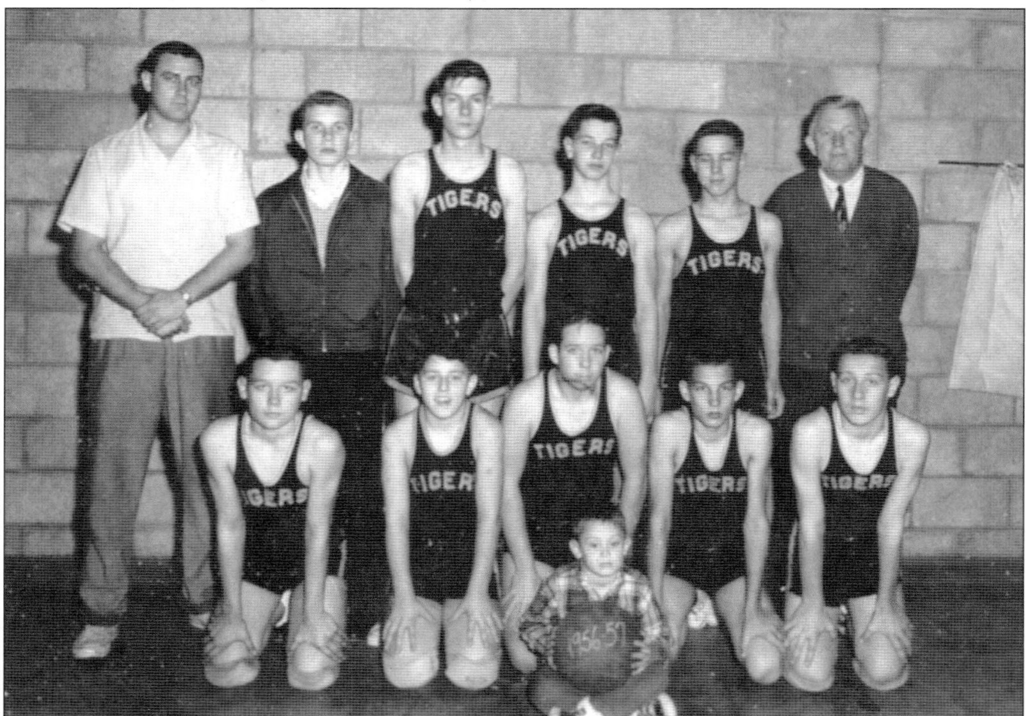

When the Tiger Club gym was built on Bee Road, the boys finally had a permanent home for basketball games. This 1956–1957 team included, from left to right, (first row) Dickie Knight, Walter Garvin, Julian Sipple, unidentified, and Tony Mesaras; (second row) coach Bill "Kowboy" Campbell, Fred Vetter, Pat Kleinpeter, Billy Kleinpeter, Matt Miller, and coach Fred Garis. The little boy holding the basketball is unidentified. Rick Belford, who lived nearby, said Garis paid him 50¢ a week to clean the gym floors with sawdust and linseed oil. (Courtesy of the Garis family.)

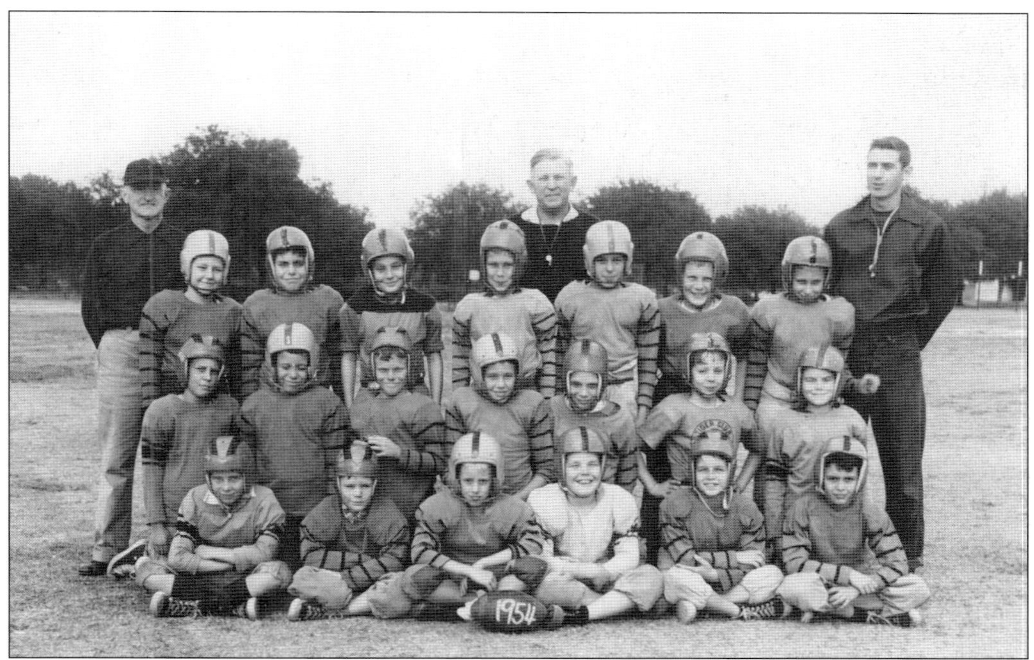

Boys on the 1954 Tiger Athletic Club team wore old-school helmets. Director Fred Garis is at center in the rear, and Bill "Kowboy" Campbell is the coach on the right. Campbell acquired the nickname "Kowboy" because he was bowlegged, his daughter said. (Courtesy of the Garis family.)

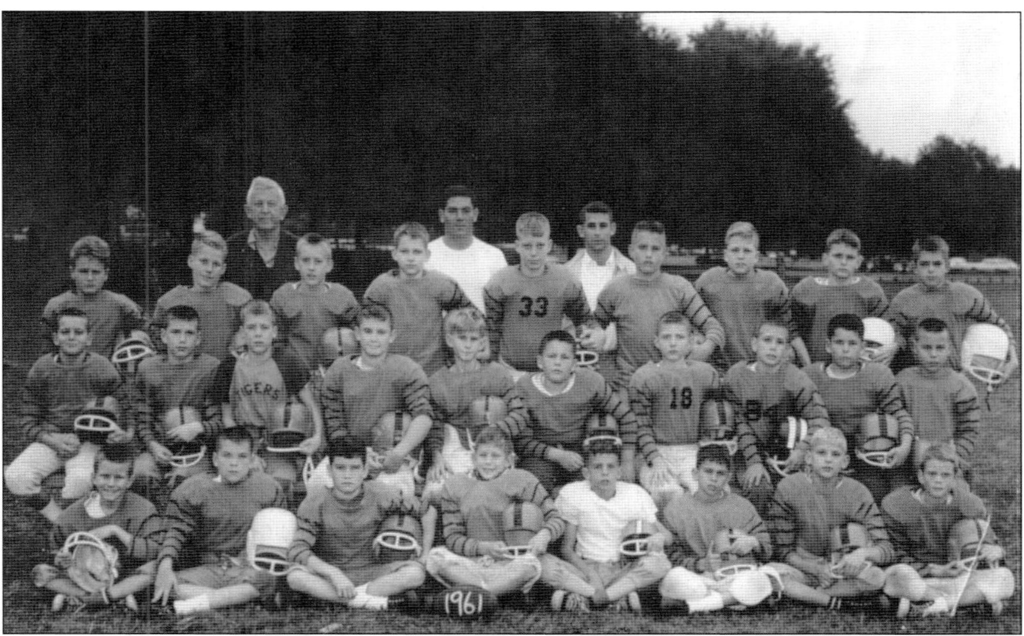

Players on the 1961 Tigers team are, from left to right, (first row) Tommy Adams, Scott Connolly, Strud Blun, two unidentified, Chip Robertson, Robbie DePue, and John Lyons; (second row) Walter Dasher, unidentified, Lee Page, Richard Sears, five unidentified, and Frank Streiff; (third row) Frank McNeal, Freeman Wright, unidentified, Tommy Gilbert, Jim Lynah, Claiborne Lewis, Billy McIntosh, unidentified, and Jimbo Walker. (Courtesy of the Garis family.)

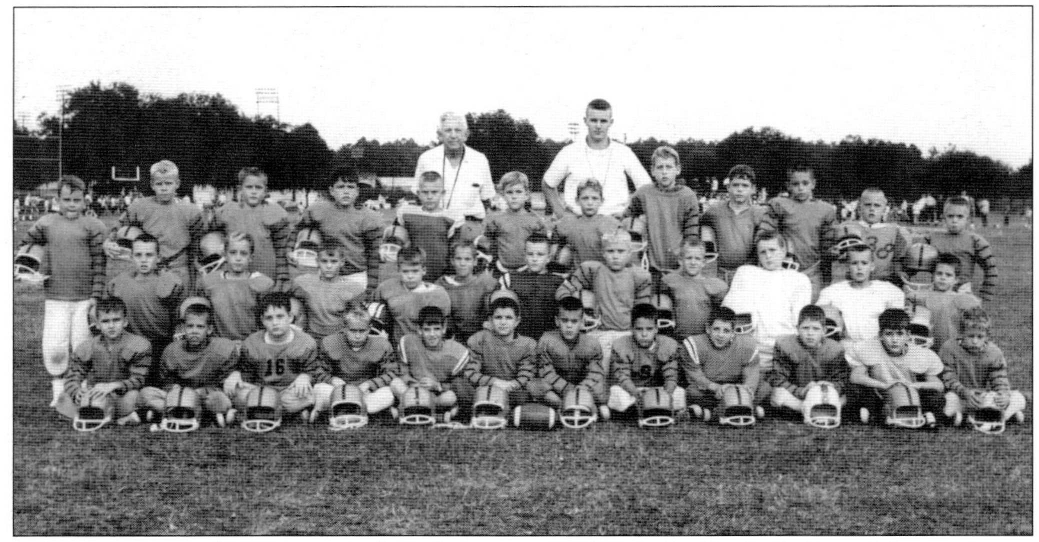

More Tigers from the early 1960s had their picture taken in Daffin Park. From left to right are (first row) Carl Roebling, four unidentified, Bill Tullis, Mike Bousquet, Neil Mingledorff, two unidentified, Buzzy Brennan, and Randy Ormond; (second row) unidentified, Reece Shellman, Kirk Schwalbe, Steve Schirm, Howard Reeve, unidentified, Frank McTeer, Billy Kehoe, and three unidentified; (third row) T. Stanley, Steve Harris, Chuck Sipple, Henry Morgan, unidentified, Tommy Adams, Chip Compton, Cooper Stults, Cooper Glenn, Harvey Granger, Spanky Schley, and Dennis Pierce. (Courtesy of the Garis family.)

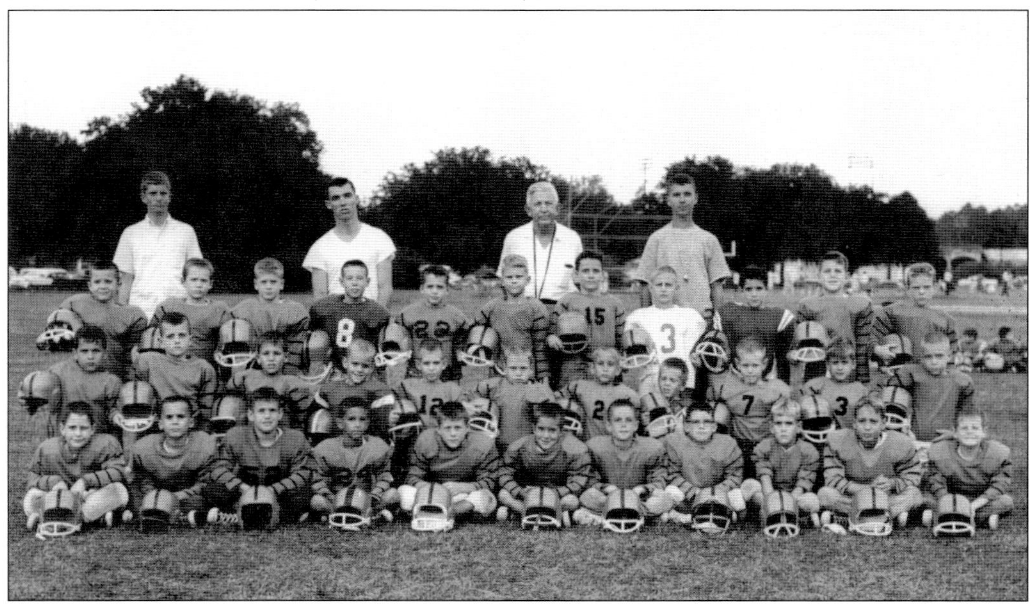

These Tigers had their picture taken in the early 1960s in Daffin Park. From left to right are (first row) Ricky Traub, Harry Howard, three unidentified, Brother Logan, Matt Granger, Ronnie Knight, two unidentified, and John Angell; (second row) Mark Hollingsworth, two unidentified, Stephen Lee, Mark Smith, George Mercer, Beaver Felton, unidentified, Bill Robertson, Hugh Papy, and Mike Alberino; (third row) unidentified, Lee Sparkman, Lawrence McGoldrick, unidentified, Wesley Espy, Tom Stalvey, Lloyd Hopkins, Ray Rogers, Bobby Adler, and two unidentified. The coaches are unidentified except for Fred Garis, second from right. (Courtesy of the Garis family.)

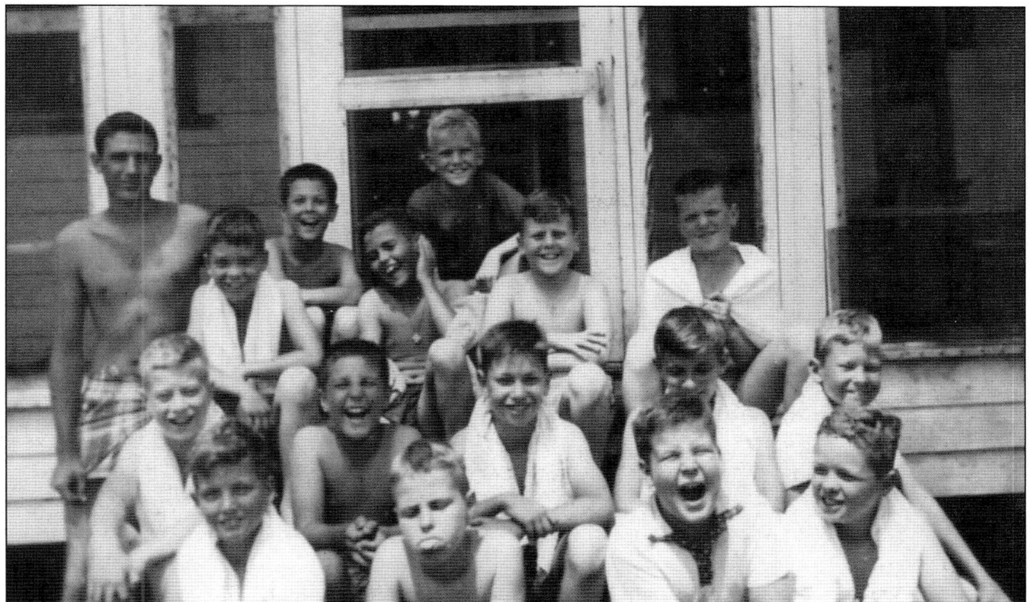

During the summer, the Tigers took time off from practice in Daffin Park to go to the beach for a bit of rest and relaxation. The Garis family's Tybee Island camp for Tigers was known as SABECA (an acronym for Savannah Beach Camp). These boys posing for a picture during the 1950s at SABECA certainly look like they are having loads of fun. At the very top is Harrell Murray. In the second row at center with a towel around his neck is Billy Kleinpeter. (Courtesy of the Garis family.)

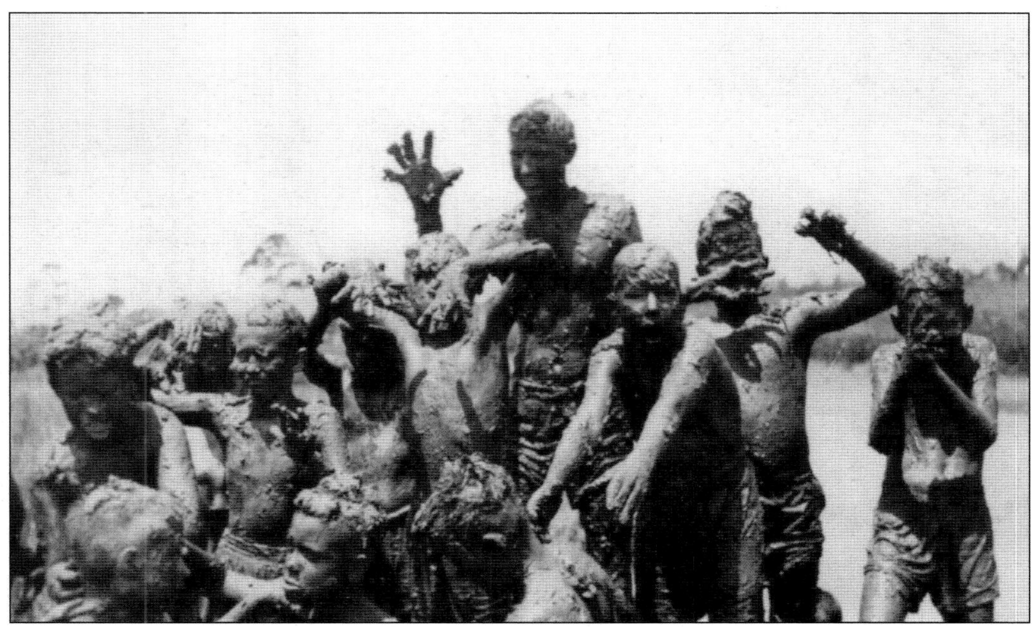

At SABECA, which was off Jones Street near its intersection with Eighth Street, Tiger Club boys swam, dropped crab lines, and played in the saltwater creek behind the facility. This c. 1950s photograph shows the boys letting loose in the muddy waters. (Courtesy of the Garis family.)

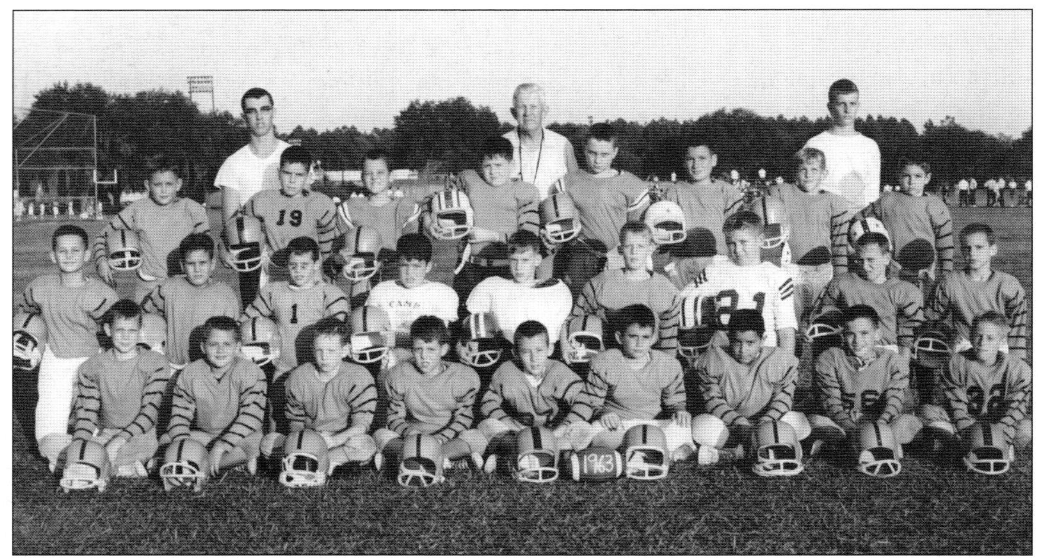

Some of these 1963 Tigers look as if they were reluctant to have their pictures taken. From left to right are (first row) Kenny McDonald, unidentified, Duncan Pindar, Philip Morgan, Corky Jones, Wip McCuen, unidentified, Kirk Victor, and unidentified; (second row) unidentified, Lee Adler, Earl Dempsey: Henry Morgan, three unidentified, George Patterson, and unidentified; (third row) unidentified, Bernard Doyle, unidentified, Frank Arden, Bill Lattimore, Brian Nagy, possibly Tommy Adams, and George Mingledorff. (Courtesy of the Garis family.)

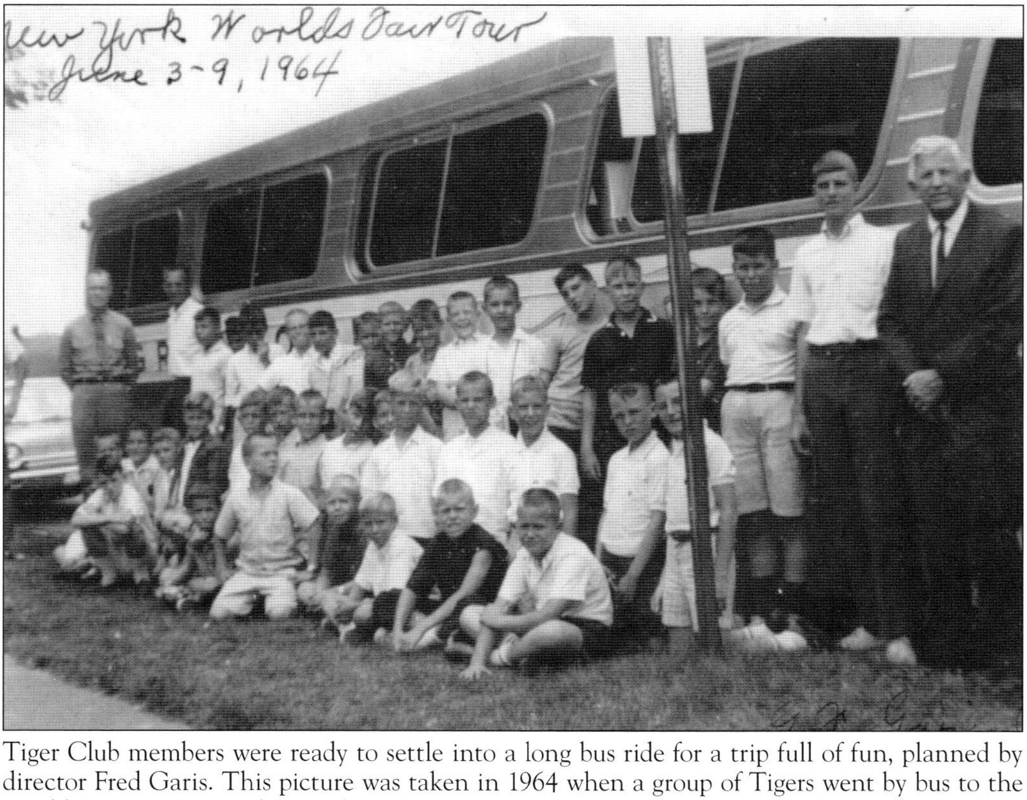

Tiger Club members were ready to settle into a long bus ride for a trip full of fun, planned by director Fred Garis. This picture was taken in 1964 when a group of Tigers went by bus to the World's Fair in New York City. (Courtesy of the Garis family.)

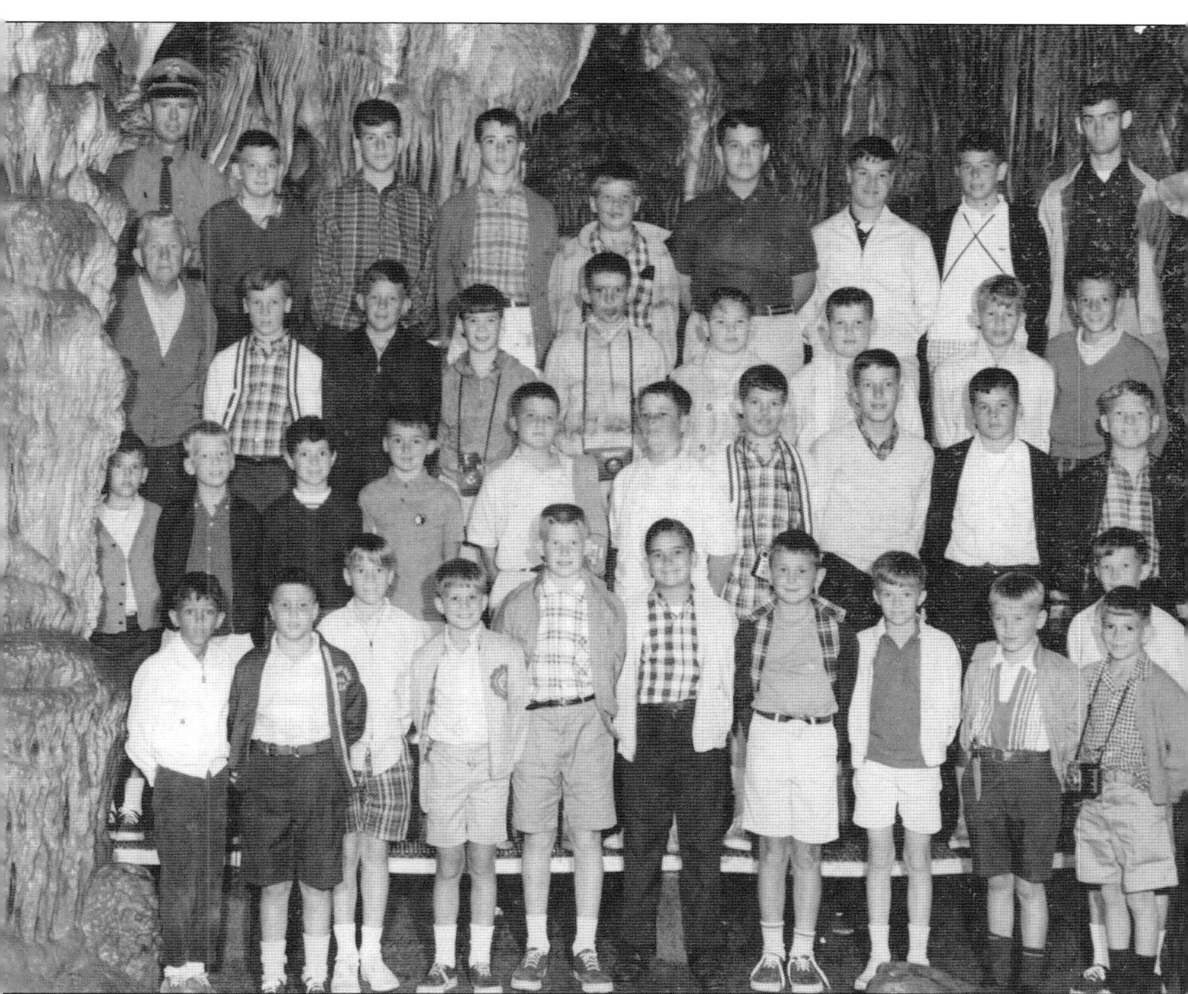

In addition to playing sports, the boys in the Tiger Athletic Club went on trips that were meticulously planned by club director Fred Garis. This 1965 photograph was taken when some of the Tigers visited the caverns of Luray, Virginia, en route to New York City. From left to right are (first row) Matt Sanders, David Jelks, Howard Reeve, Billy Winburn, Tim Harriott, Steve Hester, Sherrod Patterson, Edward Brown, Harry King, Mark Smith, and Lloyd Brown; (second row) Bobby Buechner, Campbell Coxe, Thomas Scardino, Carl Roebling Jr., Alan Williams, Matt Barfield, Walter Lewis, Gregg Propst, Billy Mordecai, and Thomas Coxe; (third row) Garis, Curtis Lewis III, Bill Campbell, Ricky Timms, Frank Durkin, Will Burgstiner, Millard Long, Kirk Campbell, and Billy Bond; (fourth row) bus driver C.B. Cox, Gene Brogdon, Bruce Ladson, Tommy Bond, Olin McIntosh, Howard Smith, Tony Fine, Ricky Buechner, and Ford Ewaldsen. (Courtesy of the Garis family.)

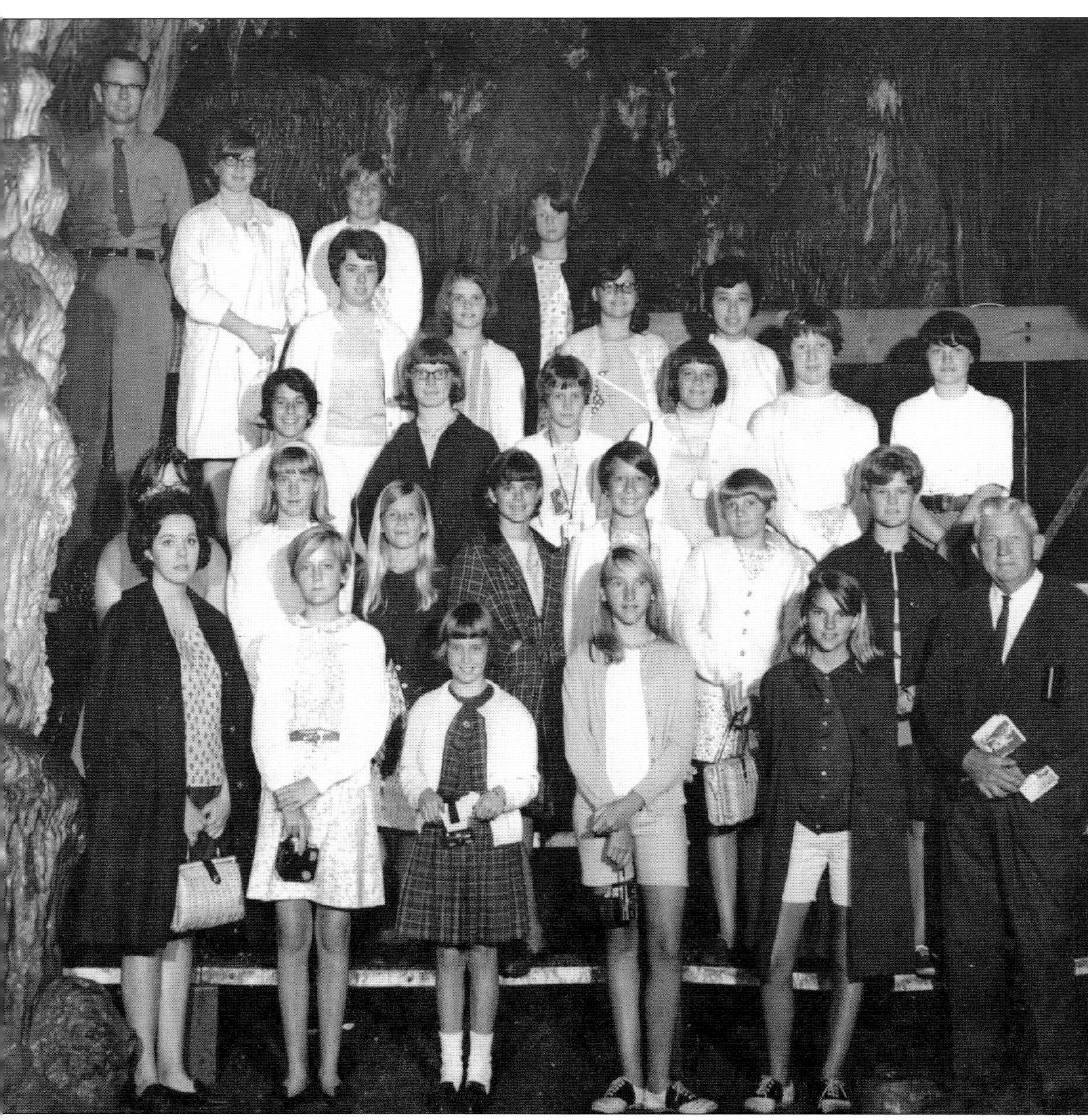

In the summer of 1967, Tiger Club director Fred Garis planned the first girls' trip. From left to right are (first row) Marsha Miller, Judy Daniel, Helen Lynah, Debra Williams, Cindy Sanders, and Garis; (second row) Monica Logsdon, Cindy Saunders, Marie Powers, Nancy Skipper, Carolyn Rudd, Bessie Mercer, and Caroline Sparks; (third row) Debbie Oelsner, Jan Peterson, Donna Jones, Bonnie Mileski, Kay Lynah, and Edith Nichols; (fourth row) Carol Cox, Marcea West, Anne Roebling, and Nancy Chiles; (fifth row) bus driver C.B. Cox, Peggy Davidson, Lysa Dixon, and Lynda McGinty. (Courtesy of Donna Jones Tuten.)

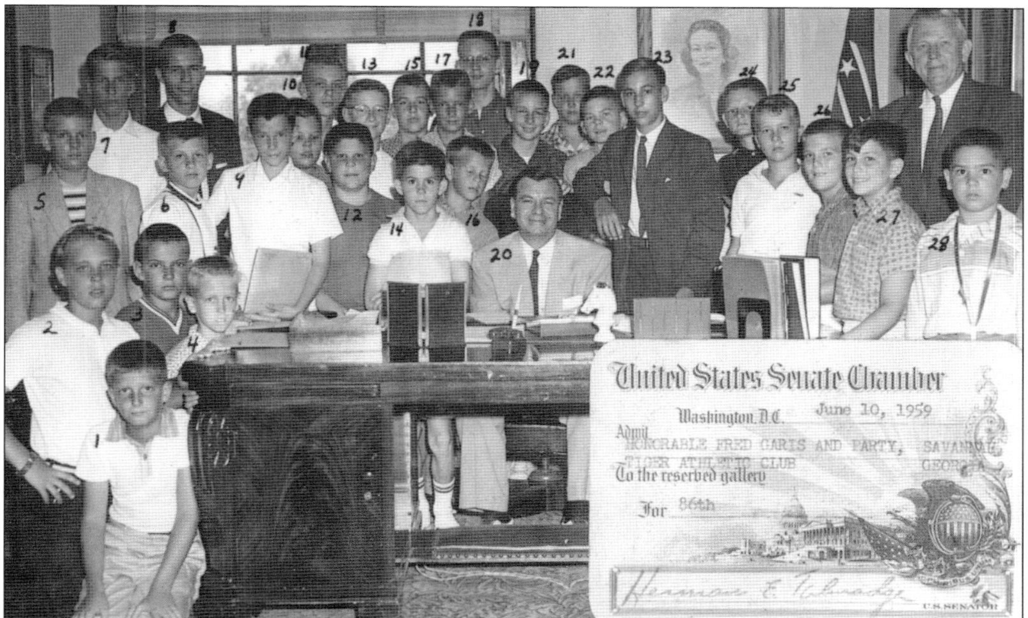

This picture was taken in the Washington, DC, office of US senator Herman Talmadge during a Tiger Club trip. One of the boys remembers the cost being $100 for the bus, lodging, food, and fees. Each boy could bring $10 spending money, which Garis portioned out each day. Pictured are 1. Chuck Davis, 2. Roby Hester, 3. Lee Belford, 4. Harry Bowyer, 5. Jackie Miller, 6. Marion Dantzler, 7. Bobby Bowyer, 8. Fred Garis Jr., 9. Jay Bradley, 10. Brinson Williams, 11. Ron Newman, 12. Bernie Slotin, 13. Robert Shuman, 14. Edward Schirm, 15. David Elmore, 16. Bobby Groves, 17. Ricky Belford, 18. Leiston Shuman, 19. Jimmy Heidt, 20. Senator Talmadge, 21. Grady Overstreet, 22. Barrett Benton, 23. Frank McGee, 24. Peter Hendry, 25. Johnny Hoffman, 26. Randy Dasher, 27. Ricky Segall, 28. Tommy Hollngsworth, and 29. Fred Garis. (Courtesy of the Garis family.)

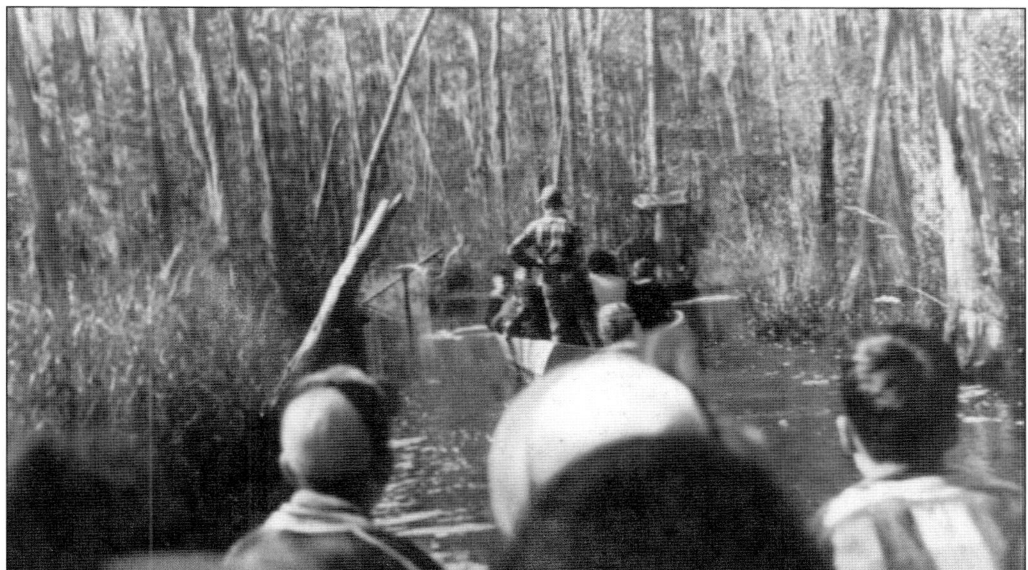

The Tigers also took short trips throughout the state of Georgia. This picture was taken during an excursion to the Okefenokee Swamp, nicknamed the "Land of the Trembling Earth," outside of Waycross. (Courtesy of the Garis family.)

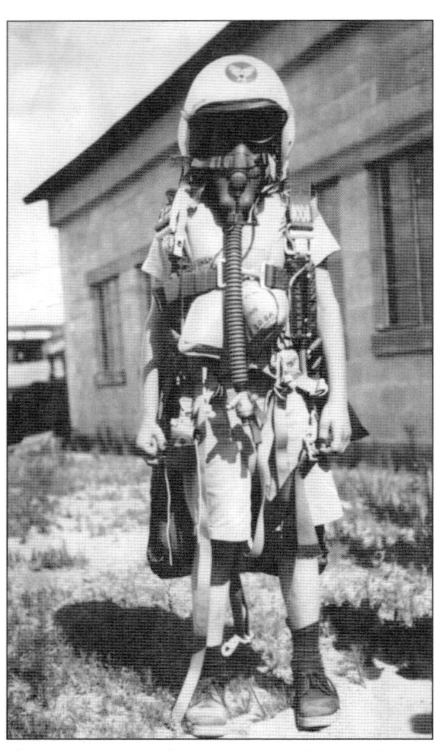

This little member of the Tiger Club tried on a US Air Force pilot's helmet and parachute during the late 1950s outside of the Tiger Gym on Bee Road. (Courtesy of the Garis family.)

In the early 1970s, Chris Beckmann, Charles Seiler, and Gifford Usher proudly show off their Tiger Club awards presented by club director Fred Garis. Garis died in 1979 and is buried in Savannah's Hillcrest Abbey East Cemetery. (Courtesy of Sonny Seiler.)

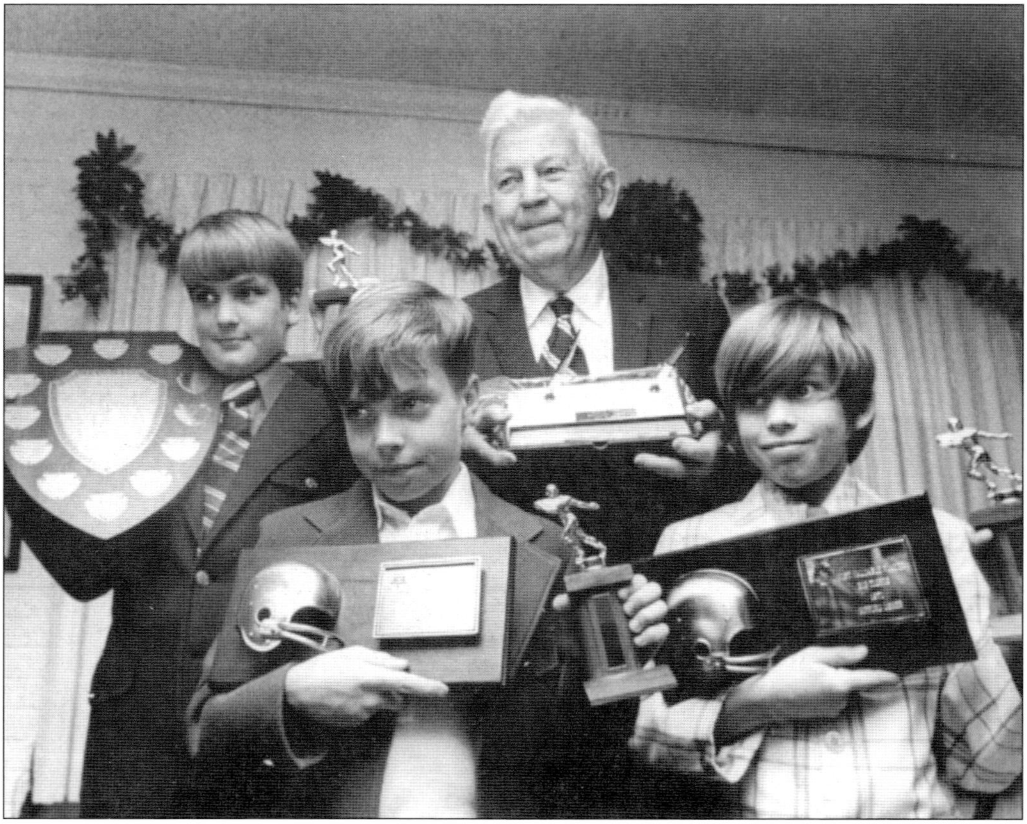

Four

THE PANTHERS AND WILDCATS

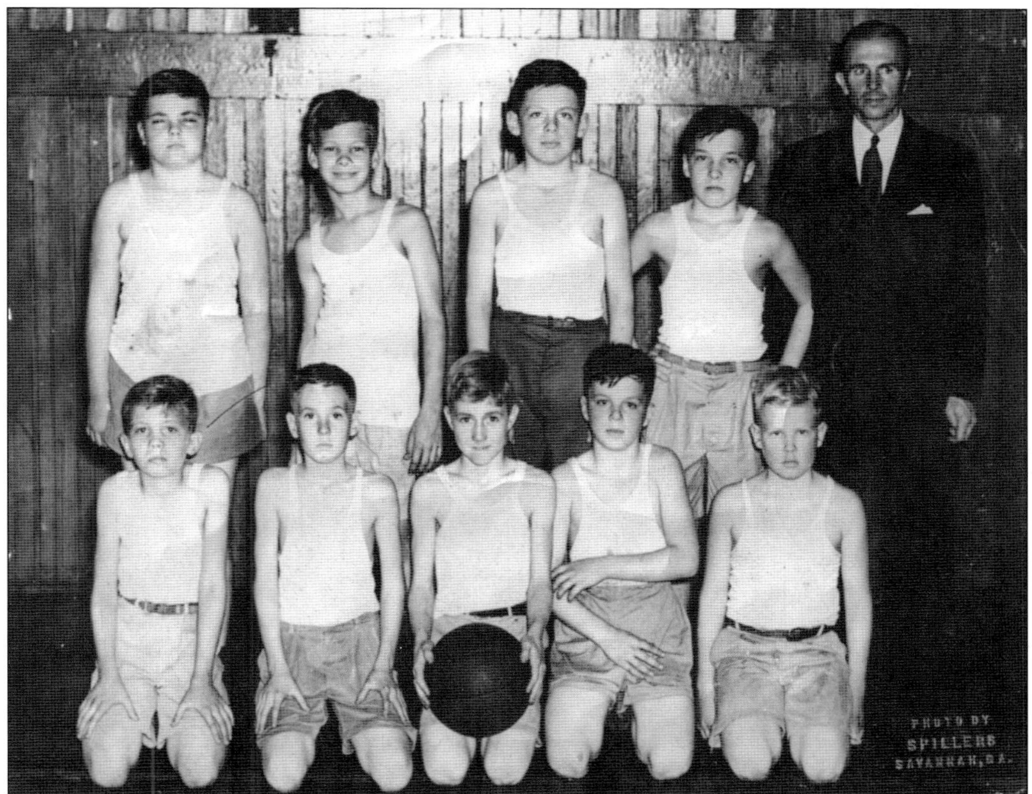

The first Panthers team was organized in 1944–1945 by Tom Moore to rival the Tiger Athletic Club with football, basketball, and other sports for boys ages 10 to 14. In this picture of that Panthers team, from left to right are (first row) unidentified, Alex Lawrence Jr., Cuyler Cline, Melvin Adler, and Norton Black; (second row) Walter Muller, Stetson Fleming, Richard Norsworthy, Sonny Seiler, and Tom Moore. (Courtesy of Sonny Seiler.)

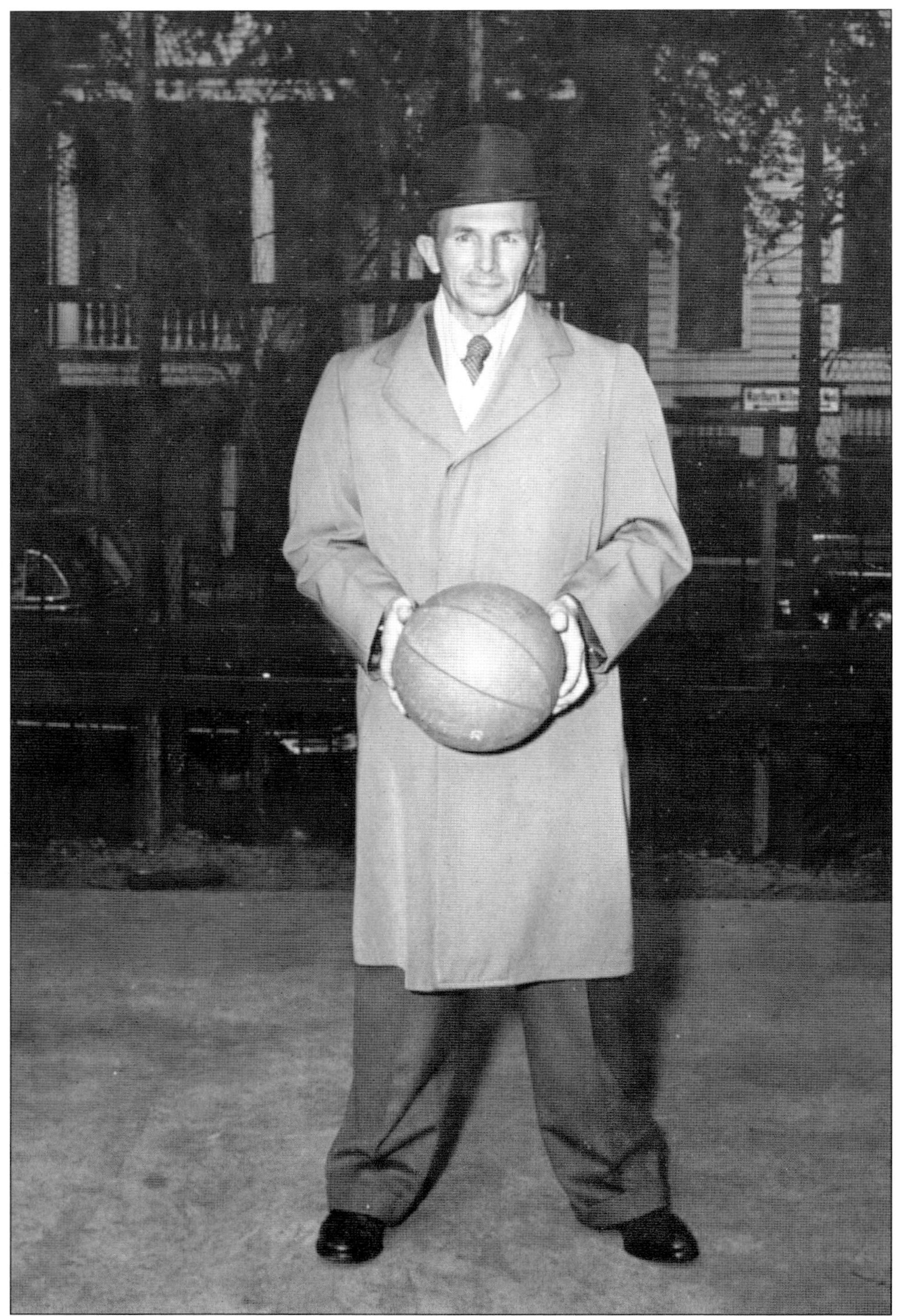

Panther director Tom Moore grew up at Bethesda Home for Boys and had a special place in his heart for youth. He coached the Panthers from 1940 until around 1970 and the Pantherettes beginning in 1951. This picture of Moore was taken in the early 1950s in front of the Pape School in downtown Savannah. (Courtesy of the Sims family.)

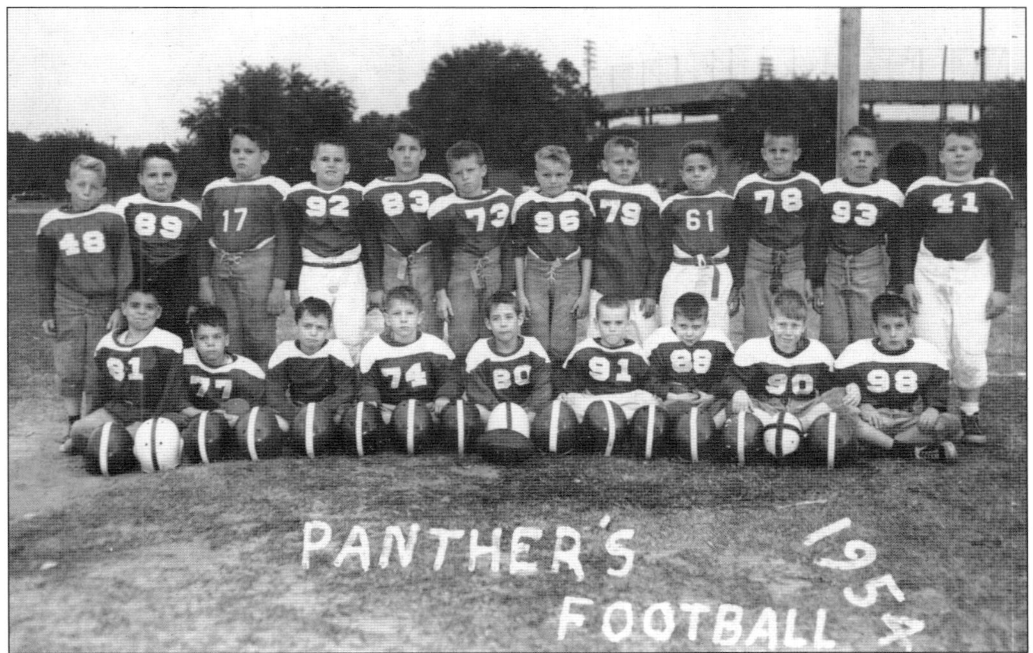

This 1954 Panthers football squad was photographed in front of Grayson Stadium in Daffin Park. From left to right are (first row) Wick Ashburn, Pat Kennedy, unidentified, Joe Saffold, Joe Inglesby, Hollis Puckett, Danny Brown, and two unidentified; (second row) Morton Wright, Robert Constantine, Ralph Kennickell, Corky Fleming, unidentified, Raddie Zittrauer, Bill Harris, unidentified, Steve Harris, Bill Canady, unidentified, and Randy Winburn. (Courtesy of the Sims family.)

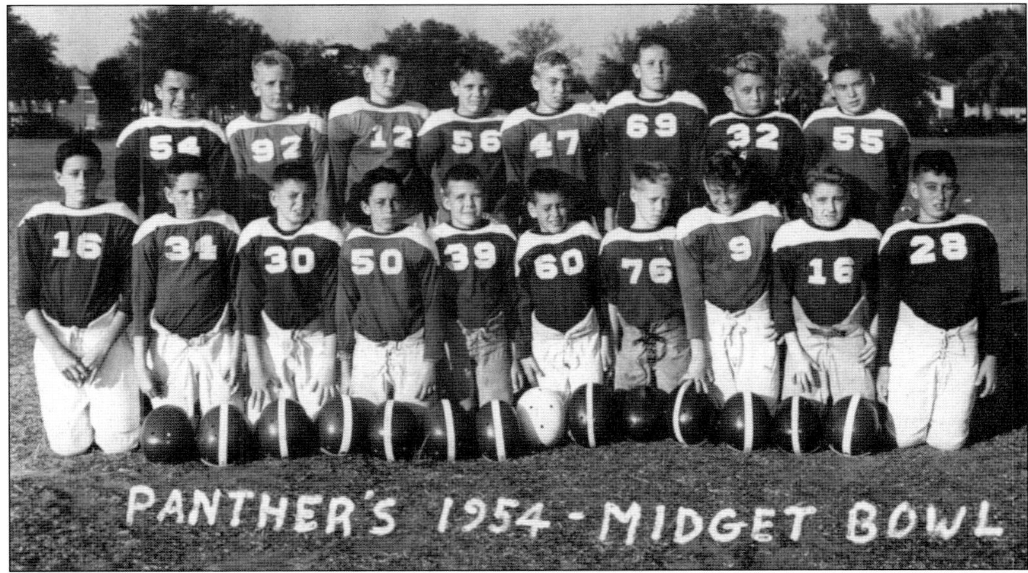

This 1954 Panthers football team advanced to the Midget Bowl, which was a tournament sometimes played in Waycross. From left to right are (first row) two unidentified, Ricky Smith, Jimmy Logan, Bill Ellis, unidentified, Harry Hitch, unidentified, Ray Chamberlain, and Danny Falligant; (second row) Jim Kelley, John Fishback, Charlie Westerfield, Fred Sullivan, Carl Jackson, and three unidentified. (Courtesy of the Sims family.)

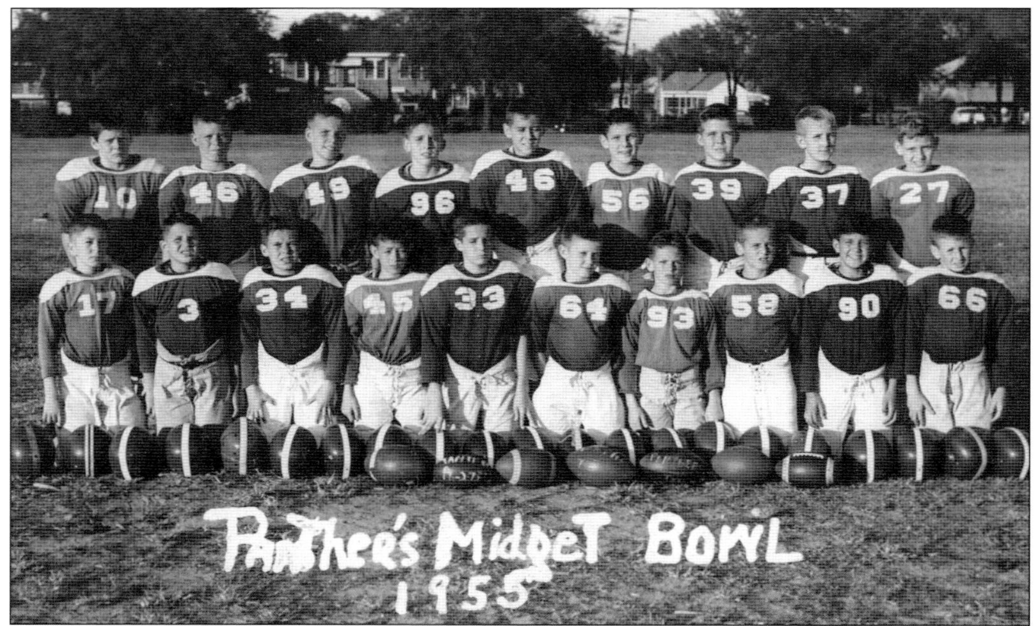

Daffin Park is the backdrop for this 1955 picture, which shows Victory Drive and the Triple X Thirst Station above the head of the boy wearing No. 39. From left to right are (first row) Mike Brannen, Richard Berry, unidentified, Billy Jones, G. Olmstead, Arthur Frapps, Bubba Linton, Lukie Sims, D. Platt, and Randy Zittrauer; (second row) Murray Marshall, Paul Hansen, Ken Young, Lane Hatcher, Ray Chamberlain, Fred Sullivan, Bill Ellis, Johnny Fishback, and B. Berry. (Courtesy of the Sims family.)

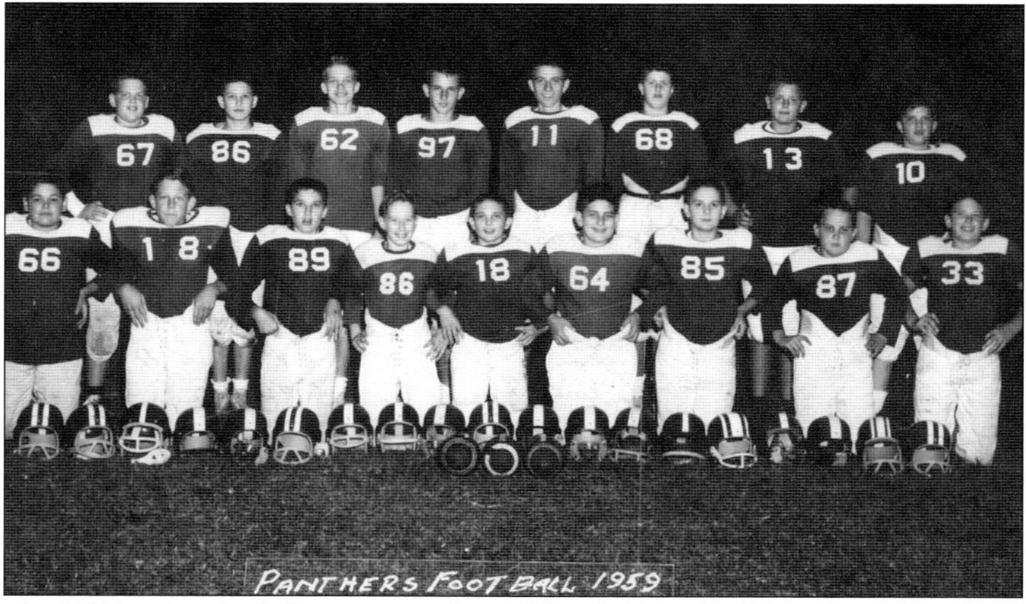

This 1959 Panthers football team was made up of, from left to right, (first row) Brooks Stillwell, Ken Burke, Spencer Dempsey, Robert Fennell, Mike Smith, Allen Tenenbaum, Jimmy Clayton, Tommy Christopher, and Steve Smith; (second row) Bert Oelschig, Henry Pruitt, Gary Moore, Eddie Yates, Larry Spell, Johnny Gammert, Jimmy Wiggins, and Larry Purvis. (Courtesy of the Sims family.)

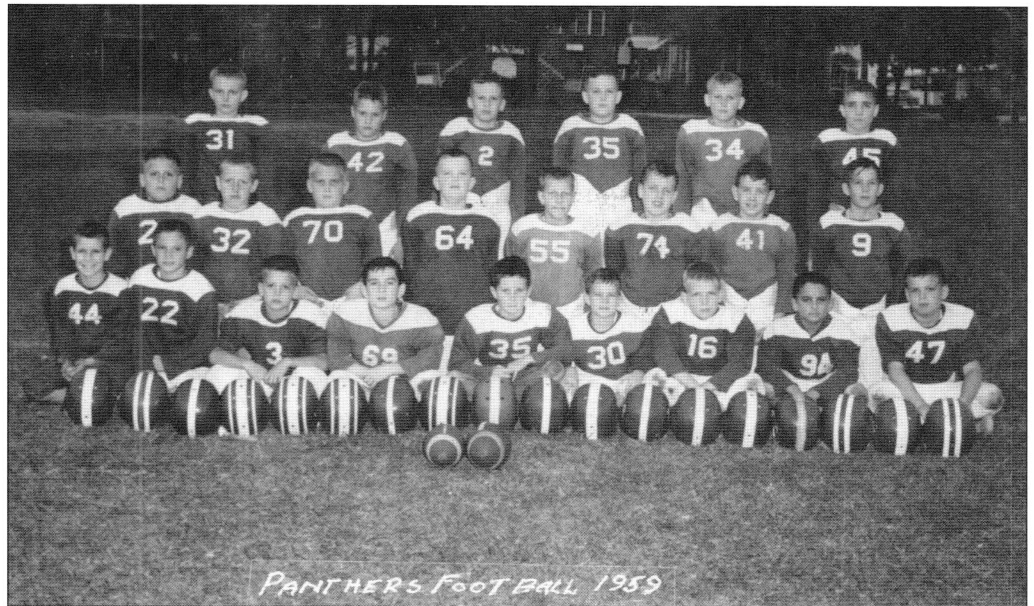

This group of young Panthers poses in Daffin Park near Victory Drive. From left to right are (first row) Johnnie McAleer, Tommy Grayson, David Peterson, Donnie Peveler, Chris Williamson, Robert West, David Vaughn, Bobby Herman, and Stephen Langston; (second row) Johnny Wiggins, Joe Kratzer, Rick Lantz, Joe Pope, Mickey Rountree, David Parker, Steve Willoughby, and Ken Stanford; (third row) Gregg Solms, Bill Sirmon, John Murray, Howard Smith, Clark Perry, and Steve Horton. (Courtesy of the Sims family.)

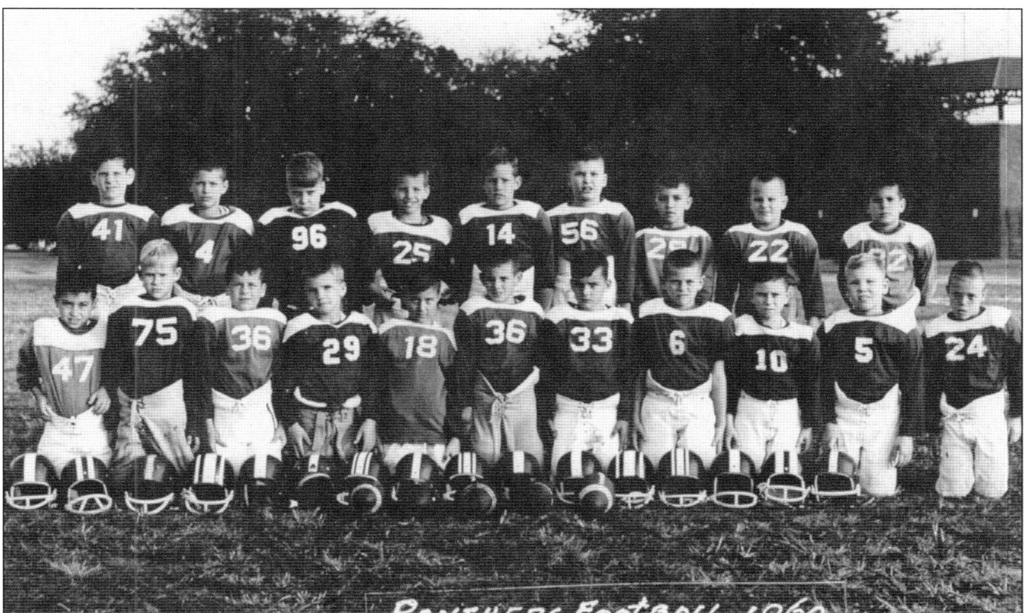

The boys on this 1960 Panthers football team were probably 9 or 10 when this picture was taken in Daffin Park. From left to right are (first row) unidentified, Bobby Freeman, Billy Mordecai, Ken Powers, unidentified, Frank Durkin, Mike Gignilliat, Glenn Hewitt, and three unidentified; (second row) Billy Morrison, Steve Becker, Frank Emile, Bill Caldwell, Ken Rudd, John McElveen, Mark Thomas, Jim Brasfield, and Tommy Myers. (Courtesy of the Sims family.)

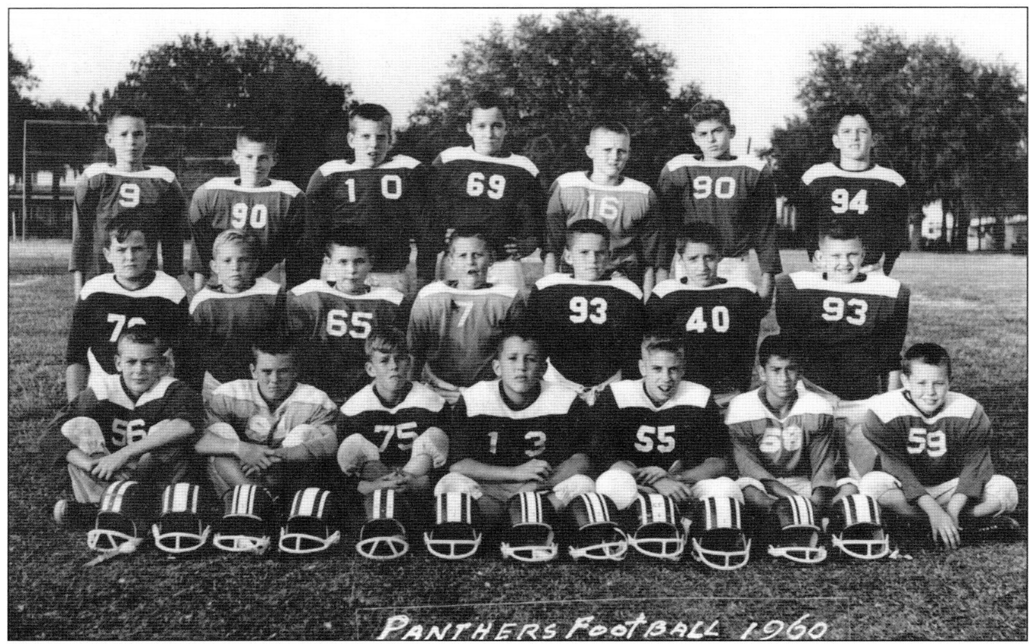

The Panthers Athletic Club was going strong in 1960 and included these older boys. Jim Mathis, who was on this team, says being a Panther is one of his great memories. He said he and his teammates spent many wonderful afternoons at Daffin Park with coaches Tom Moore and Luke Sims. (Courtesy of Jim Mathis.)

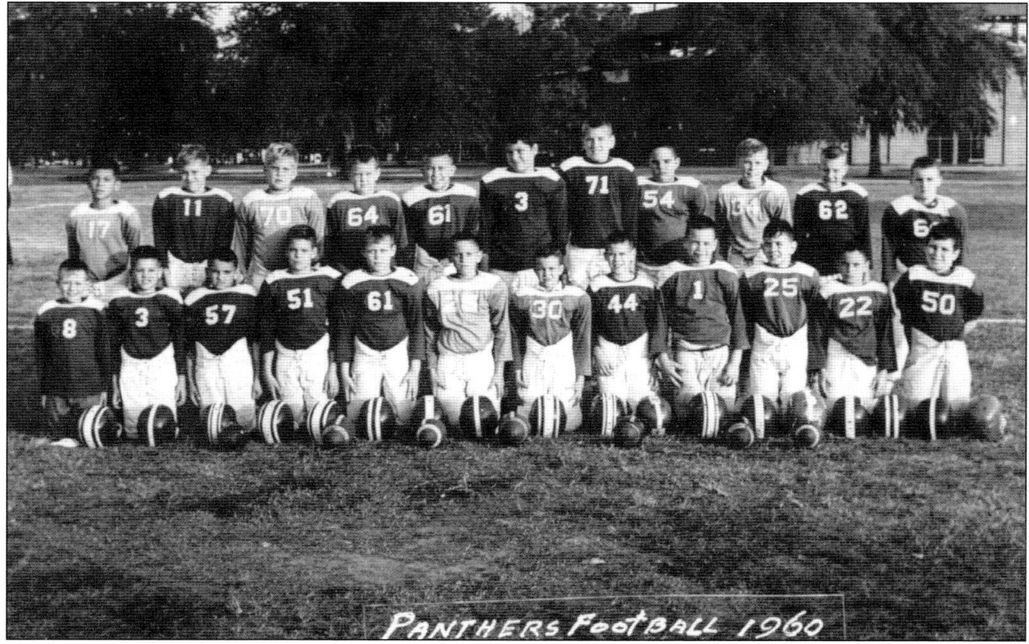

This 1960 Panthers team poses in front of Grayson Stadium. From left to right are (first row) unidentified, David Peterson, Bobby Herman, Bill Baker, Calvin Weeks, Larry Sims, unidentified, possibly John McAleer, unidentified, Steve Willoughby, and two unidentified; (second row) Bill Morgan, unidentified, Rick Lantz, unidentified, Mike Willoughby, two unidentified, Claude Shore, Clark Perry, and two unidentified. (Courtesy of the Sims family.)

These 1962 basketball players are, from left to right, (first row) unidentified, Tommy Freeman, Brent Burroughs, Rickey Epstein, Tommy Bond, and Clark Perry; (second row) Steven Lucie, George Humphries, Calvin Weeks, George Porter, Will Weeks, Jack Sims, Tommy Ewaldsen, and Johnny Thompson. (Courtesy of the Sims family.)

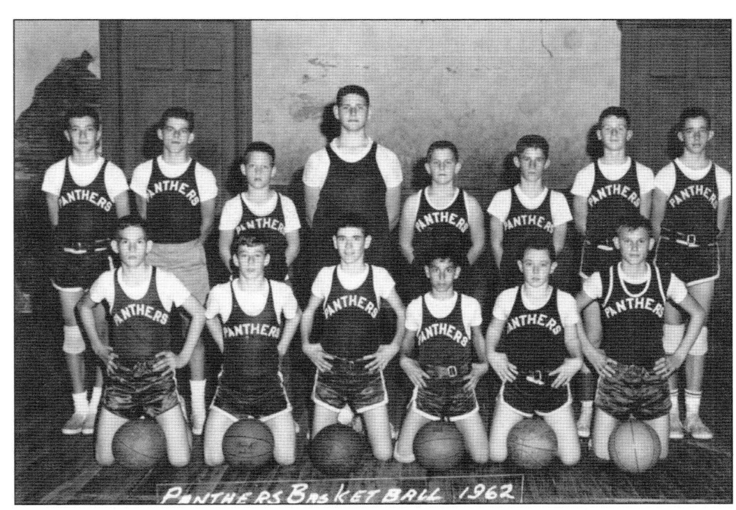

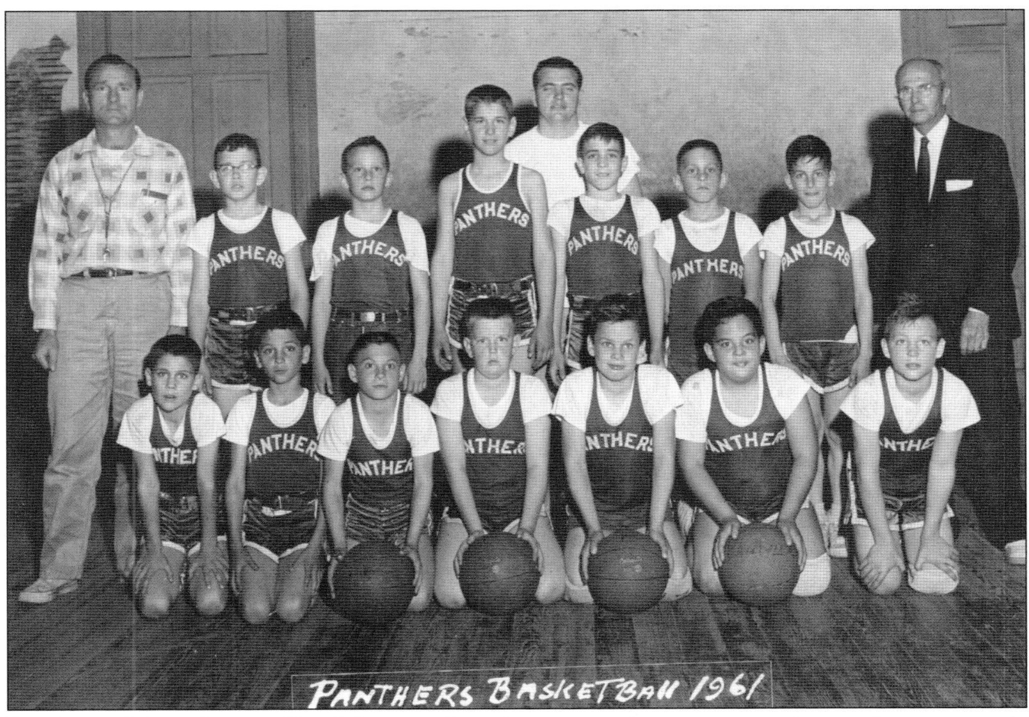

Panthers athletic director Tom Moore, at far right, was not in many team pictures, but apparently he decided to be in this 1961 photograph. From left to right are (first row) John McAleer, George Thomas, Tommy Grayson, Joe Pope, David Hinely, Claude Shore, and Calvin Weeks; (second row) coach Luke Sims, S. Willoughby, John Murray, Norman Fries, Steve Horton, Lukie Sims, and Bennie Eicholz. The coach in the middle is Joe Smith. (Courtesy of the Sims family.)

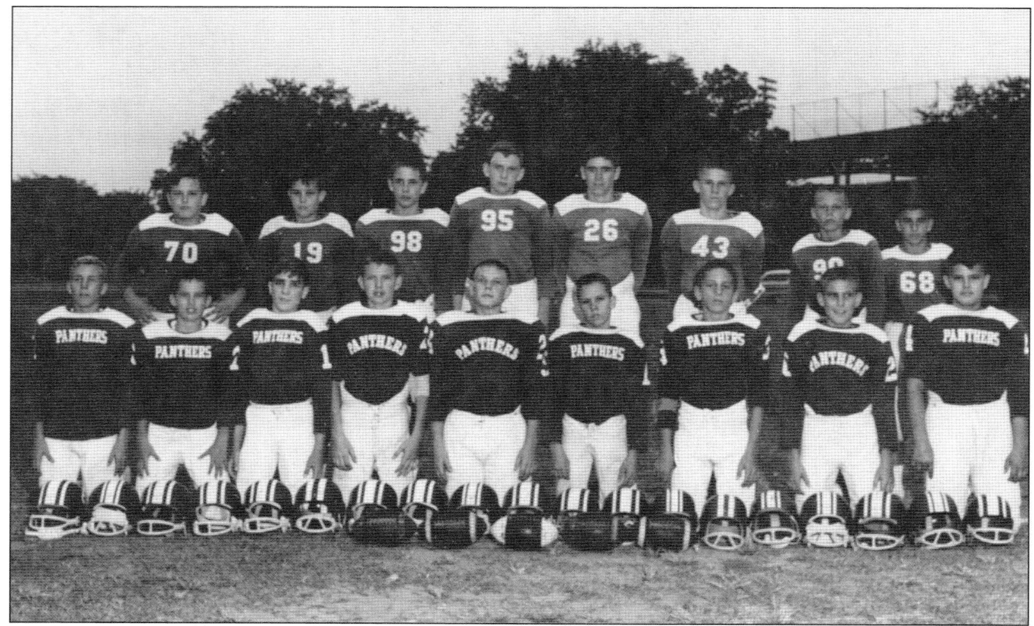

In 1962, the Panthers ages 12–14 football team posted a 16-2 record under the coaching of Tom Moore and Luke Sims. From left to right are (first row) Howard Jarrott, Jim Mayfield, Steve Horton, Al Kelley, David Vaughn, Vic Miltiades, Larry Sims, Philip Yonge, and Charles Broome; (second row) Howard Smith, George Peagler, Jim Mathis, Richard Wilson, Bill Burroughs, Jake Sims, Daryl Walker, and Rickey Epstein. (Courtesy of Jim Mathis.)

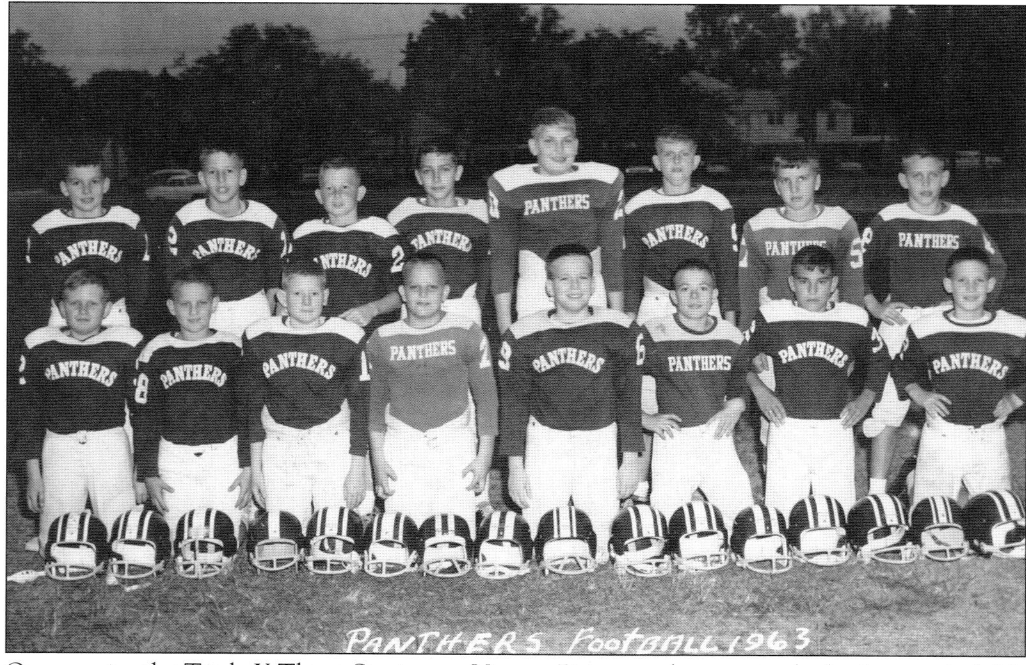

Once again, the Triple X Thirst Station on Victory Drive can be seen in the background of this 1963 Panther squad. Among the players were Arthur Peagler, Bob Williams, Jim Brasfield, Bob MacLaurin, Bill Caldwell, Mark Thomas, Ricky Smith, Ken Powers, and Glenn Hewitt. (Courtesy of the Sims family.).

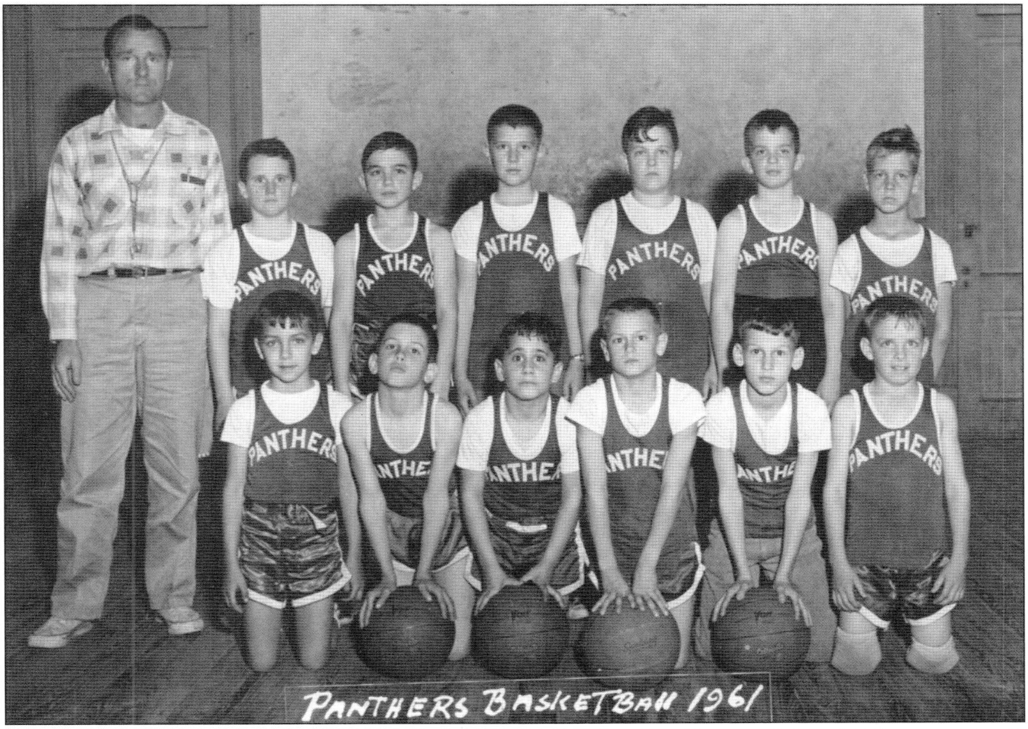

These 1961 Panthers basketball players are, from left to right, (first row) Mark Thomas, Frank Durkin, Chuck Sussman, Eddie Whelan, unidentified, and Bubba Hughes. Third from left in the second row is Marvin Grimm. The boys played under the watchful eye of coach Luke Sims, pictured at left. In 2006, Sims was posthumously named to the Greater Savannah Athletic Hall of Fame. (Courtesy of Marvin Grimm.)

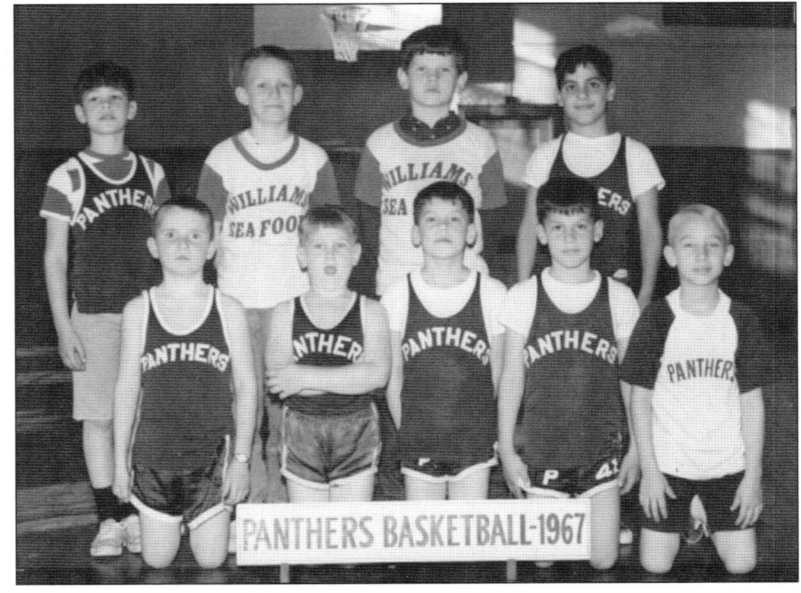

These 1967 Panthers basketball players probably were about seven or eight when this picture was taken. Among the players are Danny Sheehan, one of the Whelan boys, and Ken Griner, kneeling at far right. (Courtesy of the Sims family.)

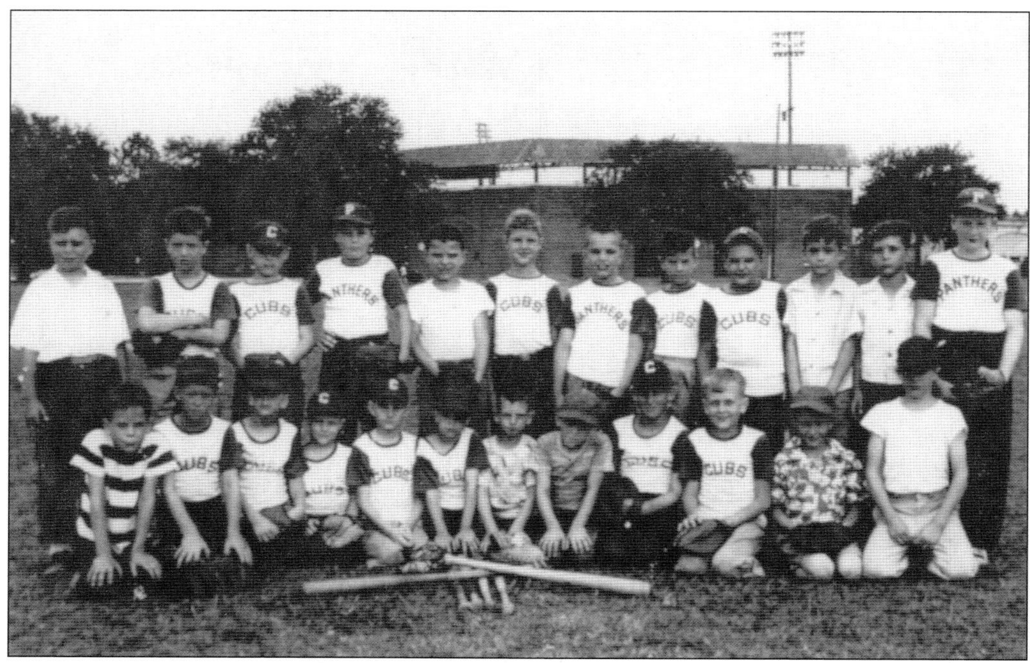

One member of this 1956 Panthers softball team was Wylly Garmany (third from right in the first row). One observer of Savannah sports history says Daffin's baseball diamonds (including No. 9) were wonderful places to play. (Courtesy of Bea Garmany Cox.)

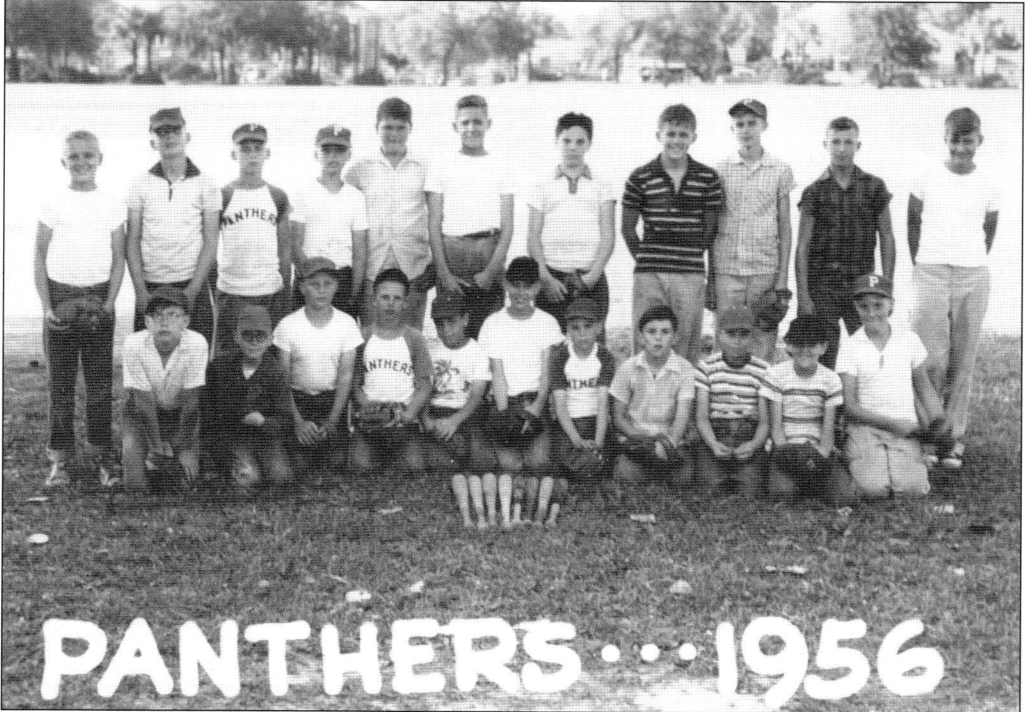

This 1956 Panthers baseball team included 22 players. Former Panthers said coaches such as Luke Sims and Tom Moore liked to win games, but they also knew the importance of allowing each boy playing time. Above all, they encouraged the boys to be good sports. (Courtesy of the Sims family.)

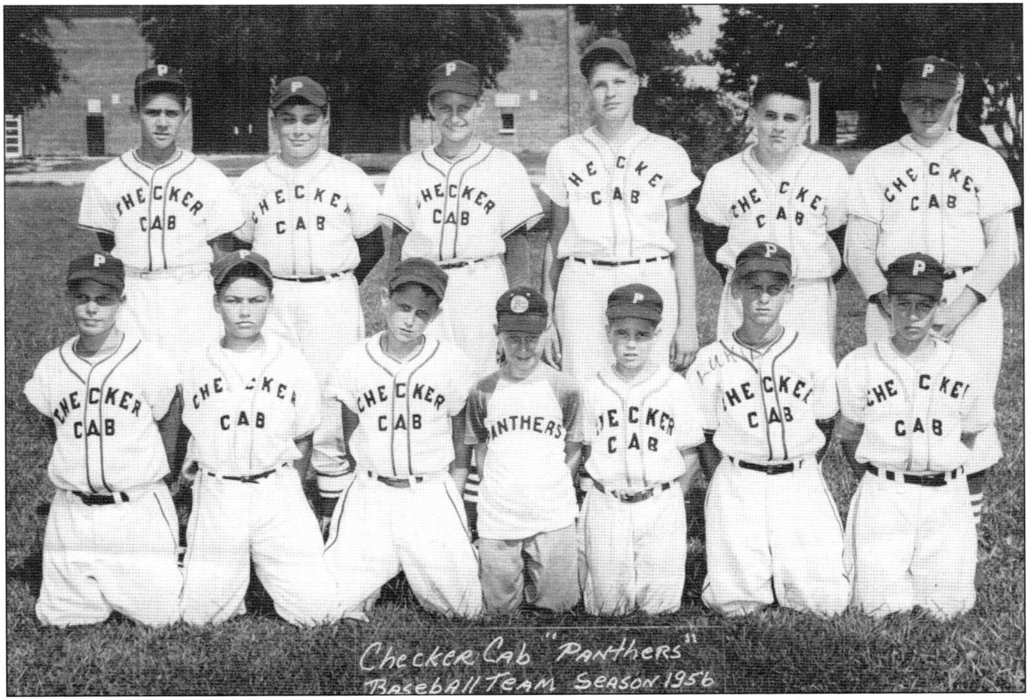

This 1956 Panther team was sponsored by Checker Cab and practiced in Daffin Park. From left to right are (first row) Ken Young, Lee Lane, Ricky Wheeles, Bob Fennell (bat boy), Lee Moore, Lukie Sims, and Billy Jones; (second row) Ray Chamberlain, Stratton Leopold, Jack Cory, Charlie Bryan, Bobby Brown, and Tony Roberts. (Courtesy of the Sims family.)

Tom Moore sent this letter to parents in 1960. Among other things, the letter explains that "sportsmanship, discipline, and other character-building qualities are taught. We are sure that you would want your boy or girl to be under good qualified leadership." (Courtesy of the Sims family.)

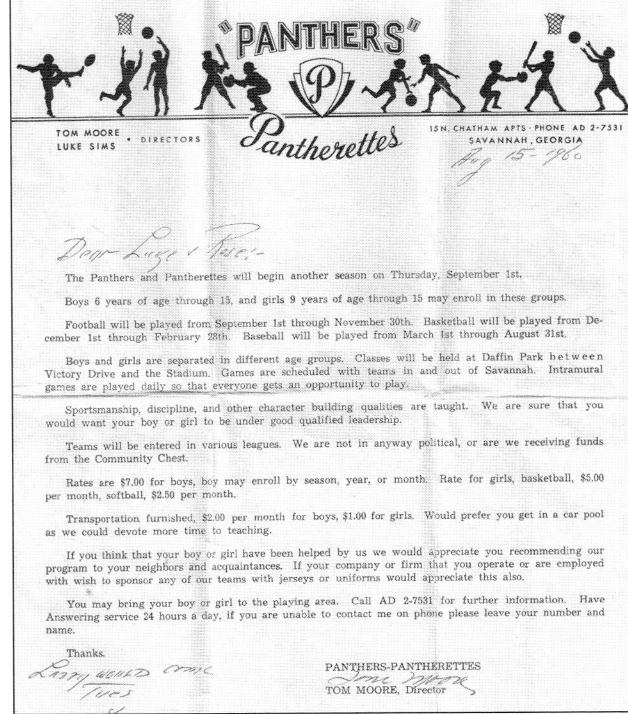

The Panthers and Pantherettes will begin another season on Thursday, September 1st.

Boys 6 years of age through 15, and girls 9 years of age through 15 may enroll in these groups.

Football will be played from September 1st through November 30th. Basketball will be played from December 1st through February 28th. Baseball will be played from March 1st through August 31st.

Boys and girls are separated in different age groups. Classes will be held at Daffin Park between Victory Drive and the Stadium. Games are scheduled with teams in and out of Savannah. Intramural games are played daily so that everyone gets an opportunity to play.

Sportsmanship, discipline, and other character building qualities are taught. We are sure that you would want your boy or girl to be under good qualified leadership.

Teams will be entered in various leagues. We are not in anyway political, or are we receiving funds from the Community Chest.

Rates are $7.00 for boys, boy may enroll by season, year, or month. Rate for girls, basketball, $5.00 per month, softball, $2.50 per month.

Transportation furnished, $2.00 per month for boys, $1.00 for girls. Would prefer you get in a car pool as we could devote more time to teaching.

If you think that your boy or girl have been helped by us we would appreciate you recommending our program to your neighbors and acquaintances. If your company or firm that you operate or are employed with wish to sponsor any of our teams with jerseys or uniforms would appreciate this also.

You may bring your boy or girl to the playing area. Call AD 2-7531 for further information. Have Answering service 24 hours a day, if you are unable to contact me on phone please leave your number and name.

Thanks.

PANTHERS-PANTHERETTES
TOM MOORE, Director

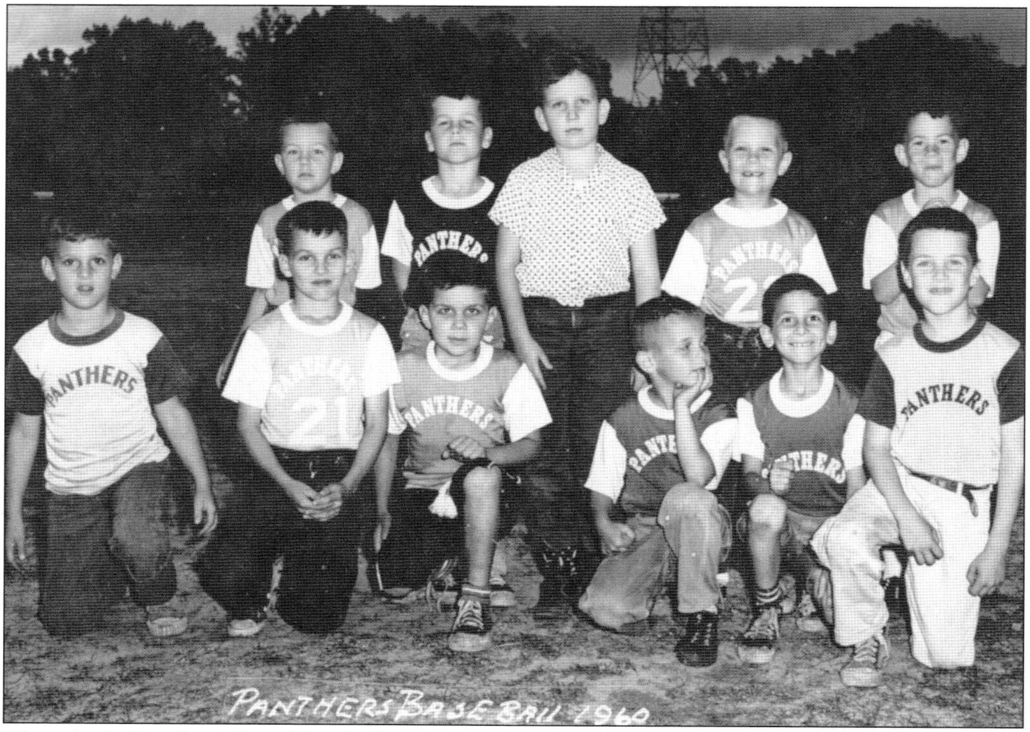

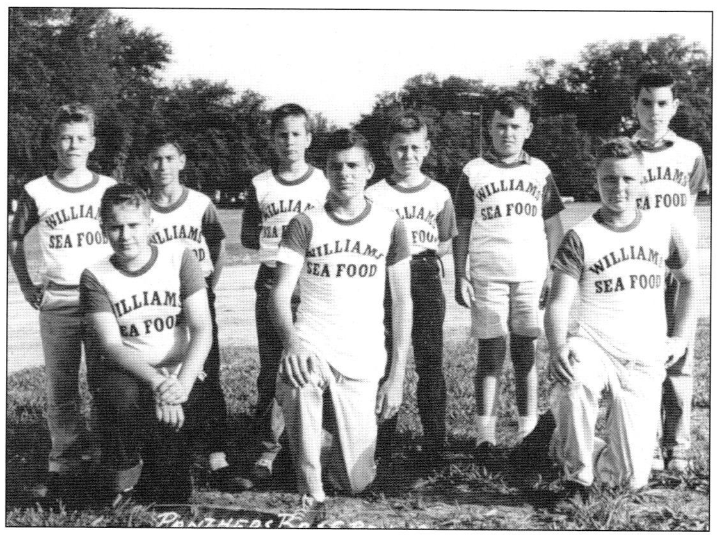

These little Panthers played baseball in 1960 and practiced in Daffin Park. This picture was taken in the park with the WSAV-TV tower on Victory Drive in the background. From left to right are (first row) Chuck Palefsky, Mike Gignilliat, two unidentified, Ricky Eicholz, and unidentified; (second row) Fred Kessler, two unidentified, Greg Odrezin, and Roy Smithberg. (Courtesy of the Sims family.)

Teams in the early 1960s that included older boys often were sponsored by local businesses, many of which have since closed their doors. The businesses helped pay for uniforms in exchange for a mention on the shirts. This squad was sponsored by Williams Seafood, a longtime favorite of Savannahians as well as out-of-towners. Joe's Drive-In sponsored another Panthers team. (Courtesy of the Sims family.)

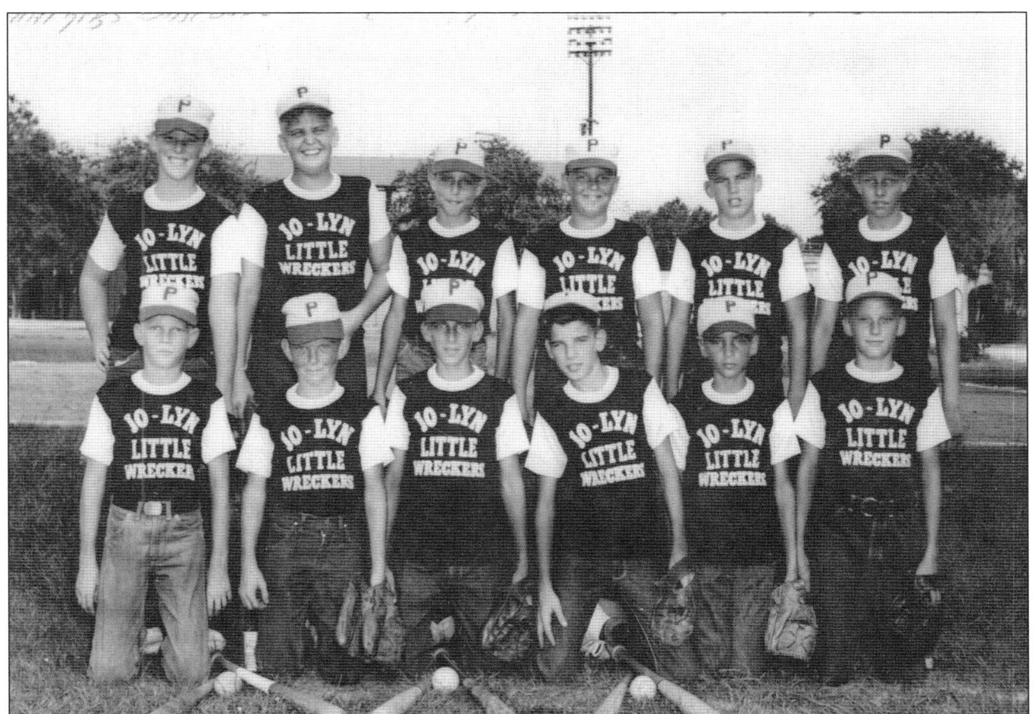

Many boys played for the Panthers year after year. This Jo-Lynn baseball team from 1963 included Benny Eicholz (first row, third from left) and John Murray (first row, far right). Standing from left to right are Harvey Gray, Rick Lantz, two unidentified, Jim Mayfield, and Jay Warthen. (Courtesy of the Sims family.)

These 1960 Panthers baseball players were on a team sponsored by Henderson's Sporting Goods. From left to right are (first row) John Skinner, Jimmy Strode, David Hinely, and Clark Perry; (second row) unidentified, Bill Baker, John Murray, Tommy Lauderdale, and Jim Mayfield. (Courtesy of the Sims family.)

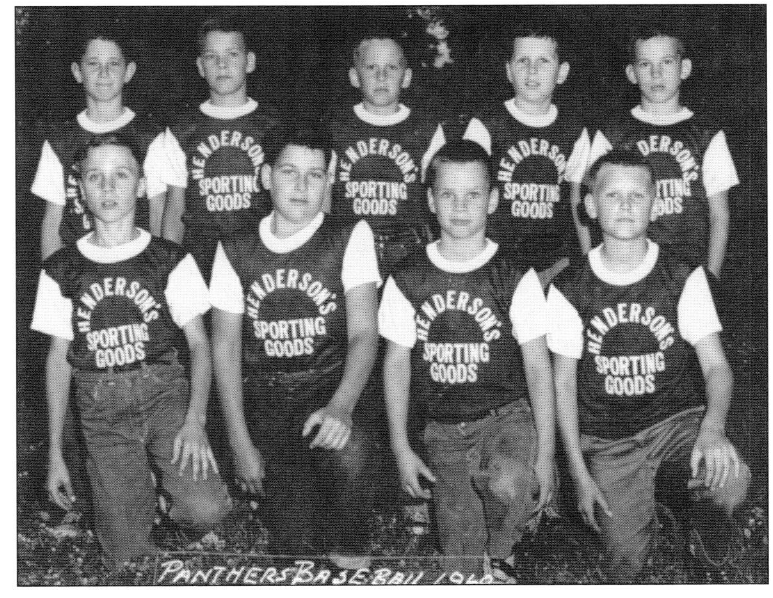

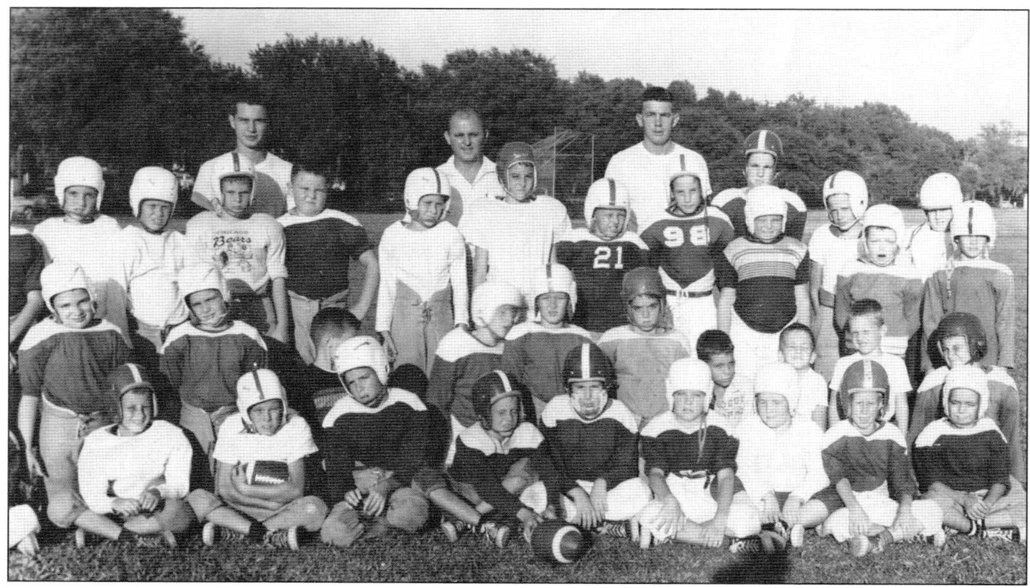

Jack Macher organized the Wildcat athletic team in the 1950s and recruited Parkside boys, those who attended nearby Blessed Sacrament Church, and other players. Members of this 1956 team are, from left to right, (first row) unidentified, Danny Corcoran, Ed Daly, unidentified, Corky Fleming, Jack Cooley, Bill Powers, Billy Braziel, and Bill Morrissey; (second row) John Oetgen, Bill Oetgen, John Ware, unidentified, Frank Baran, Cary Downing, unidentified, Michael Brower, Donald Thompson, and Joe DiNatale; (standing) Billy Adams, unidentified, Billy Bruggeman, Tony Ryan, unidentified, Tommy Stevens, Jack Macher, Bruce Barragan, Paul Weber, Bobby McManus, unidentified, Nick Thorp, Bill Harris, and unidentified. Coaches are Bubba Haupt, Jack Macher Sr., and Johnny Williams. (Courtesy of the Macher family.)

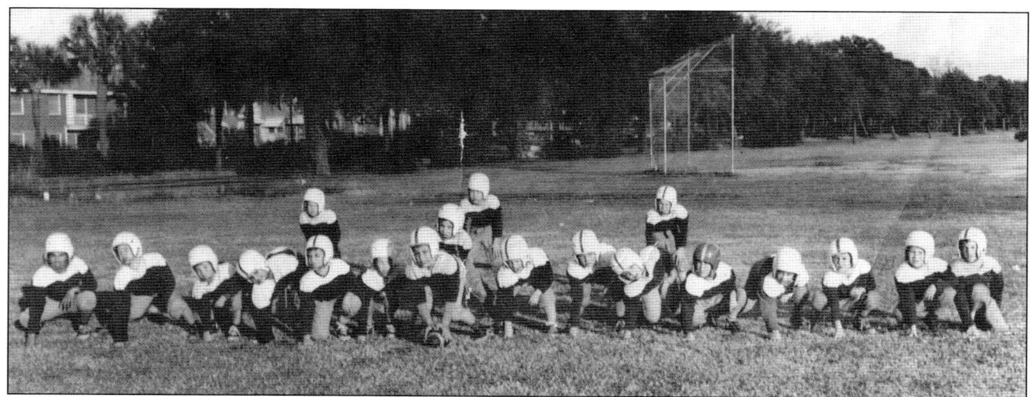

Teams like the Wildcats, shown here, as well as the Panthers and the Tigers, were dissolved in the late 1960s and early 1970s. No doubt, the young people who played for those teams have fun-filled memories of afternoon practices at Daffin Park. (Courtesy of the Macher family.)

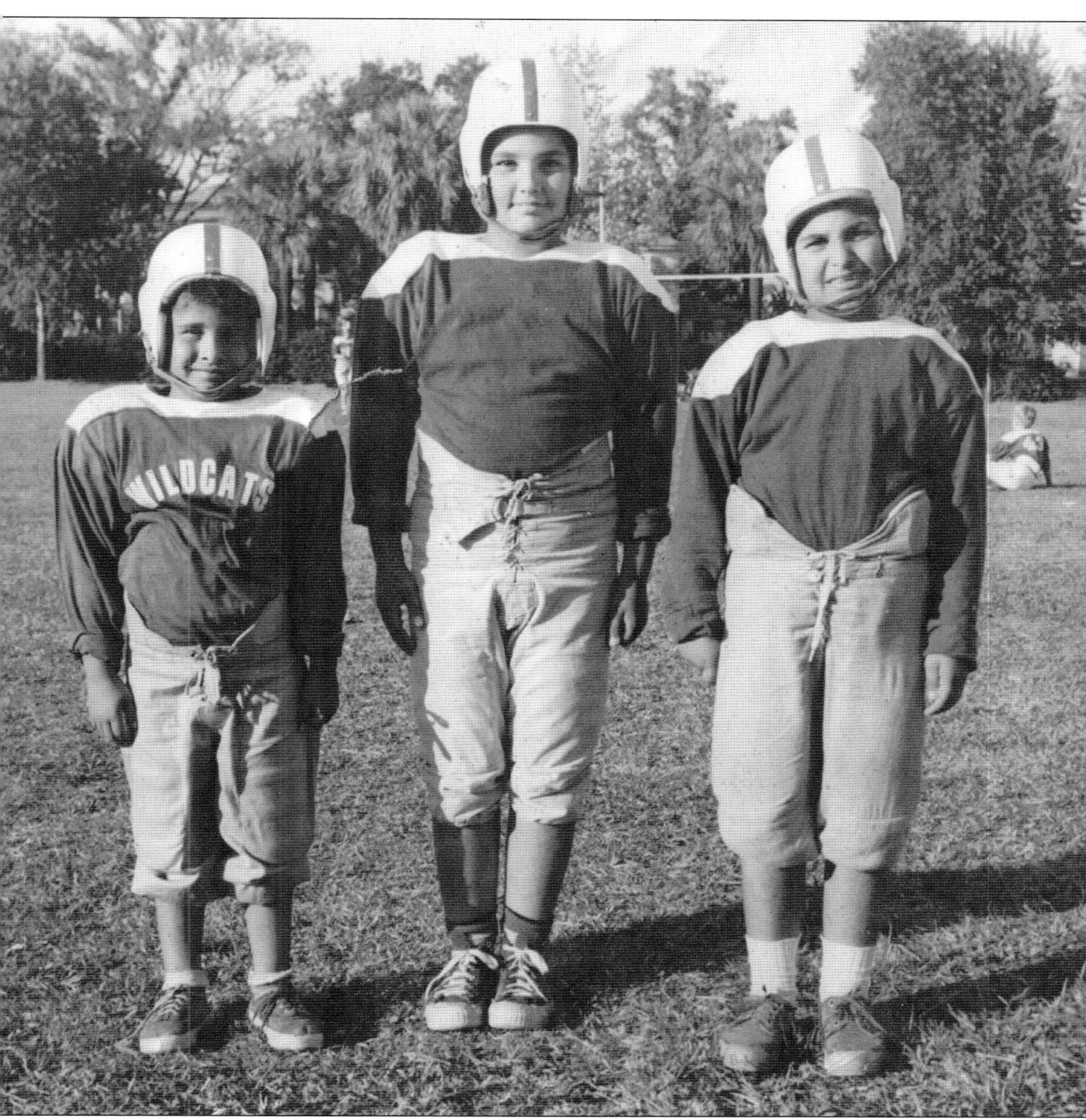

The Ganem brothers all played for the Wildcats. Here they are dressed and ready for the gridiron. From left to right are Charlie, Johnnie, and Paul Ganem. After coach Jack Macher's 1994 death, former player Jim Overstreet wrote a letter to the editor of the *Savannah Morning News*: "[Macher] taught me that a hard work ethic will eventually lead to success, no goal was too high to set and I should never underestimate my own abilities," Overstreet wrote. "His legacy surely was those many young men he helped to mold for success in life, steered in the right direction early by a man who just loved kids." (Courtesy of the Macher family.)

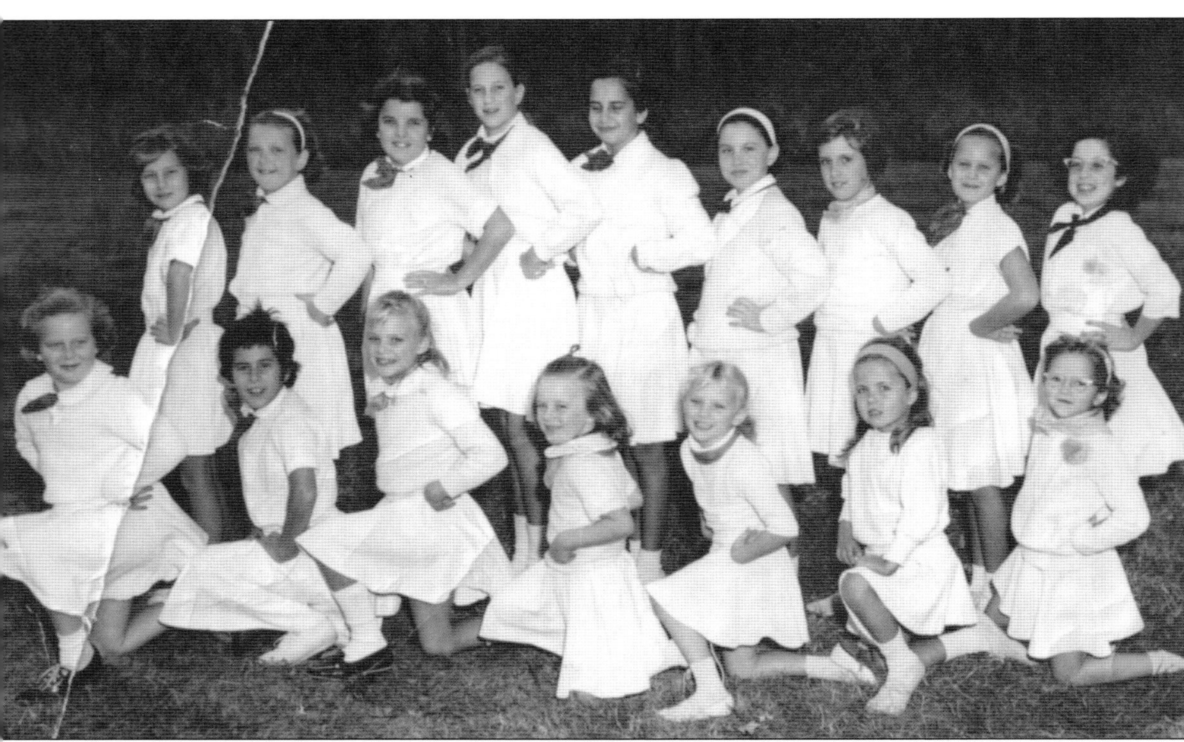

This photograph of cheerleaders for the Wildcats probably was taken in the early 1960s. From left to right are (first row) Theresa Coyle, unidentified, Marie Macher, Denise Coyle, Debbie Macher, and two unidentified; (second row) Wendy Ahrenhold, Judy Waddell, unidentified, Terry Lawless, Janie Woodward, Gail Means, two unidentified, and Carol Steinheimer. (Courtesy of the Macher family.)

Five

THE PANTHERETTES

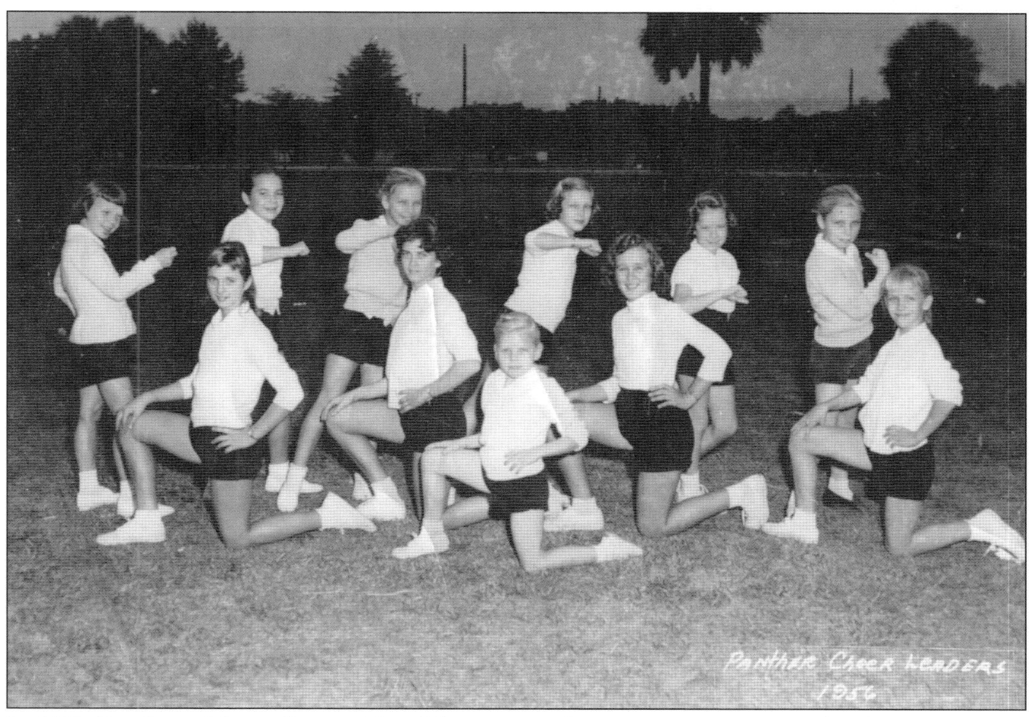

In 1951, Panther athletic director Tom Moore sent a letter to parents saying that he was starting a girls' group named the Pantherettes. "Ages will be from 12 through 15," he wrote. "There has been a need for these younger girls to begin earlier and learn the rules, fundamentals, and how to play the game correctly. . . . Rates will be $5 a month. . . . Following basketball we will play softball." This 1956 Panther cheerleading squad included, from left to right, (first row) Diane Bailey, Diane Jackson, Patty Daniels (front), Jenell Rogers, and Terry Densley; (second row) Nancy Bryan, Julie Hodges, Jean Powers, Carolyn Reiser, Patty Fennell, and Jane Powers. (Author's collection.)

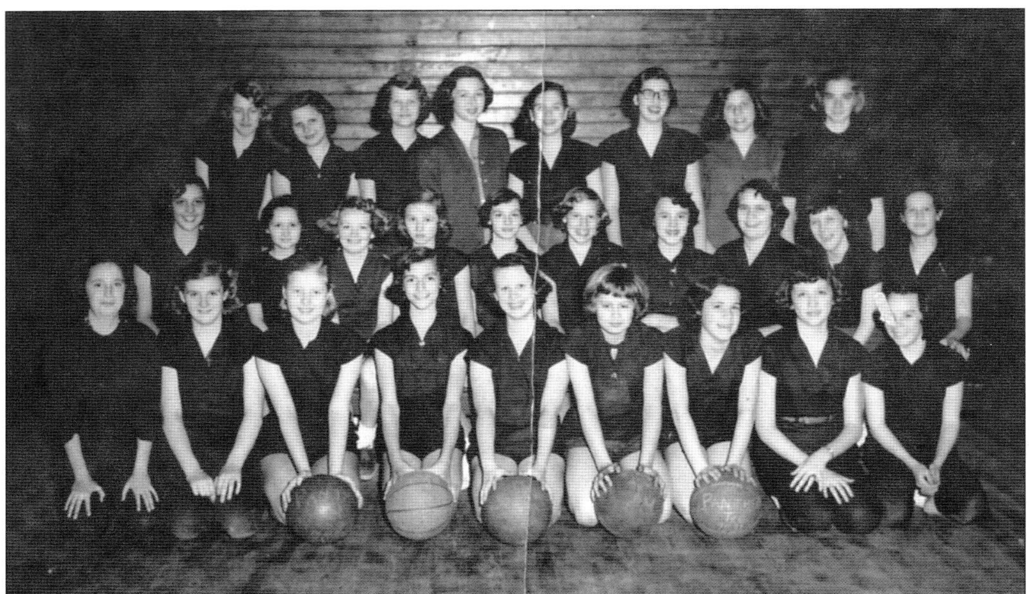

This c. 1950 Pantherette basketball team included students from the Pape School, which was the predecessor to the Savannah Country Day School. From left to right are (first row) two unidentified, Mary Pacifici, Margaret McLamb, Carlotta Cruzan, Cookie Pacifici, unidentified, Harriet Hoffman, and unidentified; (second row) Lynn Crovatt, two unidentified, Marylyn Walters, Cissy Kennard, Linda Maxwell, two unidentified, Ann Hancock, and unidentified; (third row) Louise Armstrong, Cler Colson, Julia Oliver, Ann Lazard, unidentified, Nita Morgan, Ginger Connerat, and Polly Wylly. (Courtesy of Cler Colson.)

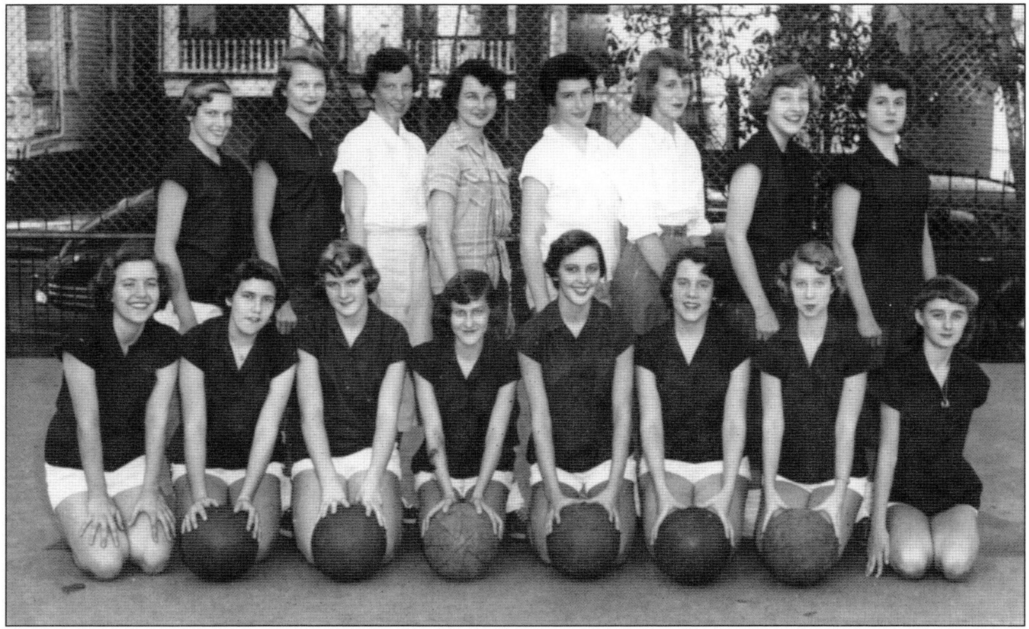

These 1954 Patherettes are, from left to right, (first row) Susan Grefe, Kay Ireland, Anne Gordon, Joan Coons, Lynn Crovatt, Margie Roberson, Kay Deese, and Carlotta ?; (second row) Linda Maxwell, Louise Oliver, unidentified, Vivian Logue, Pam Thomson, Louise Armstrong, unidentified, and Celia Williams. (Courtesy of the Sims family.)

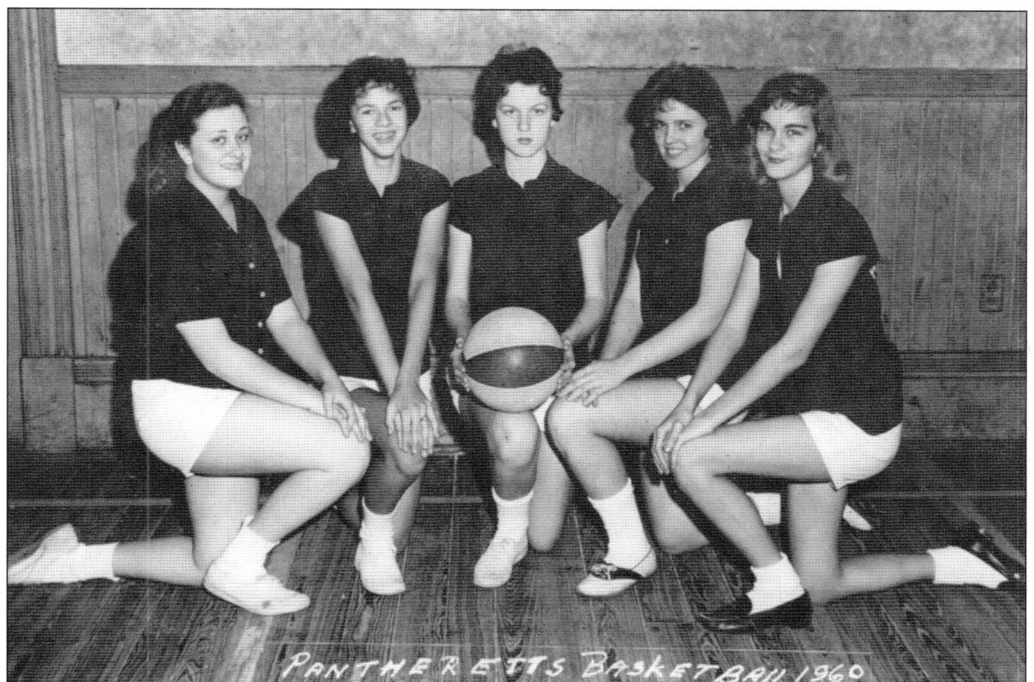

These girls played on one of the 1960 Pantherette basketball teams. From left to right are Tirzah Helmly, P. Robinson, Paula Bragg, Sandra Arnold, and V. Millikan. (Courtesy of the Sims family.)

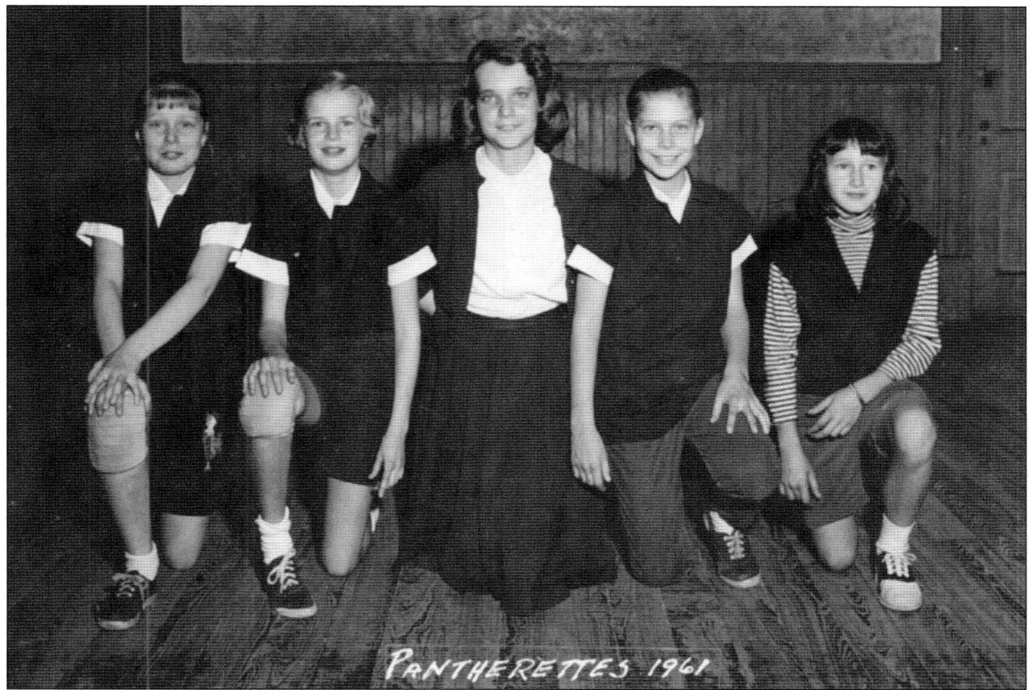

Many Pantherette basketball players recall practicing either in the Pape School gym or in the gym at the Union Bag Athletic Association on Barnard and State Streets. This 1961 team included, from left to right, Maureen Pacifici, unidentified, B. Stellar, Margaret Pacifici, and Susan Dempsey. (Courtesy of the Sims family.)

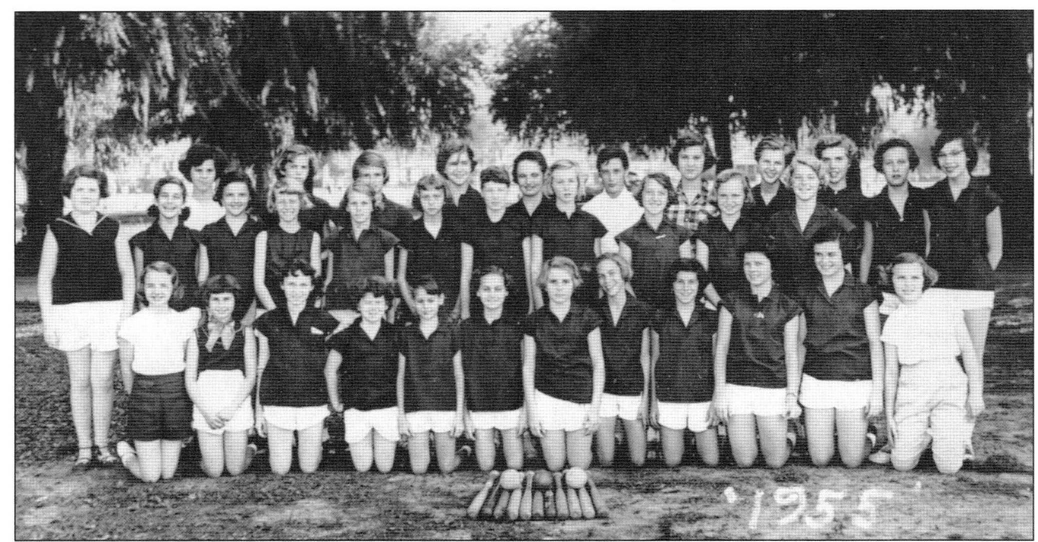

This 1955 team shown in Daffin Park included, from left to right, (first row) Carol Mahaney, Carol Liebrels, three unidentified, Sandy Rivers, Eileen Moreno, Mimi Daniel, Katharine Ellis, Connie McIntire, Anne Carson, and unidentified; (second row) Karen Hodges, Kitty Comer, Bonnie Cay, unidentified, Eleanor Inglesby, two unidentified, Nan Saussy, Harriett Lariscy, Elaine Constantine, and Sue Wylly; (third row) Kathy Calhoun, unidentified, Caroline Waller, Frida Barrow, Louisa Constantine, Margaret Close, Nina Ravenscroff, two unidentified, Dee Sharpley, and Nancy Keith. (Courtesy of the Sims family.)

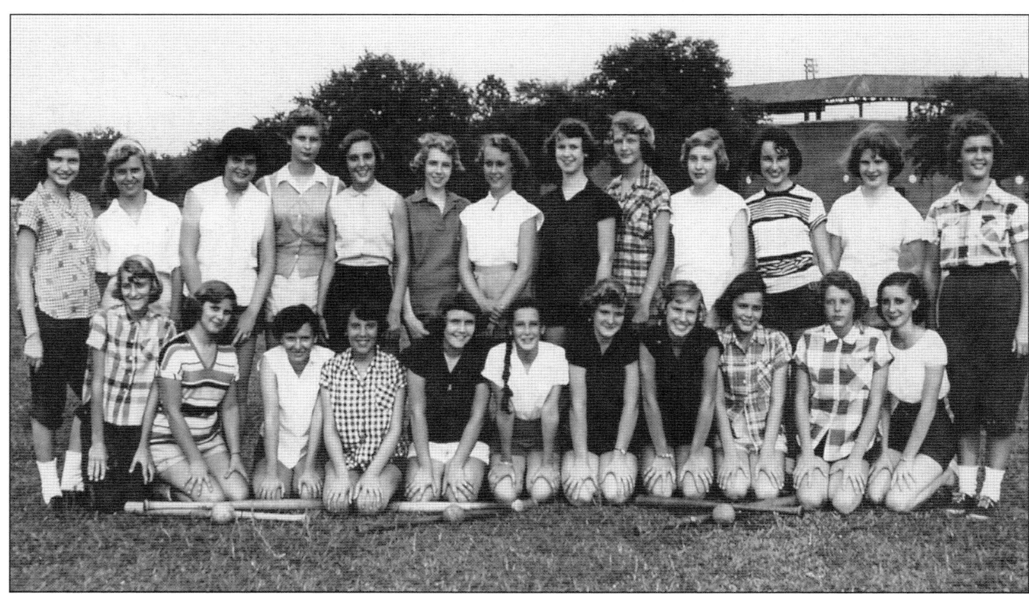

During the 1950s, these Pantherettes played softball for Panther athletic director Tom Moore. From left to right are (first row) Louise Armstrong, Cler Colson, four unidentified, Ann Gordon, Linda Maxwell, and three unidentified; (second row) Claire Hutto, Carmen Cherry, Mary Delegal, Jean Smith, Lynn Crovatt, Ann Mercer, Carlotta Cruzan, Julia Oliver, four unidentified, and Penny Espy. (Courtesy of the Sims family.)

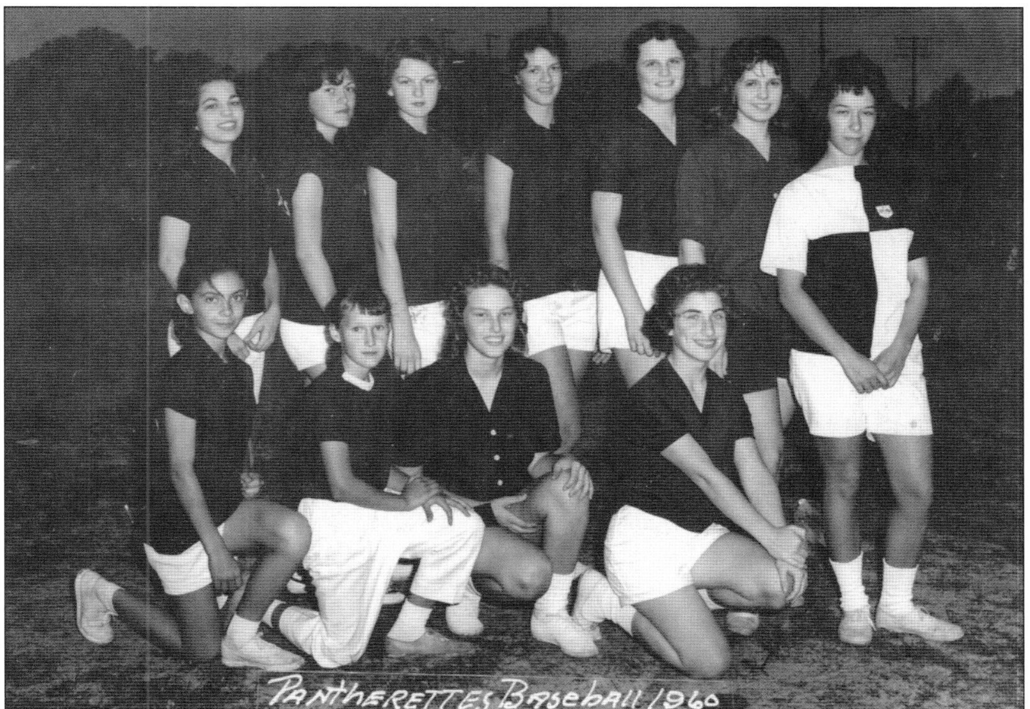

The Pantherettes 1960 softball team had its picture taken in Daffin Park by photographer Carroll Burke. From left to right are (first row) Fran Morgan, unidentified, Marcia Marvin, and Anita Kaminsky; (second row) unidentified, Sherry Anderson, Paula Bragg, unidentified, Hope Weeks, Sandra Arnold, and unidentified. (Courtesy of the Sims family.)

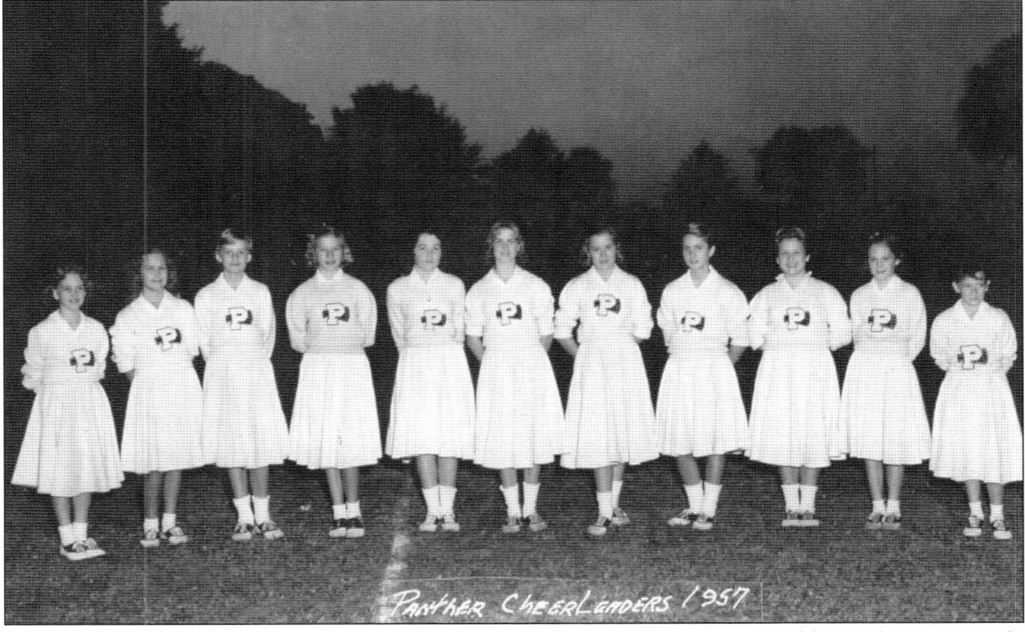

The 1957 Panthers cheer squad included, from left to right, Dale Peterson, Debbie Nelson, Amanda McLaughlin, Kay Saffold, unidentified, Diane Jackson, Jenell Rogers, Diane Bailey, Ann Robinson, Camille Puckett, and Patty Fennell. (Courtesy of Amanda McLaughlin Cannon.)

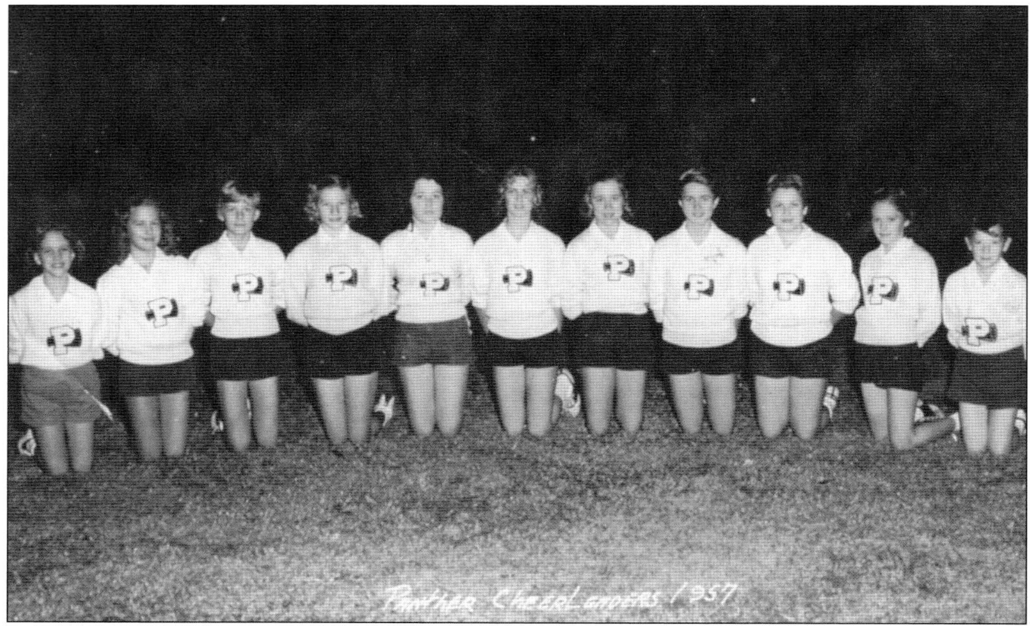

Cheering for the various Panther sports teams called for slightly different uniforms. Shown here in 1957 are, from left to right, Dale Peterson, Debbie Nelson, Amanda McLaughlin, Kay Saffold, unidentified, Diane Jackson, Jenell Rogers, Diane Bailey, Ann Robinson, Camille Puckett, and Patty Fennell. (Courtesy of Amanda McLaughlin Cannon.)

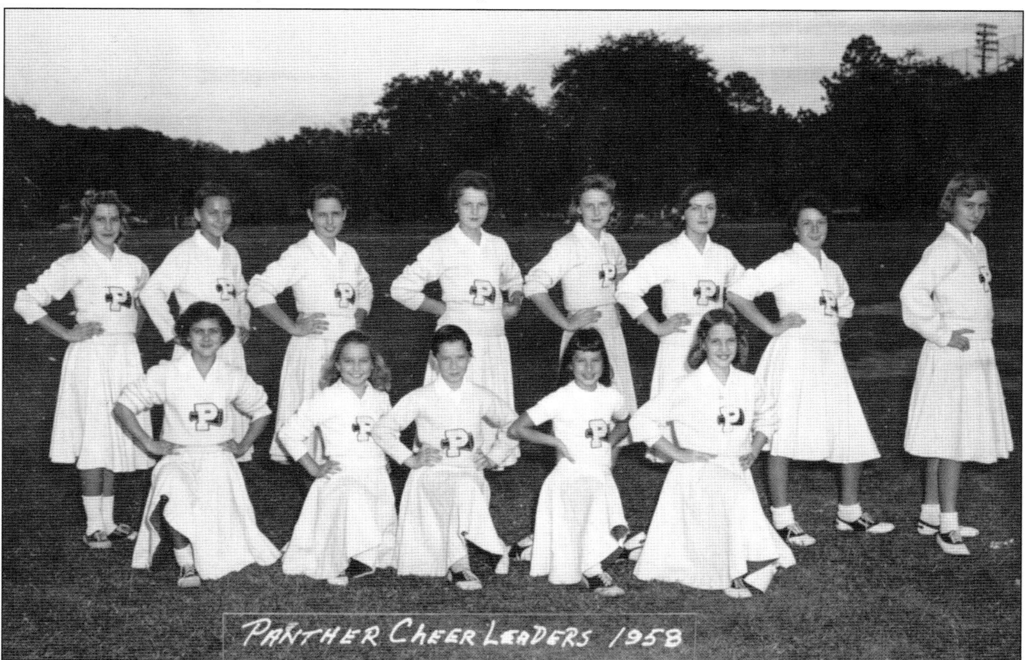

Like squads before and after them, the 1958 Panther cheerleaders practiced in Daffin Park. The girls are, from left to right, (first row) Cecile Mathews, unidentified, Patty Fennell, unidentified, and Dale Peterson; (second row) Shirley Oliver, unidentified, Sandra Arnold, Paula Bragg, Amanda McLaughlin, Sherry Anderson, unidentified, and Betty Nichols. (Courtesy of Amanda McLaughlin Cannon.)

88

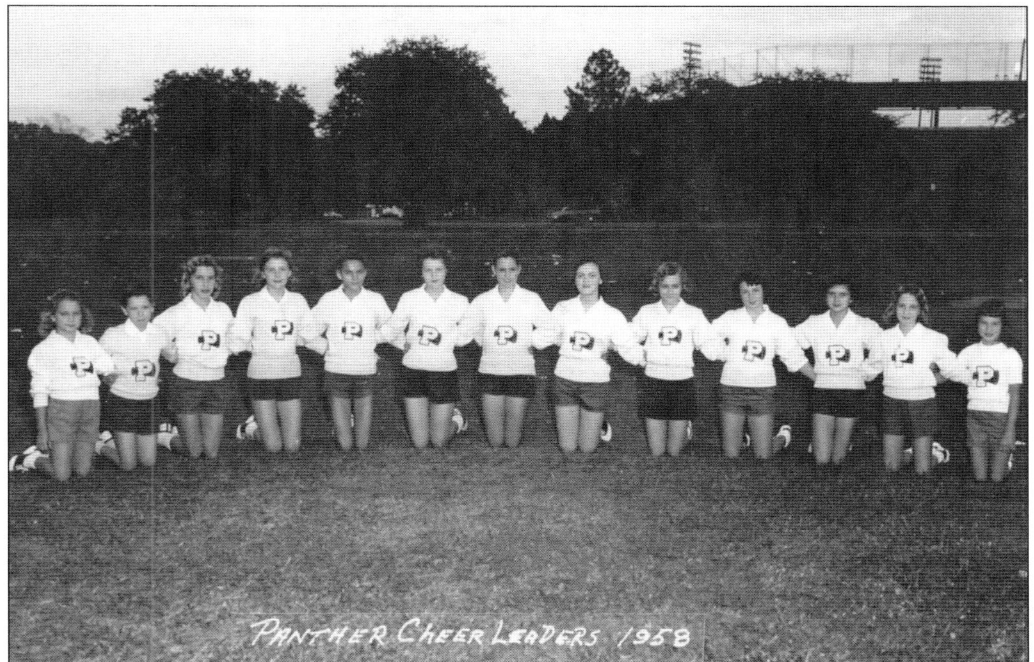

The girls seen here in 1958 are, from left to right, unidentified, Patty Fennell, Shirley Oliver, Amanda McLaughlin, unidentified, Paula Bragg, Sandra Arnold, Sherry Anderson, Betty Nichols, unidentified, Cecile Mathews, Dale Peterson, and unidentified. (Courtesy of Amanda McLaughlin Cannon)

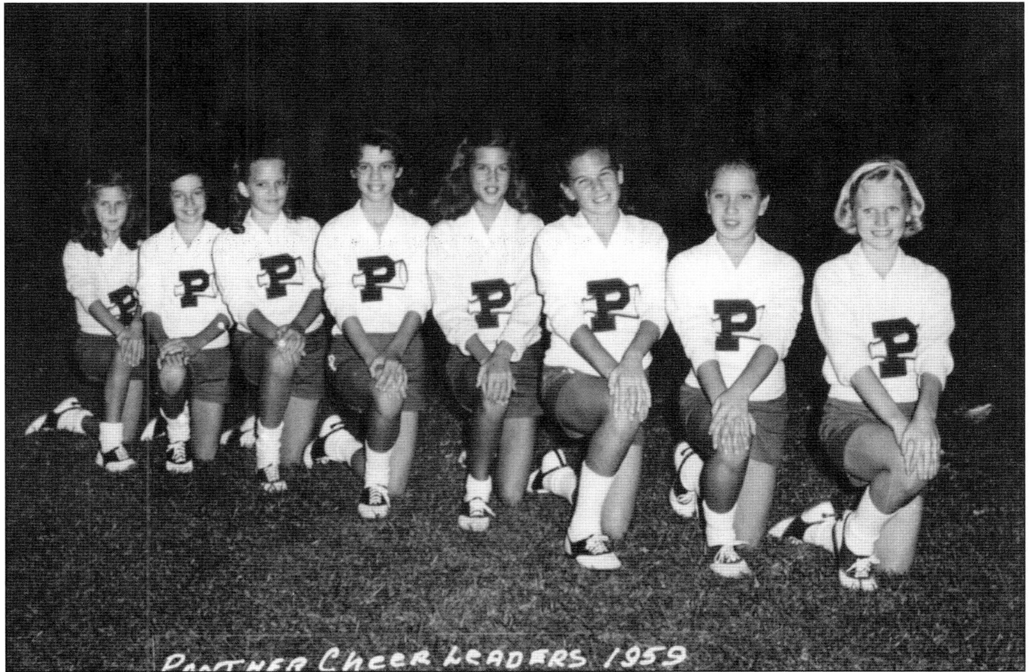

The Panthers 1959 cheer squad included, from left to right, Judy Orvin, Nancy Howle, Marilyn Hood, Susan Black, Sandra Orvin, Barbara Zittrauer, Bert Oliver, and Mary Jane Reilly. The girls practiced in Daffin Park and cheered during the games at Bethesda. (Courtesy of the Sims family.)

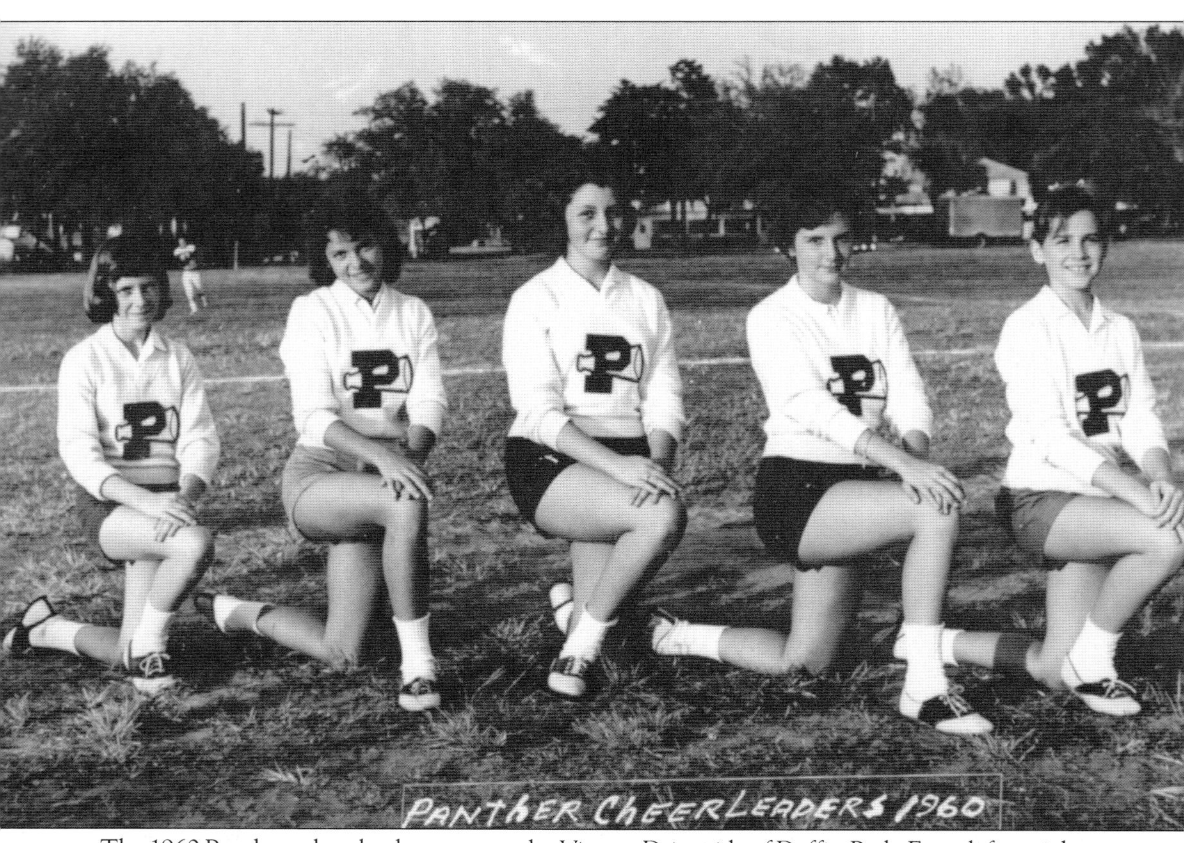

The 1960 Panthers cheerleaders pose on the Victory Drive side of Daffin Park. From left to right are two unidentified, Linda Calhoun, Nancy Causey, and Susan Adams. (Courtesy of the Sims family.)

Six

CHURCHES, SCHOOLS, AND MOMENTOUS EVENTS

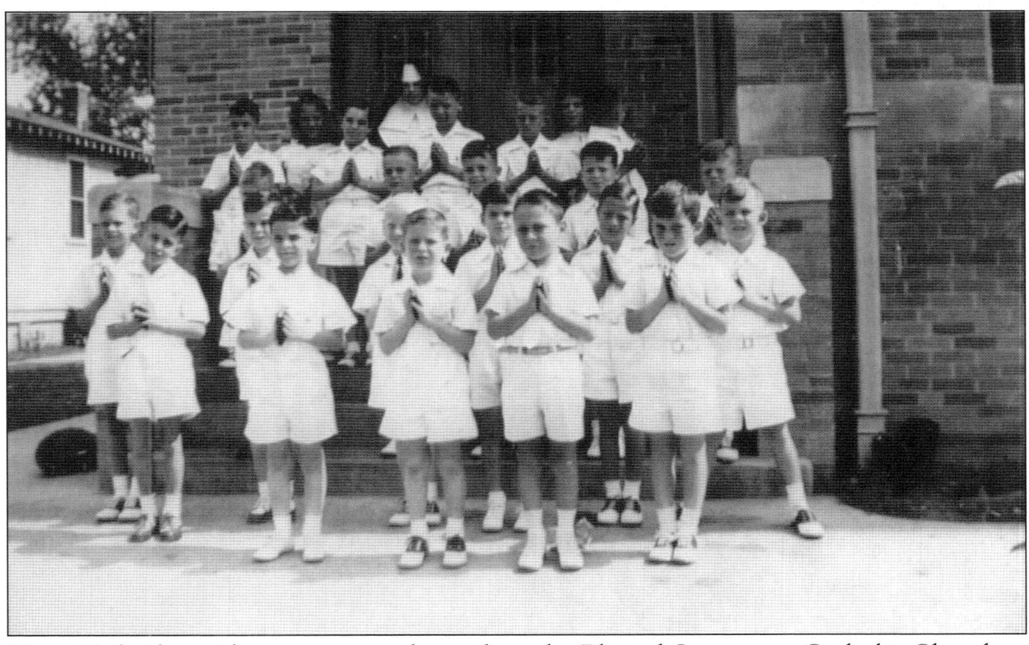

Many Parkside residents were members of nearby Blessed Sacrament Catholic Church, a landmark on the corner of East Forty-Fourth Street and Victory Drive. The church and school were within easy walking distance from the neighborhood. This 1944 photograph of children who took their First Communion that year includes Dickie Everett (first row, second from left), Jimmy Zittrauer (first row, third from left), Tony Aliffi (far right), and John Reckling. (Courtesy of Shirley Toole Reckling.)

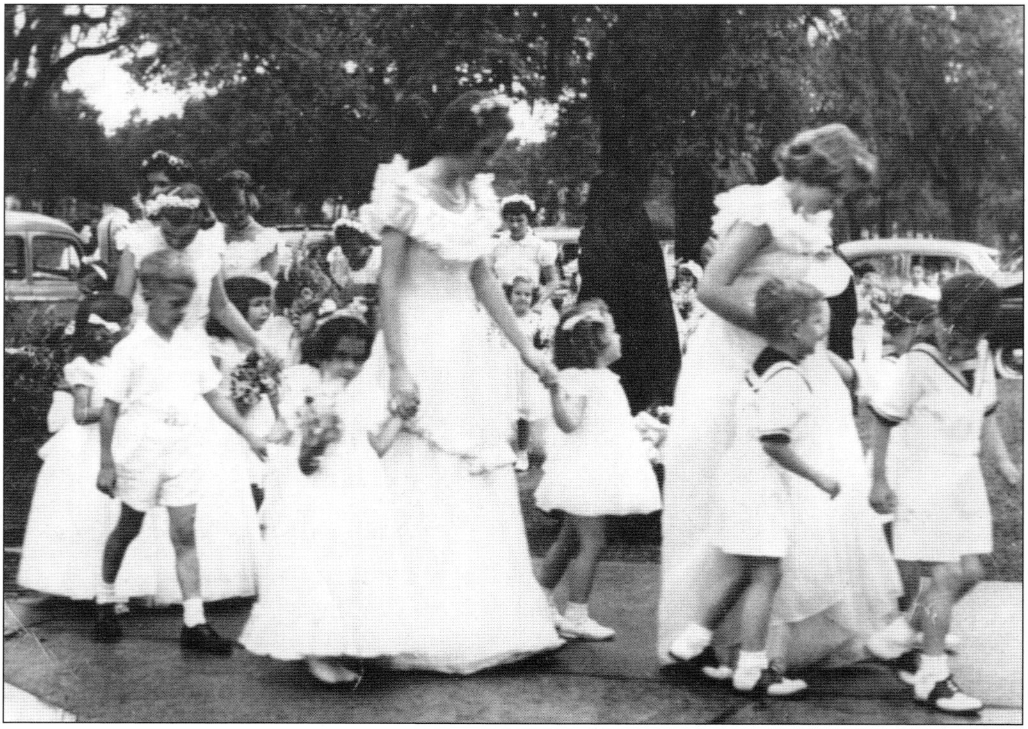

Mary Orsini, front and center with the dark hair, participated in the 1956 May Procession at Blessed Sacrament Church. Typically, in Catholic schools, the May Procession was held to honor the Virgin Mary as the Queen of May. (Courtesy of the Orsini family.)

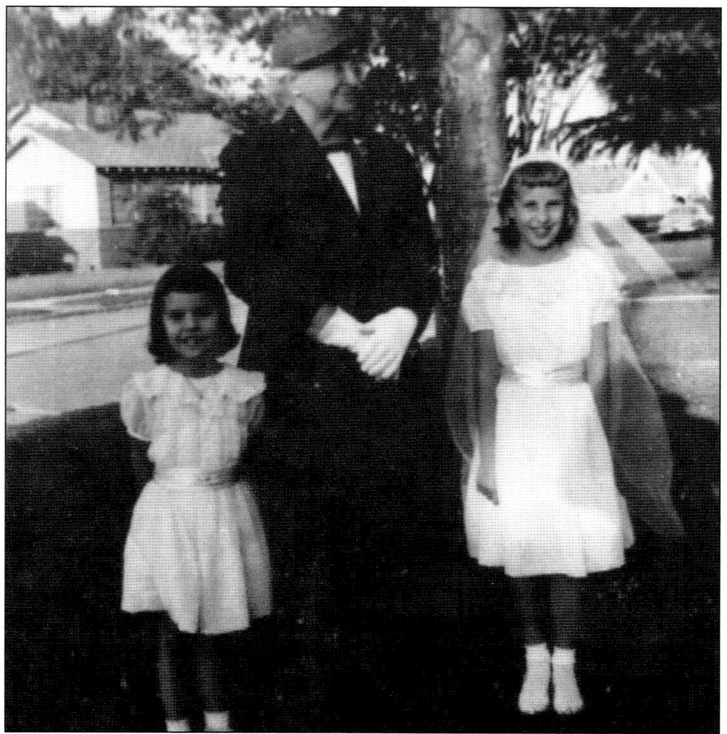

Madeleine Walker (right) was confirmed in the 1950s. She, along with her sister Natalie (left) was photographed with their great-grandmother Mrs. E. Cafiero on the Walkers' lawn at 1501 East Fiftieth Street. (Courtesy of Natalie Walker Deriso.)

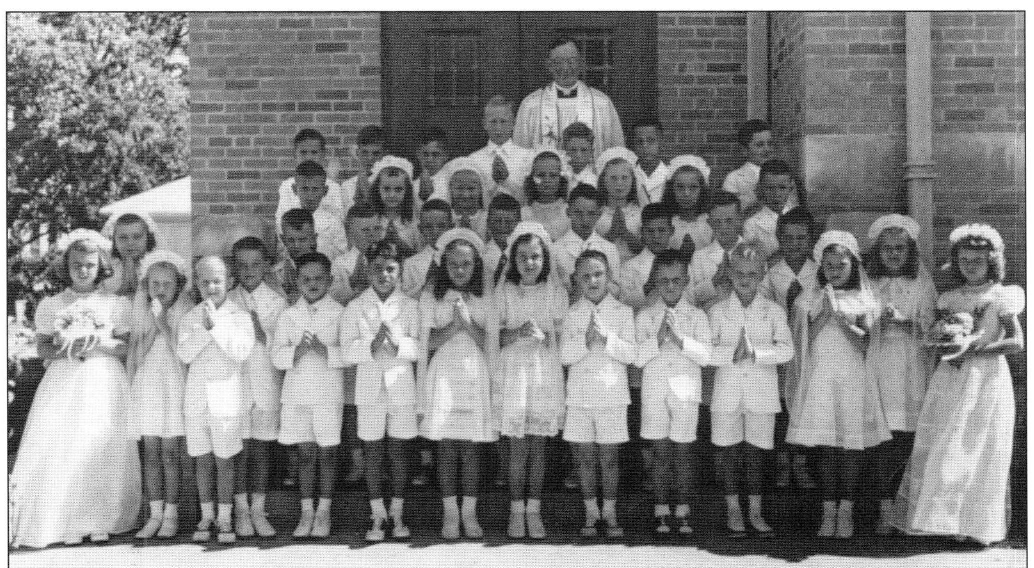

Bobby Morrissey, whose family moved to Parkside in 1950, shared this 1947 picture of his First Communion class at Blessed Sacrament School. Several other Parkside residents, including Beth Mock, also are in the picture. From left to right are (first row) three unidentified, Walter Dwyer, Gerald Fleming, unidentified, Shelia Powers, Mary Ann Brennan, unidentified, Dick Buchner, Tony Battle, Linda Bettencourt, and two unidentified; (second row) Bobby Mayes, unidentified, Morrissey, John Kennedy, unidentified, Eddie Tuttle, Bart Eason, and John Hale; (third row) Eddie Sheppard, unidentified, Mary Pacifici, Mock, Zonia Glacken, unidentified, and Hudson Wise; (fourth row) Mike McDermott, unidentified, Eddie Werntz, Louis Waldhour, Mike Campos, George Jenkins, and Buddy Register. The priest is Father Brennan. (Courtesy of the Morrissey family.)

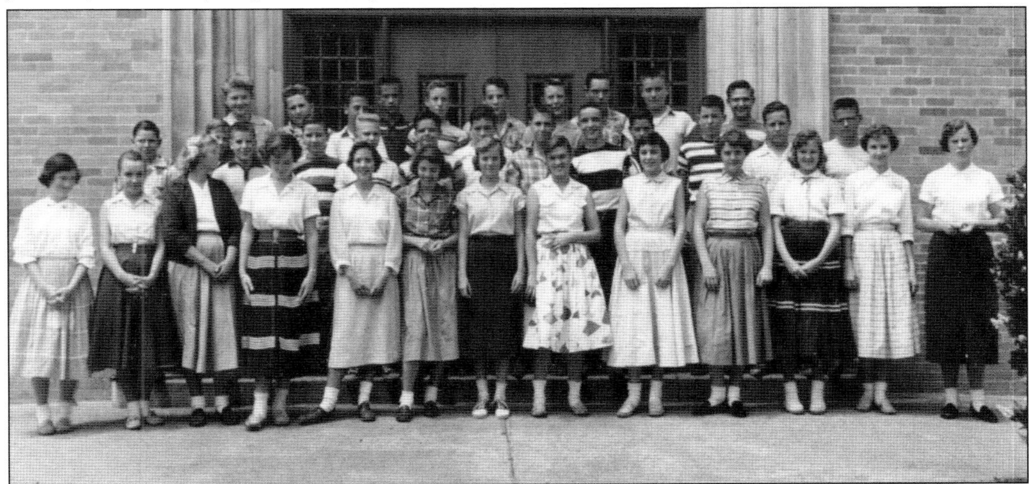

In 1954, Bobby Morrissey's eighth-grade classmates at Blessed Sacrament School gathered for a graduation picture. From left to right are (first row) Martha Corish, Shelia Powers, Mary Ann ?, Camille Dillon, Linda Bettencourt, Barbara Pinckney, Kaye Bruggeman, Ashby Connolly, Mary Ann Brennan, unidentified, Beth Mock, Margaret Stegin, unidentified, and Zonia Glacken; (second row) George Rovolis, Howard Williams, Dick Buchner, John Hale, Tony Battle, Gerald Fleming, unidentified, Eddie Werntz, Morrissey, Eddie Tuttle, Danny Floyd, Robert Martin, and Eddie Sheppard; (third row) Dickson Hamrick, Buddy Register, George Jenkins, Mike McDermott, Mike Campos, Mike Martin, Bart Eason, Hudson Wise, Denny Shimkus, and Gene Brinson. (Courtesy of the Morrissey family.)

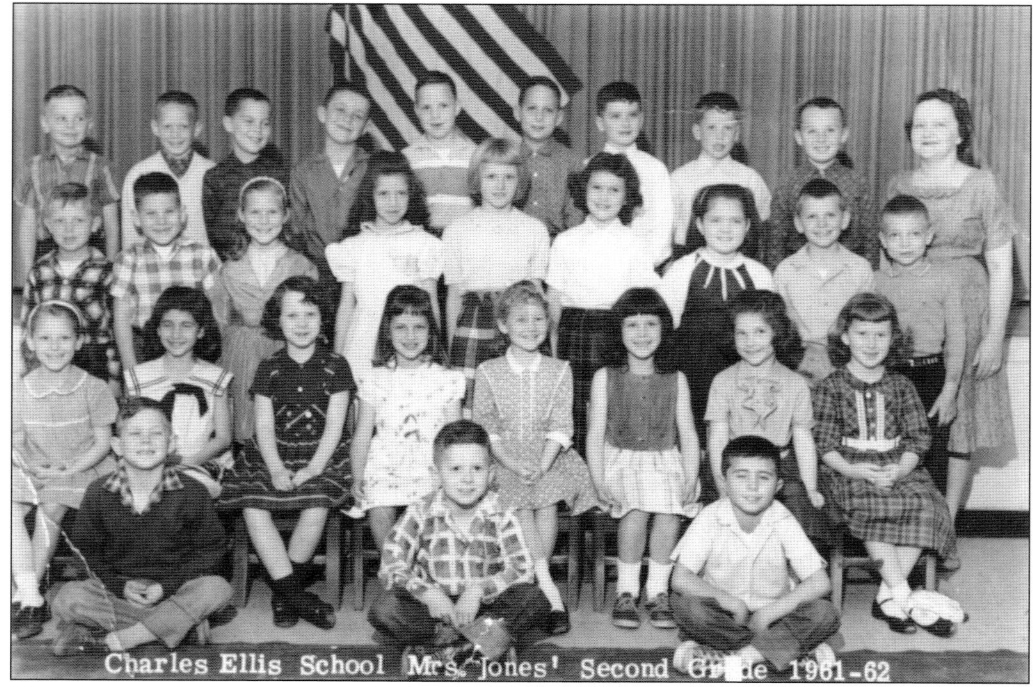

Many Parkside children attended Charles Ellis School in Ardsley Park. This 1961–1962 second-grade class included Parkside residents Johnny Smith (fourth row, fourth from left) and Charles Skinner (fourth row, fifth from left). In those days, Parkside children who attended public schools were assigned to Charles Ellis, Myers Junior High, and Savannah High. (Courtesy of the Smith family.)

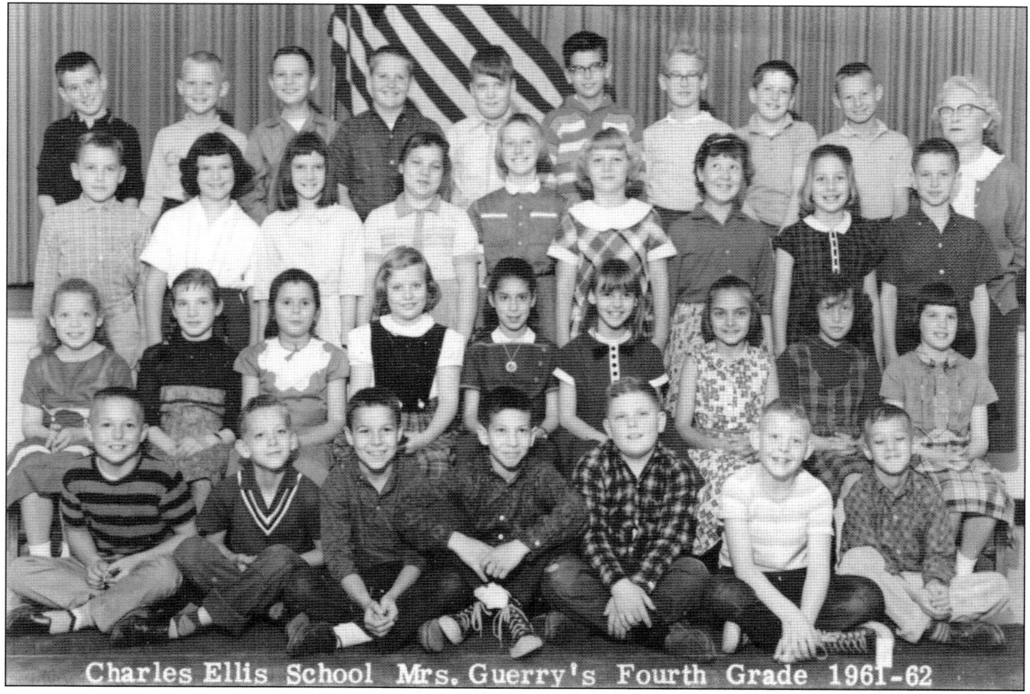

In 1961–1962, Ricky Smith of East Forty-Eighth Street was in Edna Guerry's fourth-grade class at Charles Ellis. He is at far right in the third row. (Courtesy of the Smith family.)

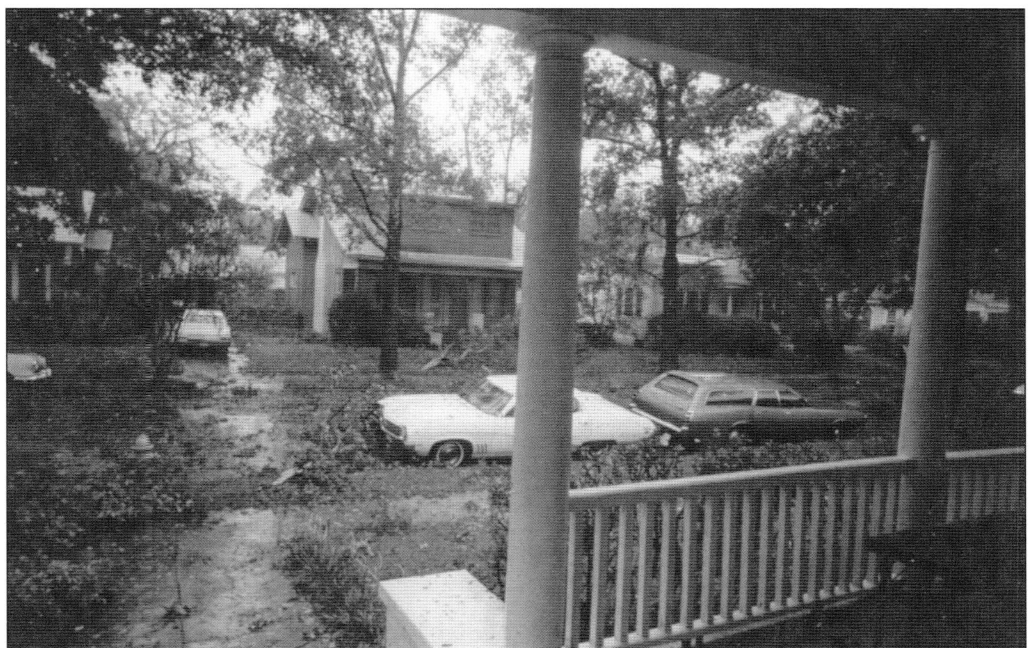

After Hurricane David roared through Savannah in 1979, many families seized the opportunity to document downed limbs and wind damage with their cameras. This photograph shows debris in the 1300 Block of East Forty-Ninth Street. (Courtesy of the DeLorme family.)

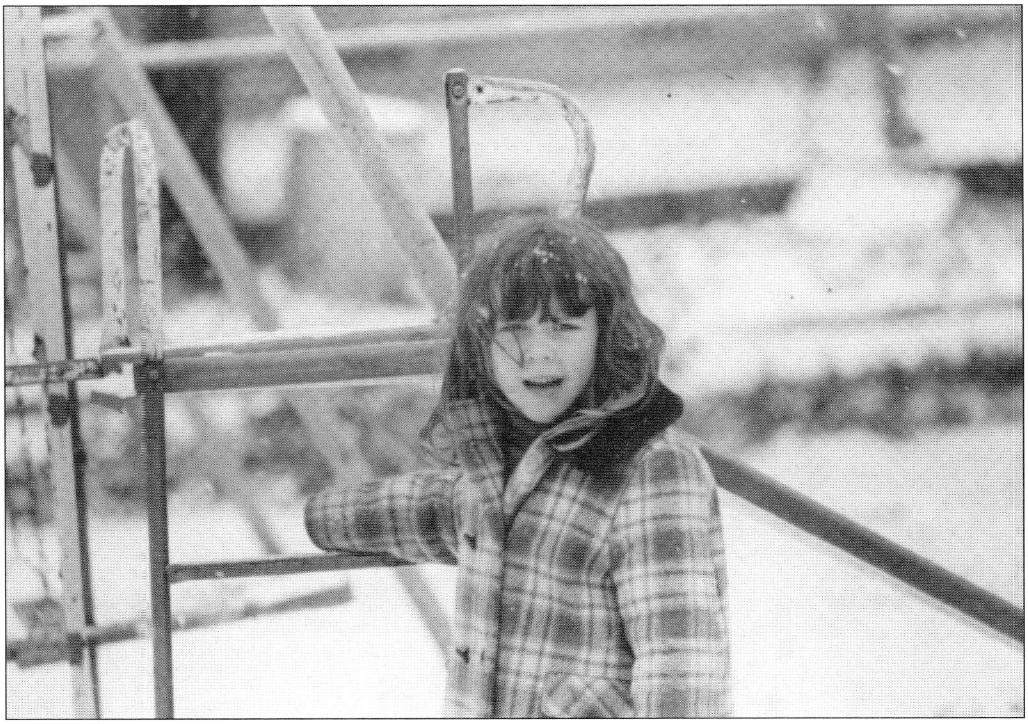

When it snowed in 1973, children throughout Savannah, including youngsters in Parkside, bundled up and hurried outside to play. This young lass poses by the slide in her yard in the 1300 block of East Forty-Ninth Street. (Courtesy of the DeLorme family.)

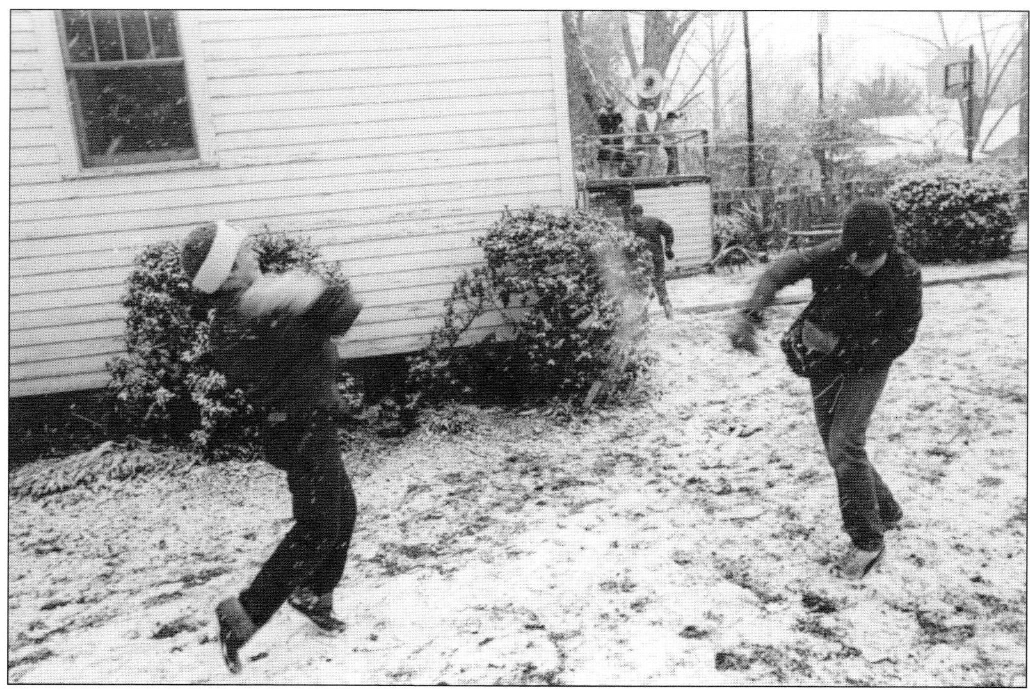

Rare snowfalls in Savannah mean it is time for a fierce snowball fight. These Parkside boys sprang into action in the 1300 block of East Forty-Ninth Street. (Courtesy of the DeLorme family.)

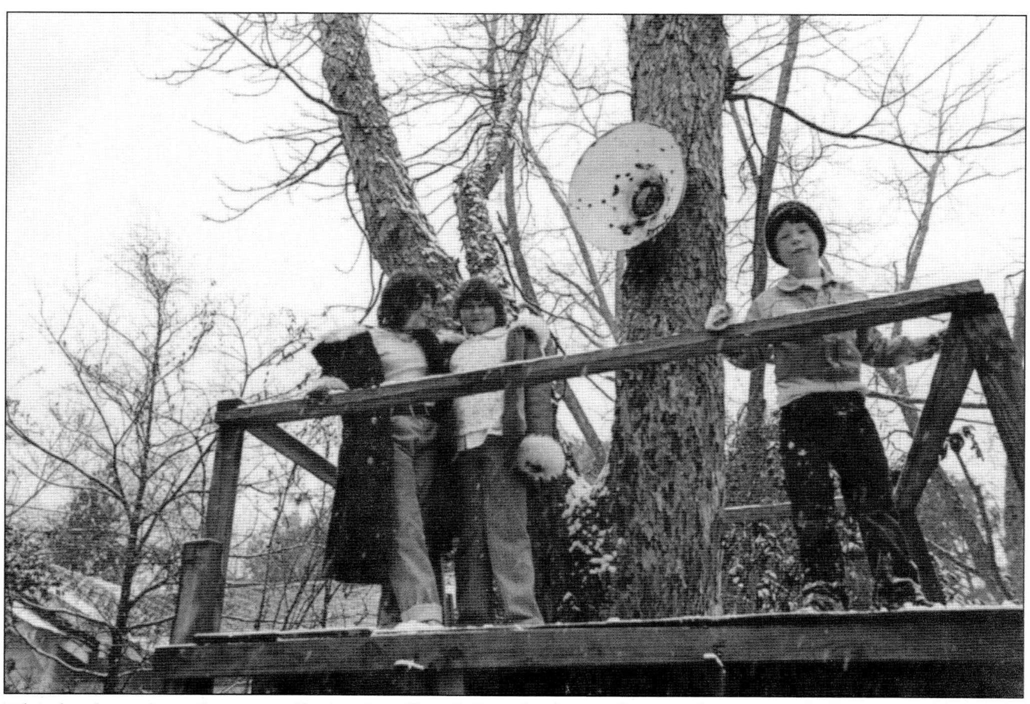

This backyard treehouse in Parkside offered the ideal spot for watching snowball fights. Watching the battle from above are, from left to right, Leonie DeLorme, Julie Johnson, and Joe DeLorme. (Courtesy of the DeLorme family.)

Seven

SPECIAL OCCASIONS

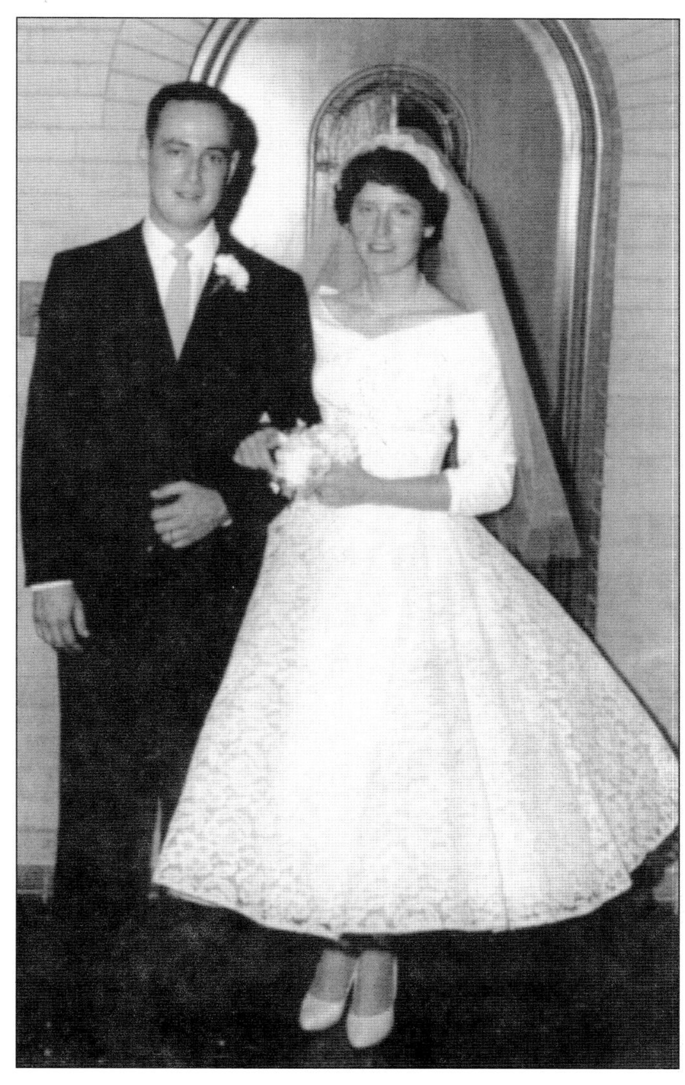

Harry DeLorme Sr. and his bride, Rita, were married at Blessed Sacrament Church in 1959 and called Parkside home for decades. (Courtesy of the DeLorme family.)

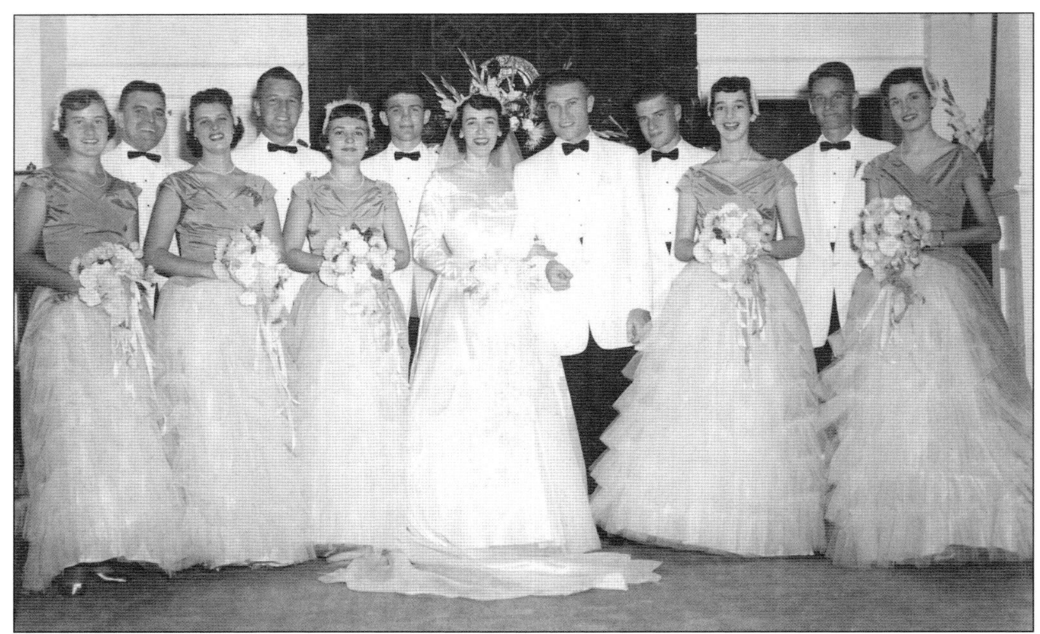

Nancy Morrissey married Bart Shea on September 12, 1953, at Sacred Heart Catholic Church. The Sheas had their wedding reception at the Morrissey home at 1109 Washington Avenue. The wedding party included, from left to right, (first row) Ann Marie Shea, Beverly Lysaught, Marjorie Morrissey, Nancy Morrissey Shea, Isabelle Powers, and Kitty Goins; (second row) Tom Dillon, Billy O'Hayer, Tom Coleman, Bart Shea, Joe Shea, and Jack Schaaf. (Courtesy of the Shea family.)

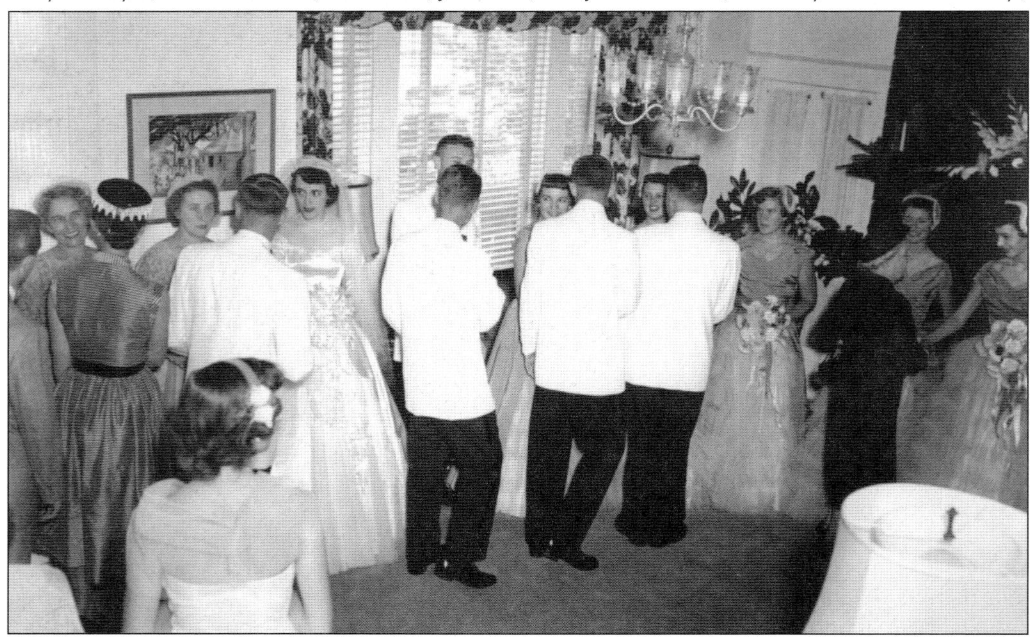

The receiving line for the Morrissey-Shea wedding reception was in the living room of the Morrissey's Washington Avenue home, which was decorated with magnolia leaves, gladioli, chrysanthemums, and ferns. Nancy was 20 when she married. After she raised seven children, she earned both bachelor's and master's degrees, taught high school, and later was principal of Windsor Forest High School in Savannah. (Courtesy of the Shea family.)

From left to right are
Billie Morrissey, Robert
Morrissey, Nancy
and Bart Shea, and
Ernestine Shea. When
the Sheas moved into
the home around
1968, they added a
swimming pool in the
side yard to the left of
the home. The house is
situated on several lots
and includes a garage
apartment where
Ernestine Shea lived for
many years. (Courtesy
of the Shea family.)

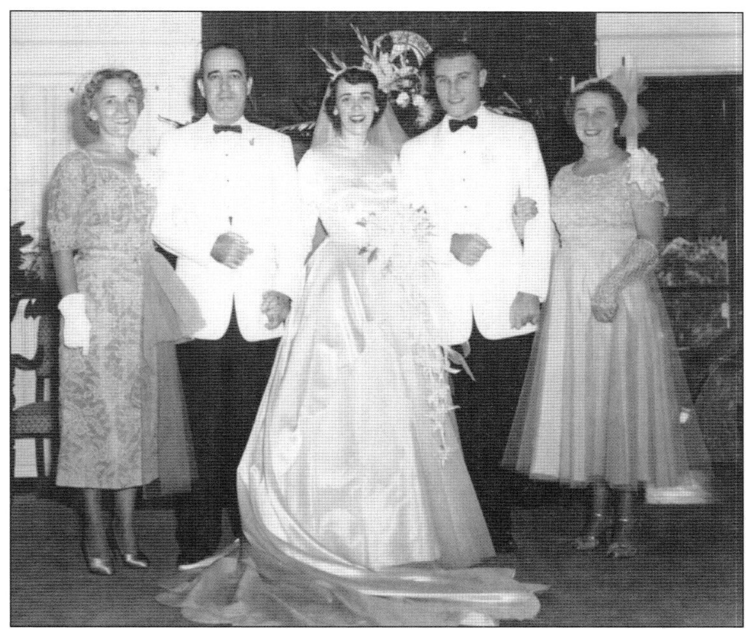

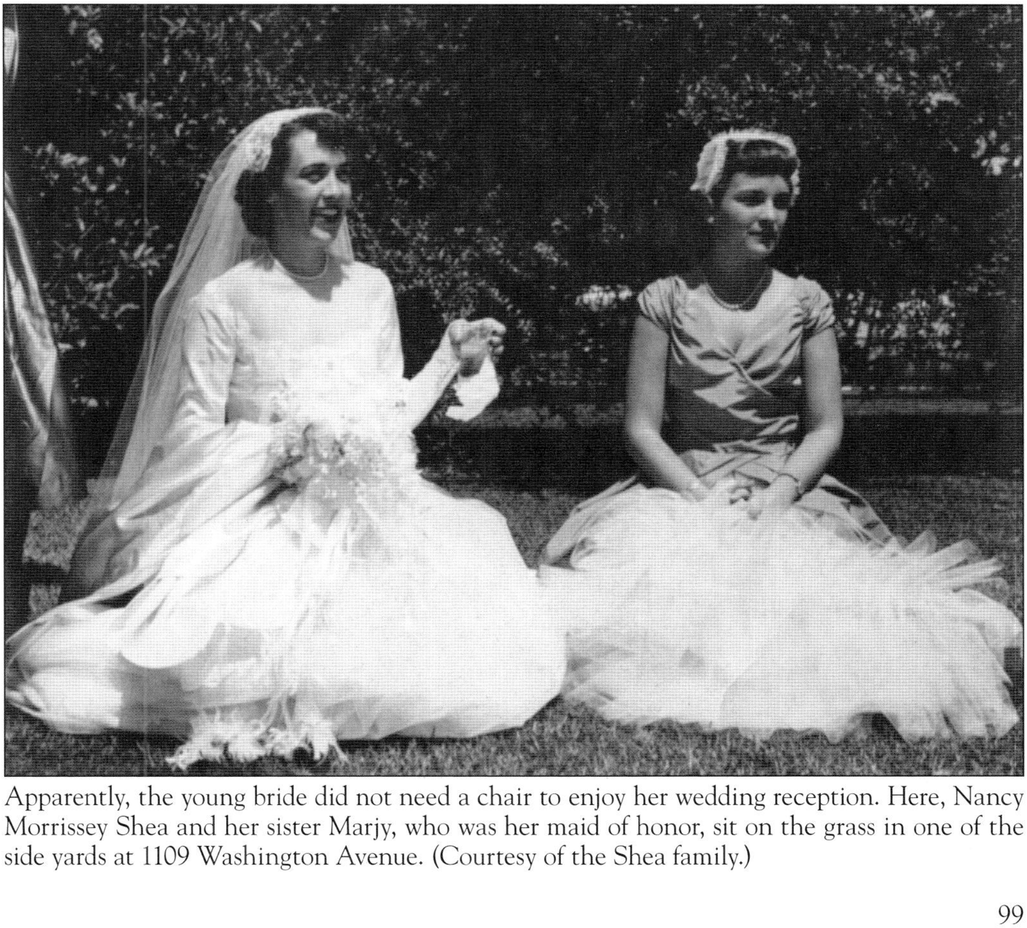

Apparently, the young bride did not need a chair to enjoy her wedding reception. Here, Nancy
Morrissey Shea and her sister Marjy, who was her maid of honor, sit on the grass in one of the
side yards at 1109 Washington Avenue. (Courtesy of the Shea family.)

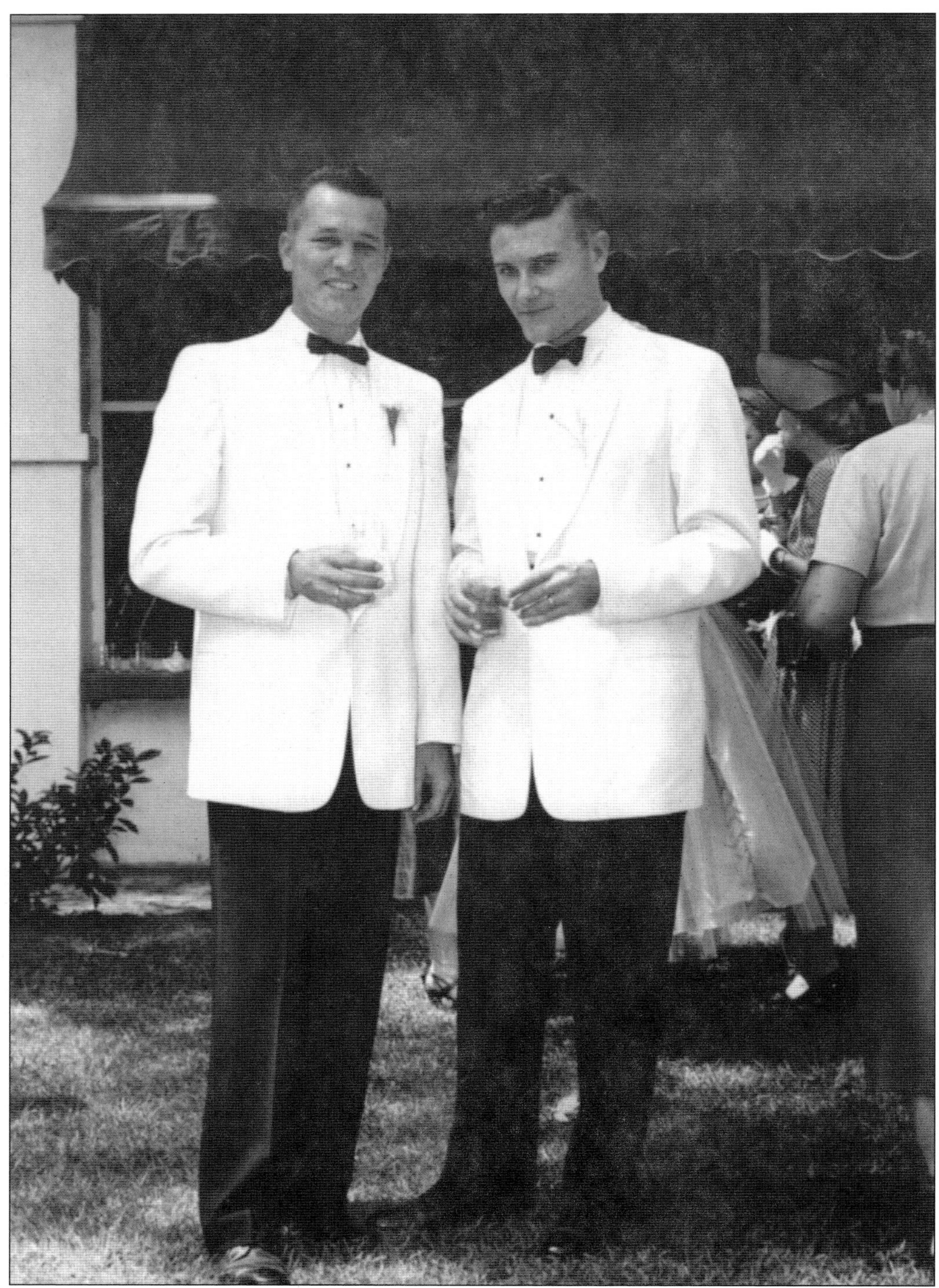

Groom Bart Shea, right, takes a break from the festivities to chat with groomsman Billy O'Hayer. Both look dapper in white dinner jackets and bow ties. In later years, Bart, who was an attorney, also served as a member of the Georgia legislature. Sadly, he died in his early 50s after jogging around Daffin Park. (Courtesy of the Shea family.)

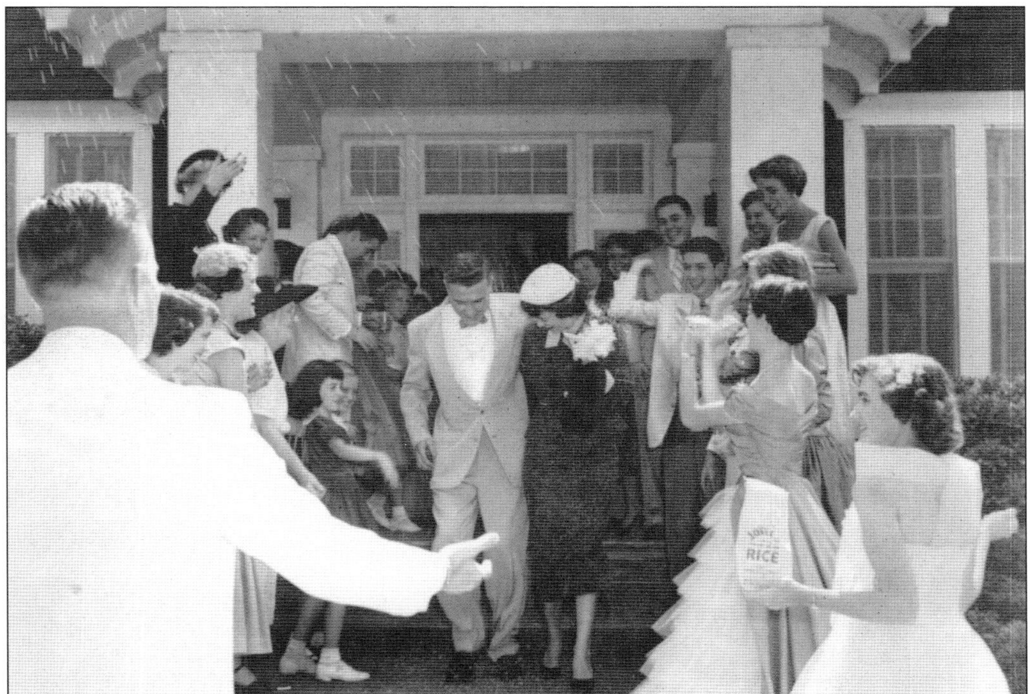

As was customary in the 1950s—as well as before and after—the bride and groom changed into going away outfits before leaving the reception at the Morrissey's Washington Avenue home. Nancy Morrissey Shea wore a beige and black wool suit, with hat, gloves, and an orchid corsage that came from her bridal bouquet. Guests at the reception showered the couple with rice as they left for their honeymoon. (Courtesy of the Shea family.)

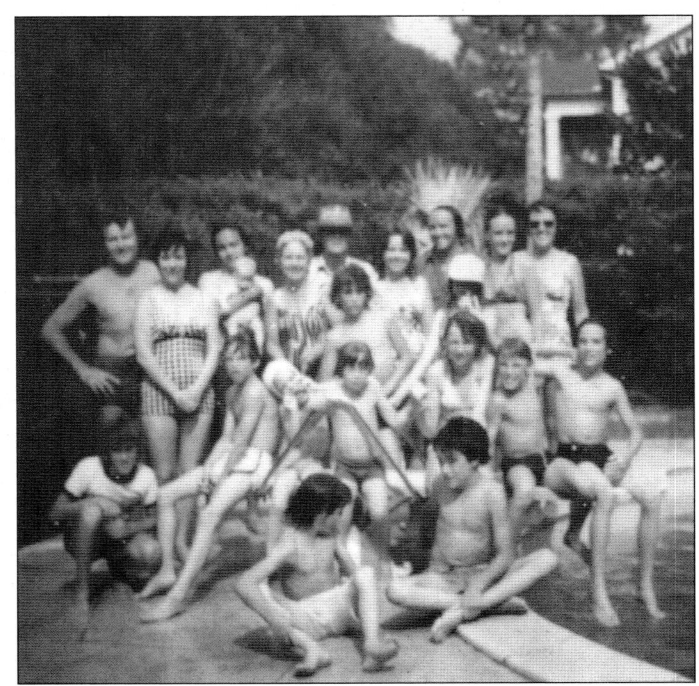

In 1959, the Morrisseys sold their Washington Avenue home to Billy and Marianna Weeks, who lived there until around 1968. When the Weekses put the house on the market, Bart Shea and his wife, Nancy Morrissey Shea, bought Nancy's former home and moved in with their family. Family members and friends are shown by the pool in the early 1970s. Bart Shea is at left with his hand on his hip. His wife, Nancy is in front of him wearing a one-piece bathing suit. (Courtesy of the Shea family.)

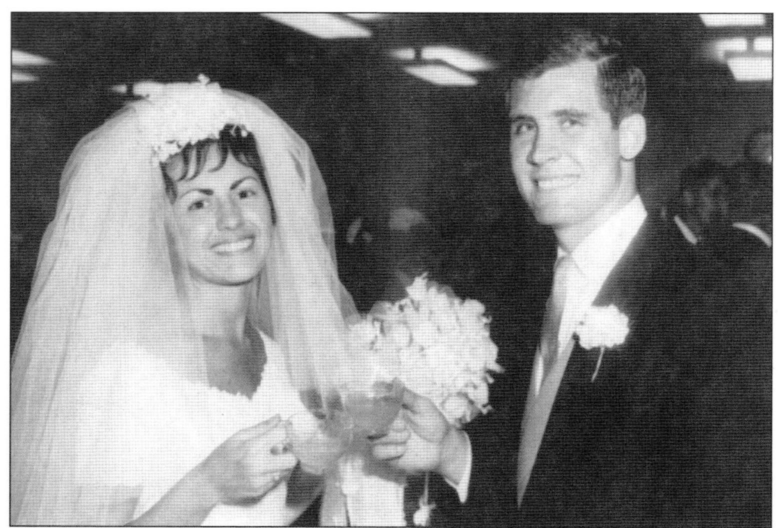

John Reckling, who grew up at 1513 East Forty-Ninth Street, and Shirley Toole, who lived at 1412 East Fiftieth Street, were married on July 7, 1962. The newlyweds are shown enjoying a cup of punch at their wedding reception. (Courtesy of Shirley Toole Reckling.)

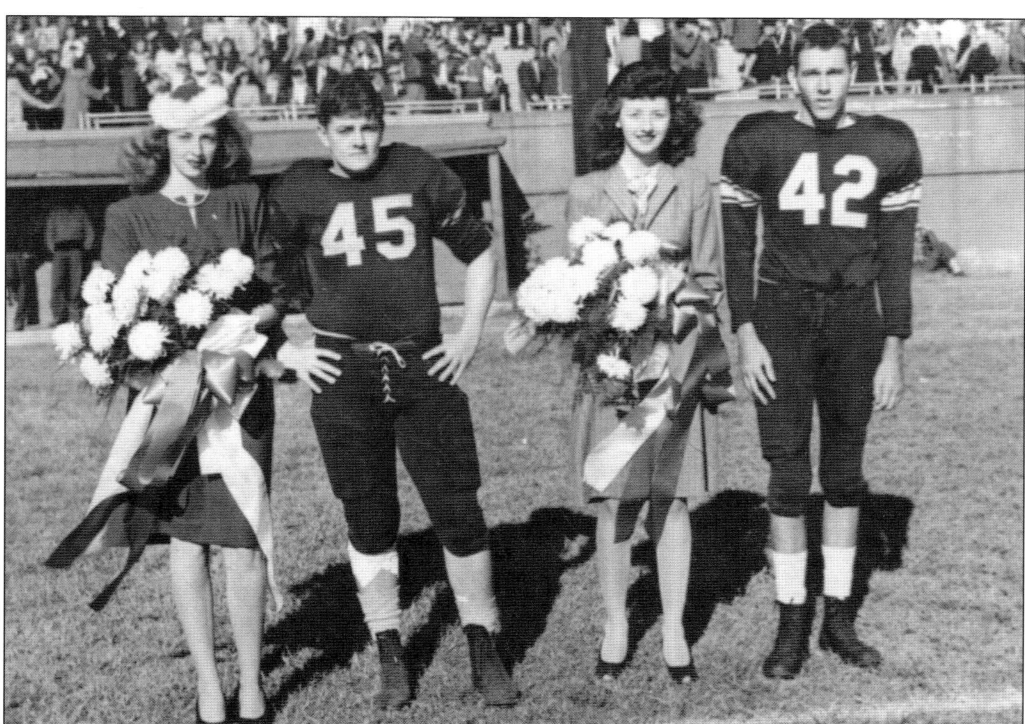

These young ladies (with their football player escorts) were named to the homecoming court during a game in the mid-1940s at Grayson Stadium. The stadium was relatively new, having been constructed to replace the old Municipal Stadium that was damaged by a hurricane. (Courtesy of the Logan family.)

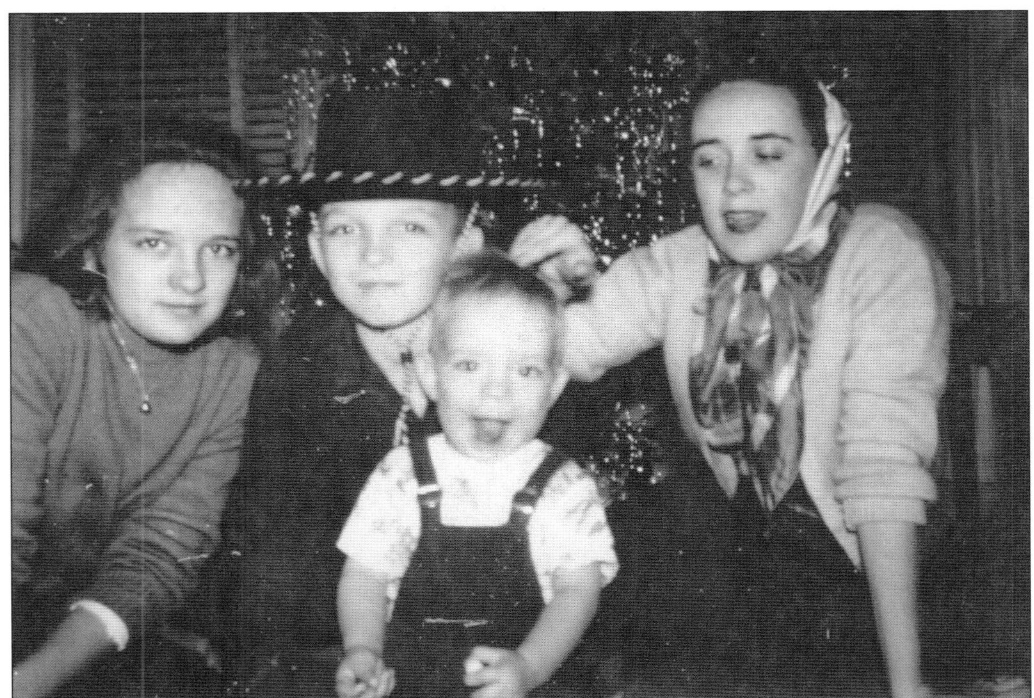

The Morrissey girls and their little brothers posed for this Christmas photograph in the late 1940s. From left to right are Marjy, Bobby, baby Billy, and Nancy. (Courtesy of the Morrissey family.)

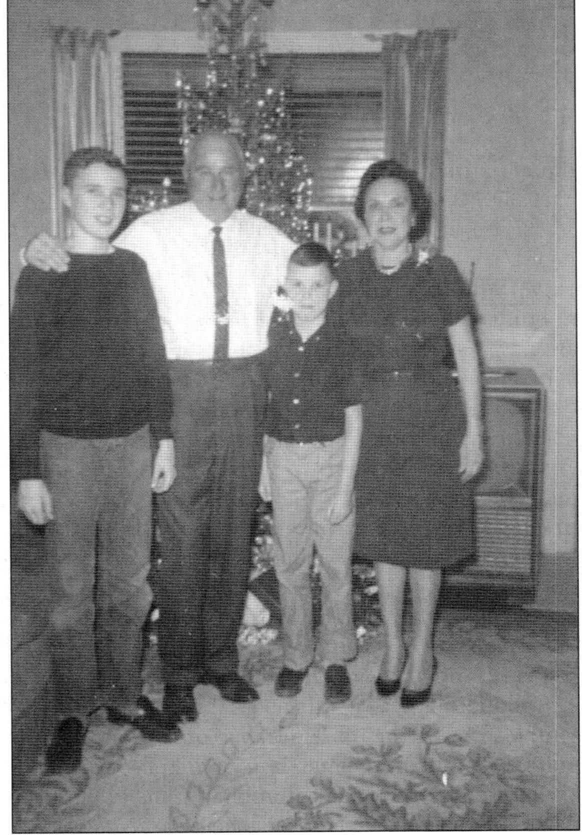

In the early 1960s, the Skinner family of East Forty-Ninth Street poses in front of their Christmas tree in the living room of their bungalow. From left to right are John, Harry, Charles, and Ola Skinner. Their console television set can be seen to the right. (Courtesy of Wallace Moye and the Savannah AMBUCS.)

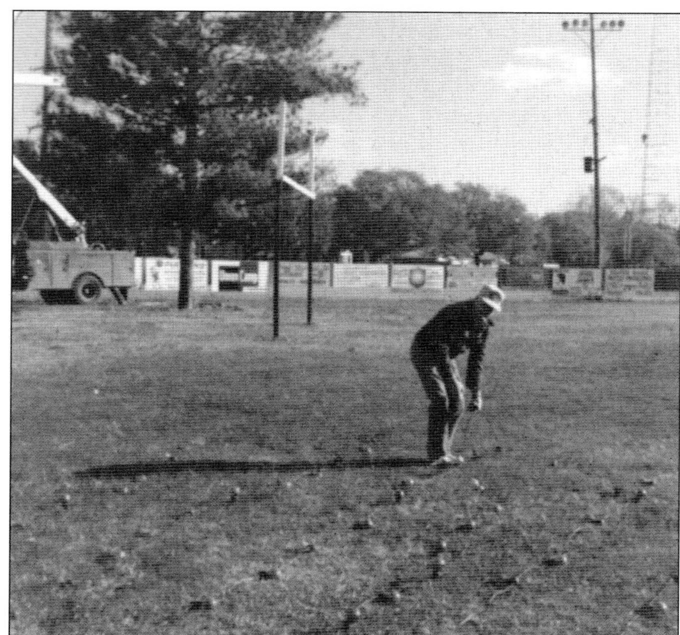

For a couple of holiday seasons in the mid-1970s, Savannah's Tree of Light was erected in AMBUCS Stadium. Decorating the tree was a labor of love for this AMBUCS volunteer, who untangles strings of lights that would go around the tree. In later years, the tree returned to Forsyth Park and other locations. (Courtesy of Wallace Moye and the Savannah AMBUCS.)

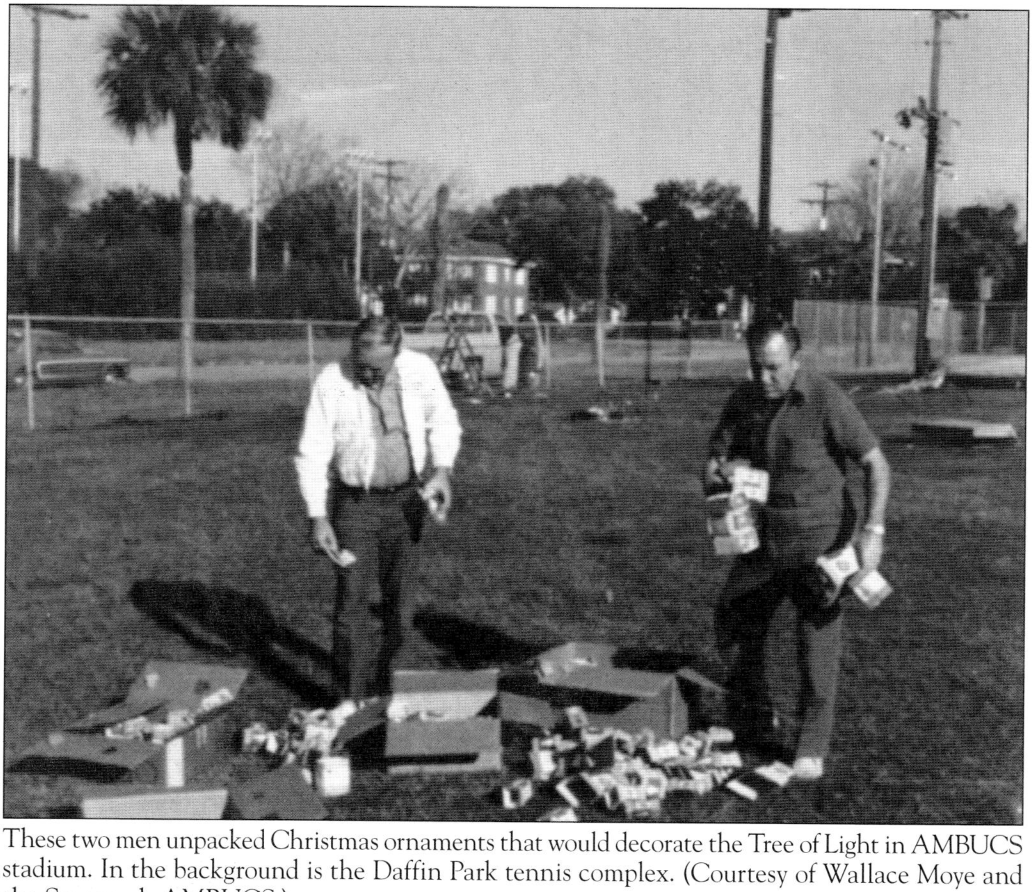

These two men unpacked Christmas ornaments that would decorate the Tree of Light in AMBUCS stadium. In the background is the Daffin Park tennis complex. (Courtesy of Wallace Moye and the Savannah AMBUCS.)

In 1962, the Easter Bunny filled up baskets belonging to Mike Burke and his brother Stephen. It is somewhat of an Easter morning tradition for many Savannah children to pose in front of blooming azaleas. (Courtesy of Mike Burke.)

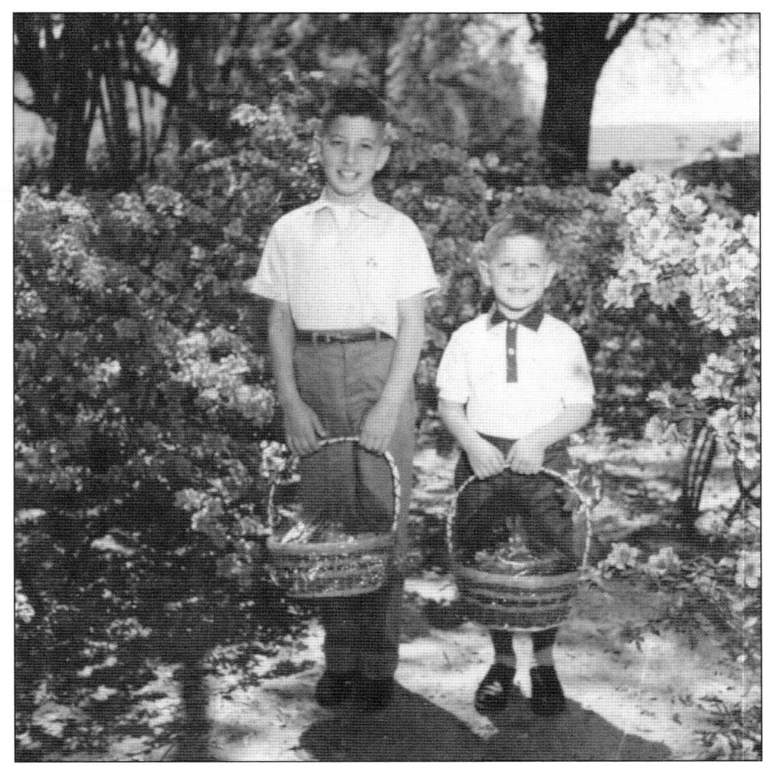

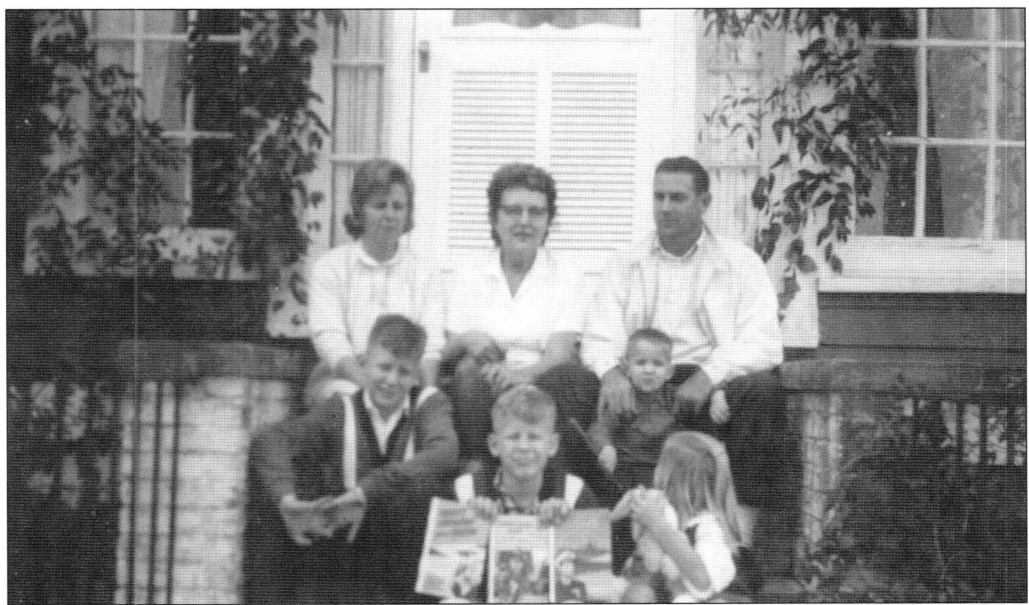

It must have been Easter in the early 1960s when Fred Garis took this picture of his wife, Katherine, with their daughter Nan's family sitting on the steps of the Garises' Washington Avenue home. From left to right are (first row) Bill, Kirk, and Pam Campbell; (second row) Nan, Katherine Garis, and Bill Campbell (holding Kerry). (Courtesy of the Garis family.)

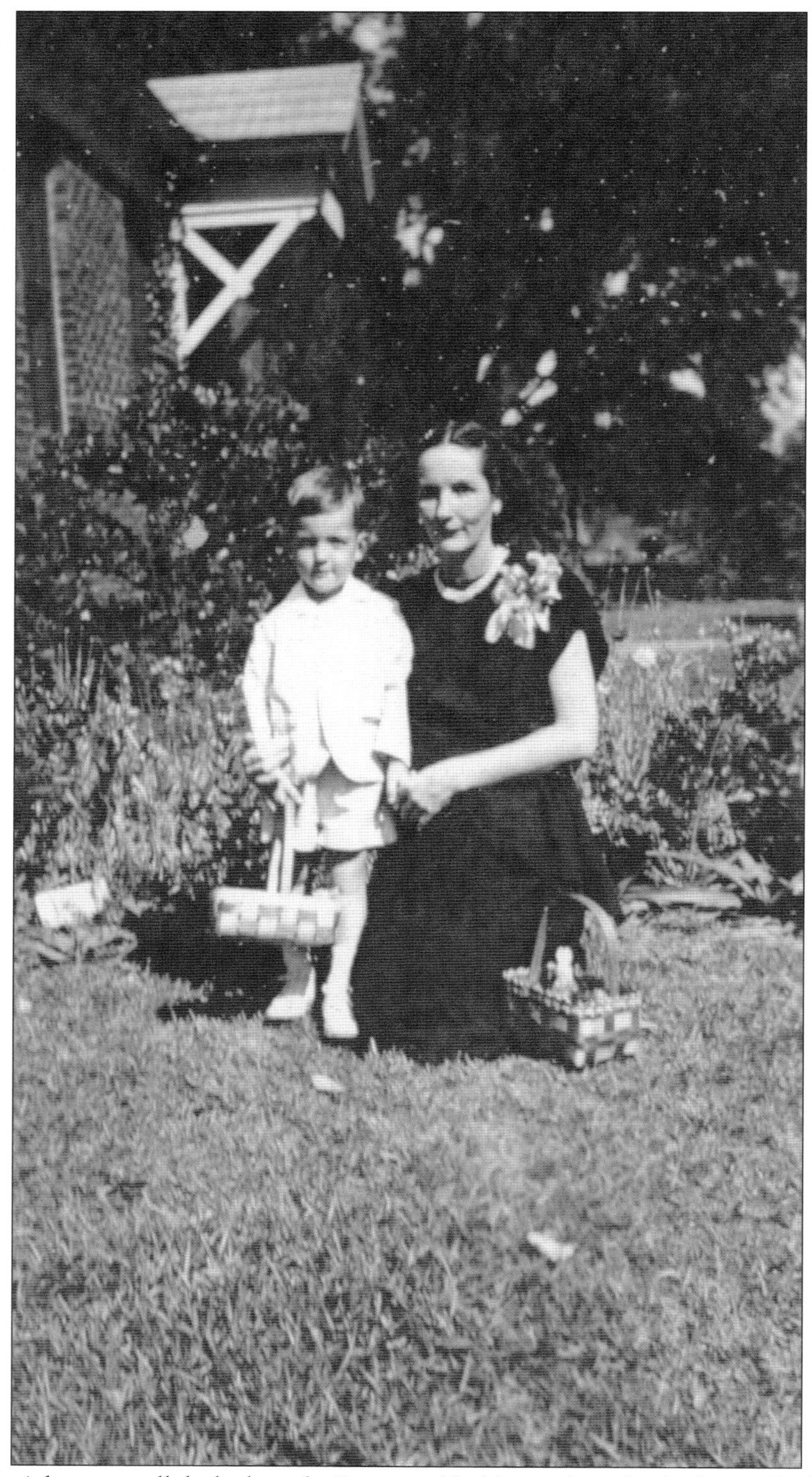

Little Billy Adams was all decked out for Easter and holding tight to his basket in the late 1940s when he posed in the 1400 block of East Forty-Eighth Street. With Billy is his mother, Florence Adams. (Courtesy of the Adams family.)

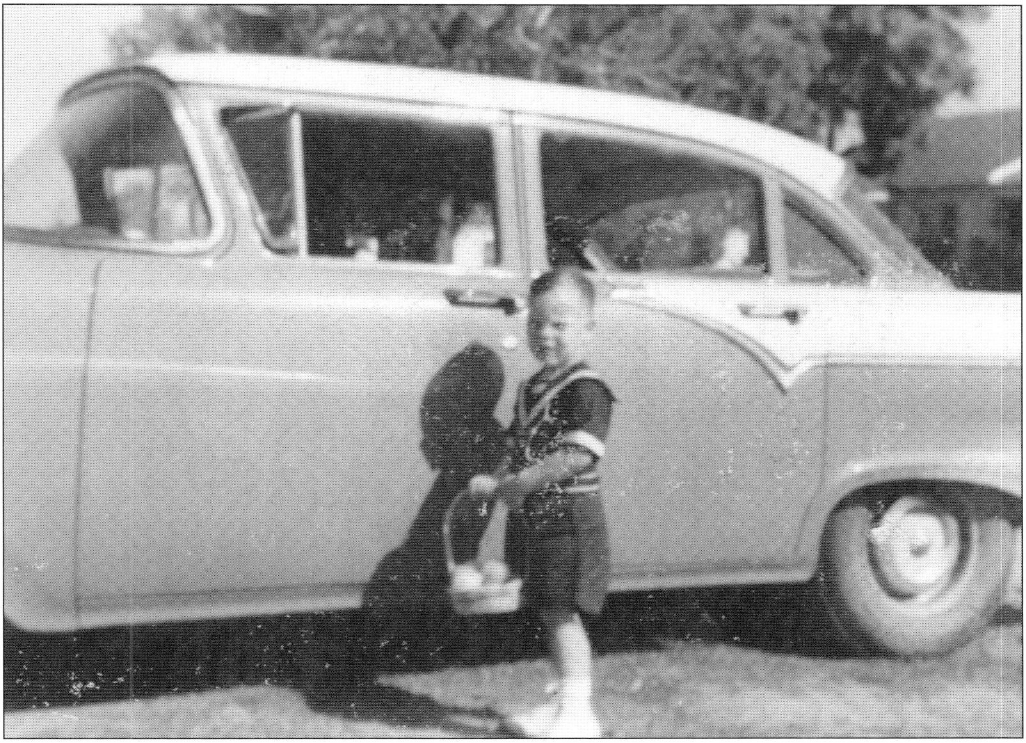

Holidays were perfect times for Parkside parents to bring out their cameras and take pictures of their children in all their finery. Pictured here is a young Charles Skinner around 1958 with his Easter basket. (Courtesy of the Skinner family.)

Helen and George Summerell Sr. celebrated their 25th wedding anniversary in February 1960. George opened Summerell Tire & Battery on Drayton Street just north of Liberty Street in 1937. The Summerells moved to Parkside in the 1940s. (Courtesy of the Summerell family.)

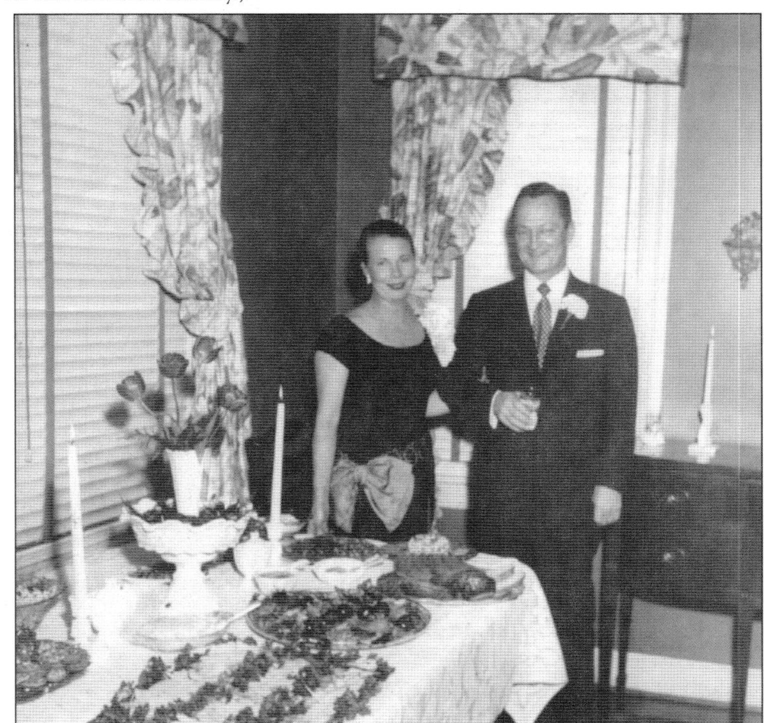

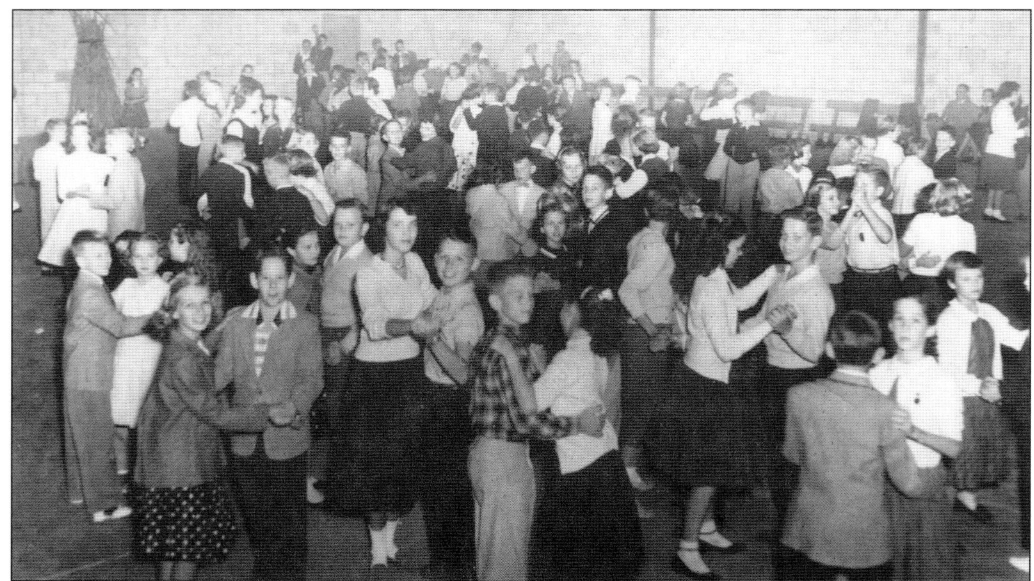

Both the Tiger Club and the Panthers Athletic Club sponsored dances or sock hops for area youth. This is a picture of one of those 1950s dances at the Tiger Gym on Bee Road across from Daffin Park. The song "Good Night, Sweetheart," was played at the end of every Panther dance. (Courtesy of the Garis family.)

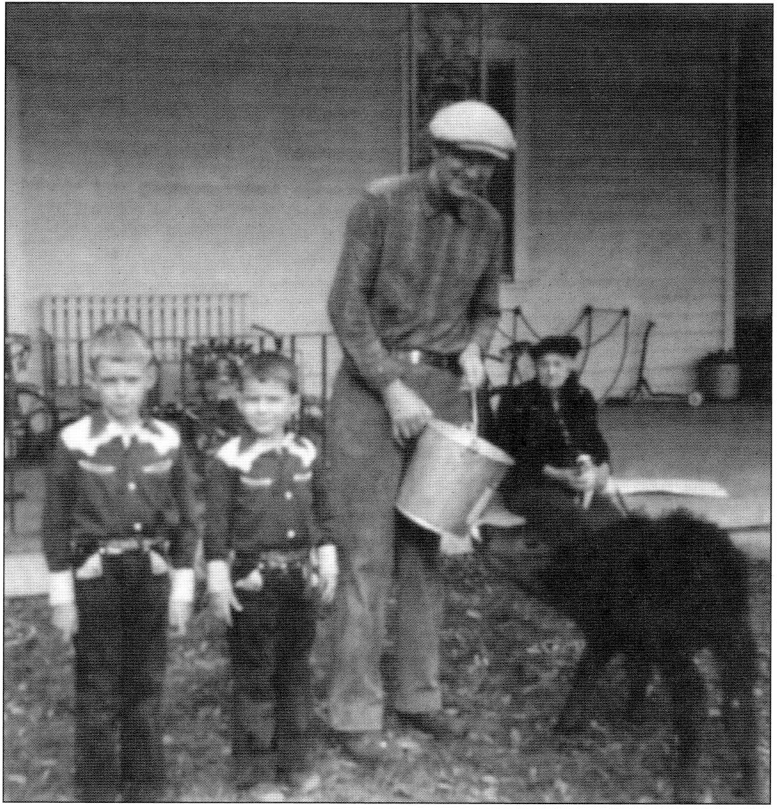

Rick Belford (left) and his brother Lee wear their favorite cowboy outfits for this picture at the family's Bee Road home. Also pictured are their father, Richard Belford, and their step-grandmother, Minnie Belford. (Courtesy of the Belford family.)

Little cowboy Billy Adams and family friend "Mr. Frank" are on the porch of the Adams home at 1426 East Forty-Eighth Street. For many years, both that block and the 1500 block of East Forty-Eighth were dirt. (Courtesy of the Adams family.)

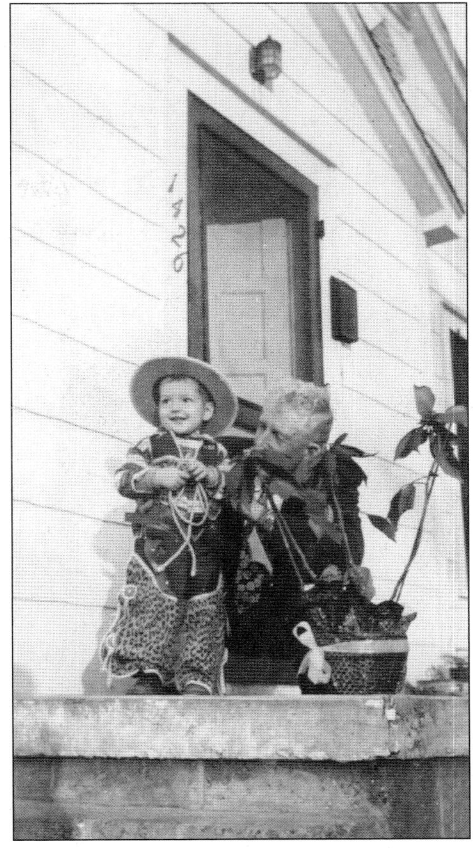

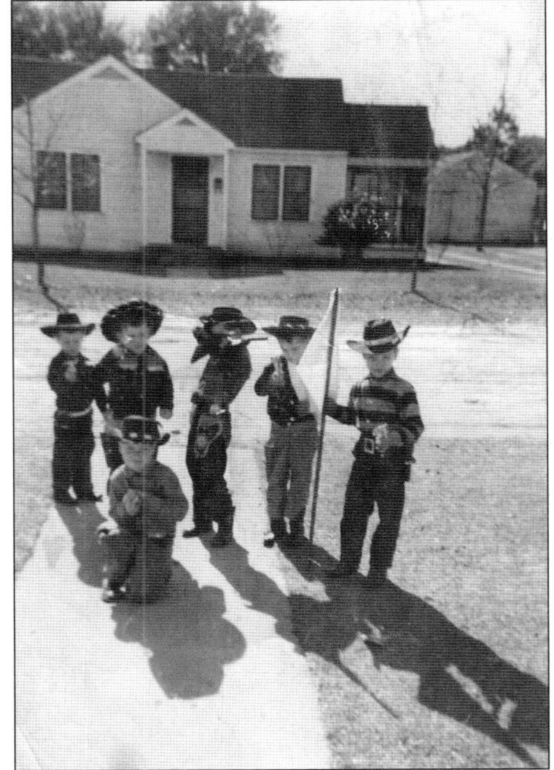

Boys who grew up in the 1950s were big fans of television Westerns and yearned to be like the cowboys they watched on the TV screen. These Parkside boys had all the gear, including a white flag they had captured from the Indians. From left to right are Paul Tuttle, Jimmy Lowery, Johnny Mulligan (kneeling), Bobby Adams, Jesse ?, and Pat Tuttle (with the flag). (Courtesy of the Mulligan family.)

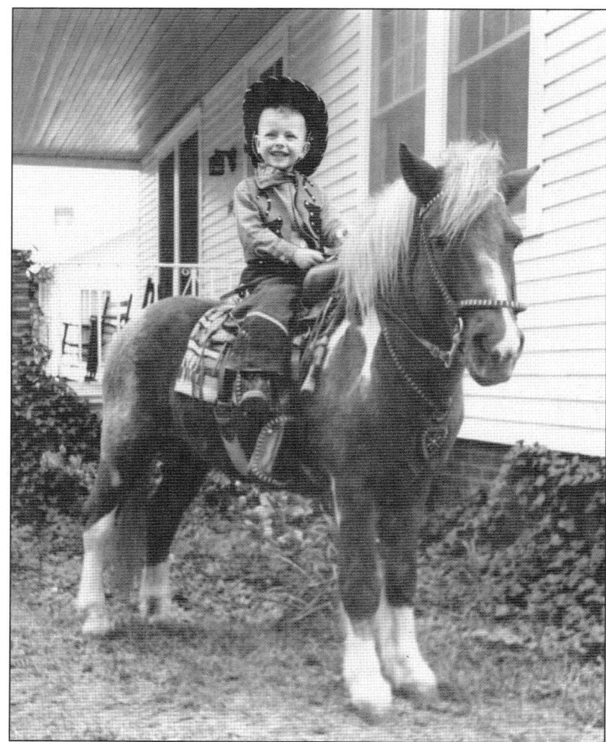

During the 1930s, 1940s, and 1950s, photographers with ponies came through Parkside and other neighborhoods to take pictures of children on the ponies. Ricky Smith put on his cowboy gear and grinned from ear to ear when he had his photograph taken on one of those ponies in the 1950s. (Courtesy of the Smith family.)

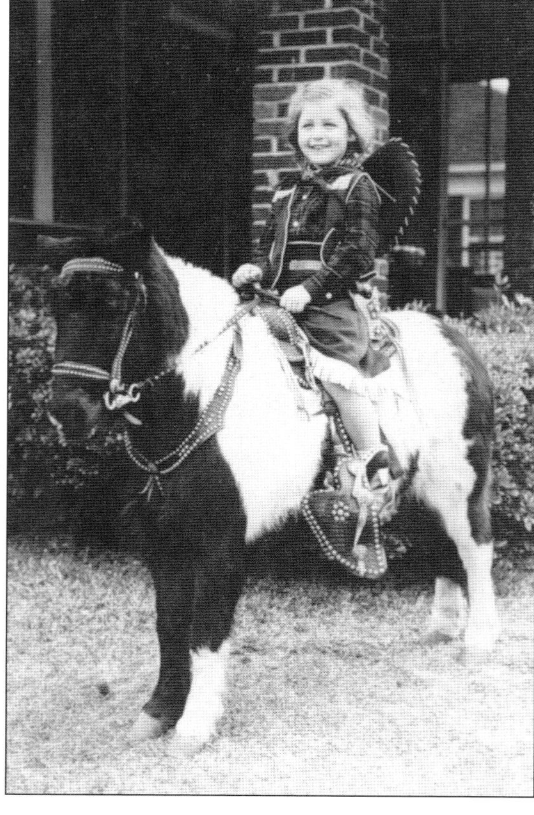

Cowgirl Linda Calhoun poses on a pony in the early 1950s in front of the Clark home at 1110 East Fifty-First Street. Linda had several friends who lived in the 1100 block of Fifty-First Street. She only had to walk across the lane from her house to make her way to her playmates' homes. (Courtesy of Linda Lynes Calhoun.)

Eight

UNFORGETTABLE NEIGHBORS

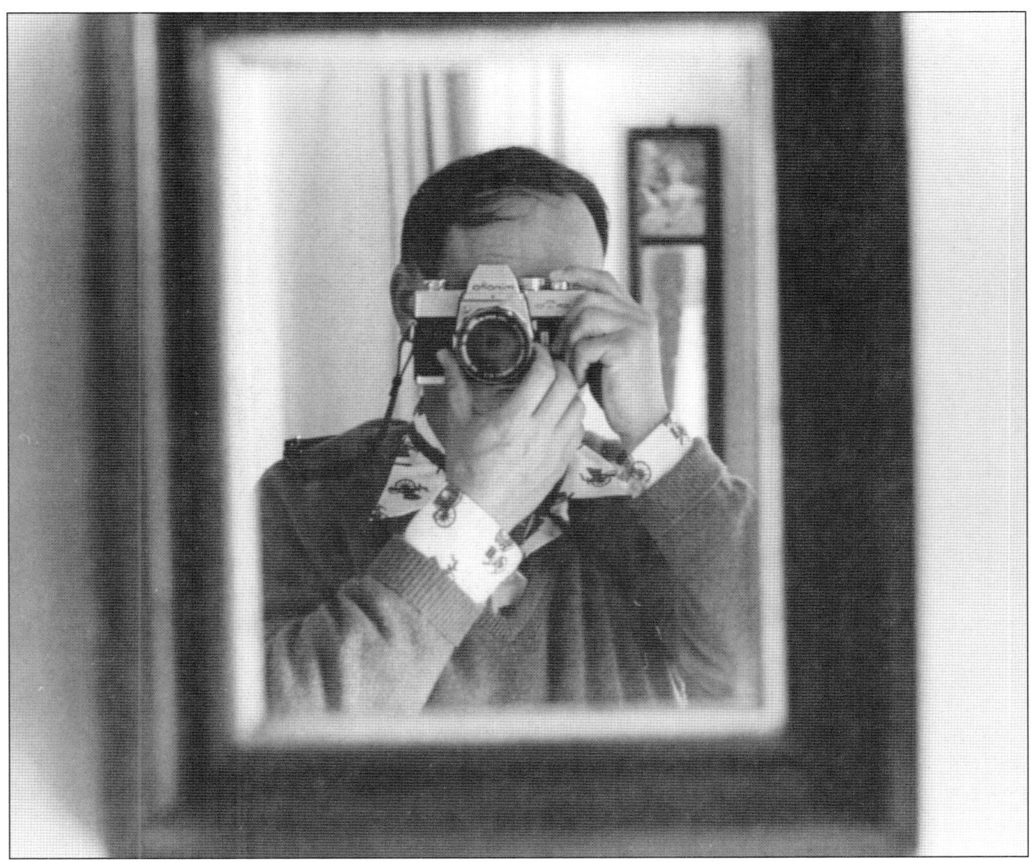

Parkside resident Harry DeLorme Sr. was an award-winning amateur photographer who snapped this self-portrait in the 1970s. He exhibited his photographs at local arts festivals and at Savannah's gallery S.P.A.C.E. (Courtesy of the DeLorme family.)

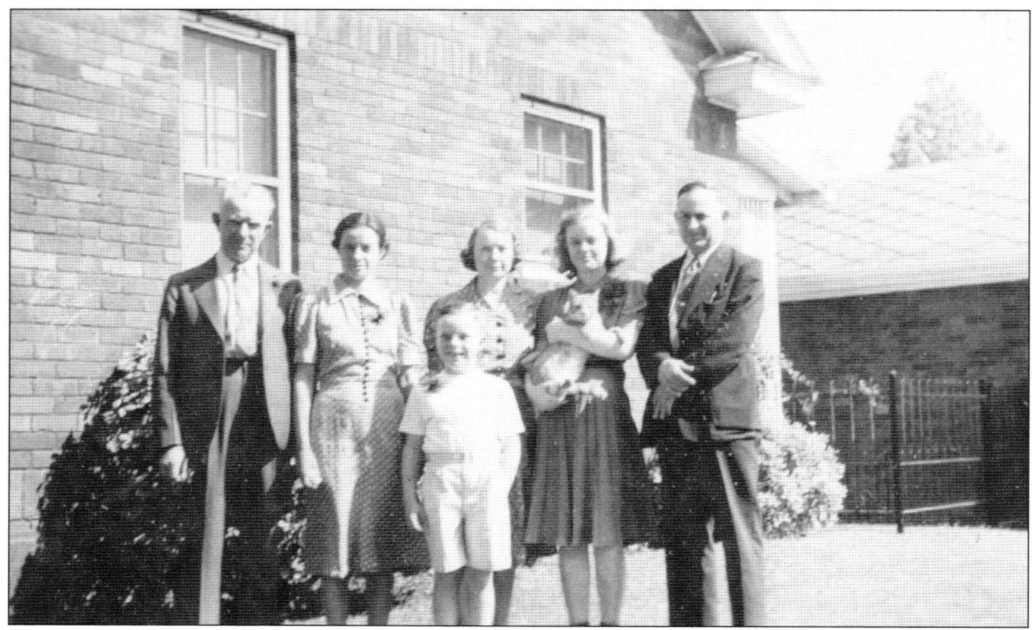

Louis and Kate Roesel built the brick home at 1301 Washington Avenue in 1930. Lou was an electrician for the Savannah Ice Company and later for Savannah Foods & Industries. The home faces Daffin Park and sits on the corner of Washington and Cedar Streets. In 1942, family members posed on the Cedar Street side of the home. From left to right are Lou Roesel, daughter Wilma Roesel, Kate Roesel, Kate's sister Florence, brother-in-law Tom, and their son Clyde in front. (Courtesy of Buz Ellis.)

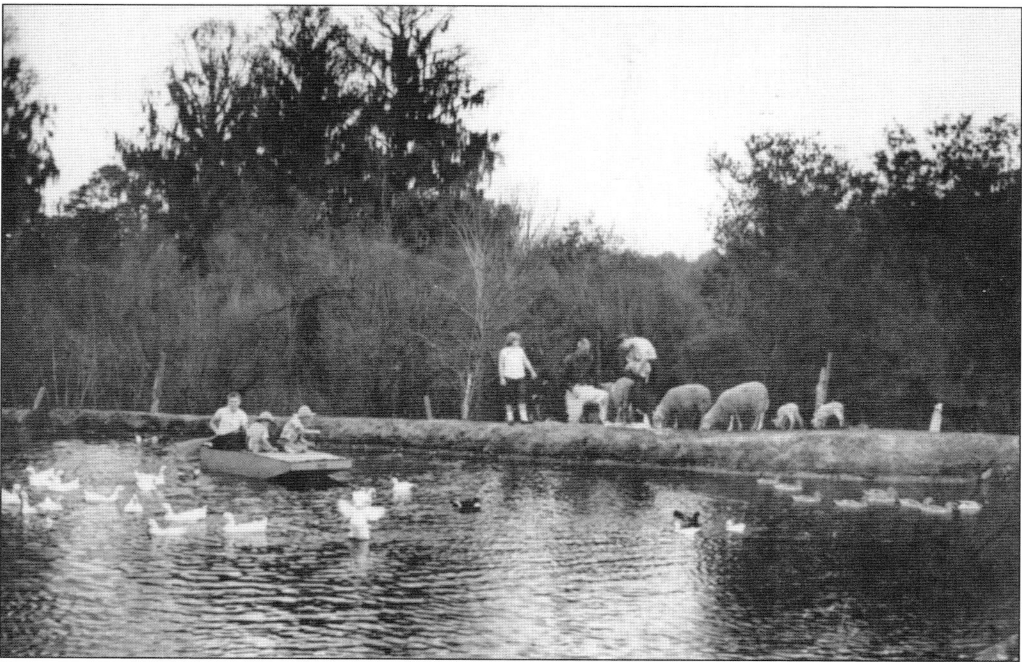

Pat Little, accompanied by two passengers, navigates a homemade boat in the Belford pond. Barbie Little stands at the edge of the pond along with two others and several of the animals that lived on the Bee Road property. (Courtesy of the Belford family.)

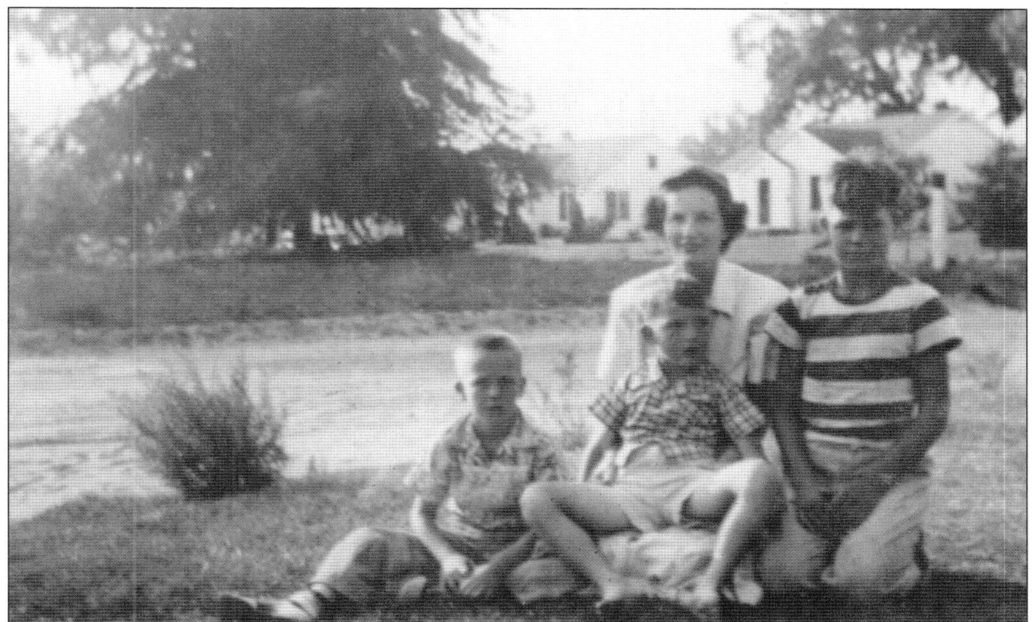

This picture was taken in the late 1940s on the lawn of the Tuttle residence at 1501 East Forty-Eighth Street. From left to right are Jimmy Dunn, Florence Adams (with son Billy in her lap), and Eddie Tuttle. (Courtesy of the Adams family.)

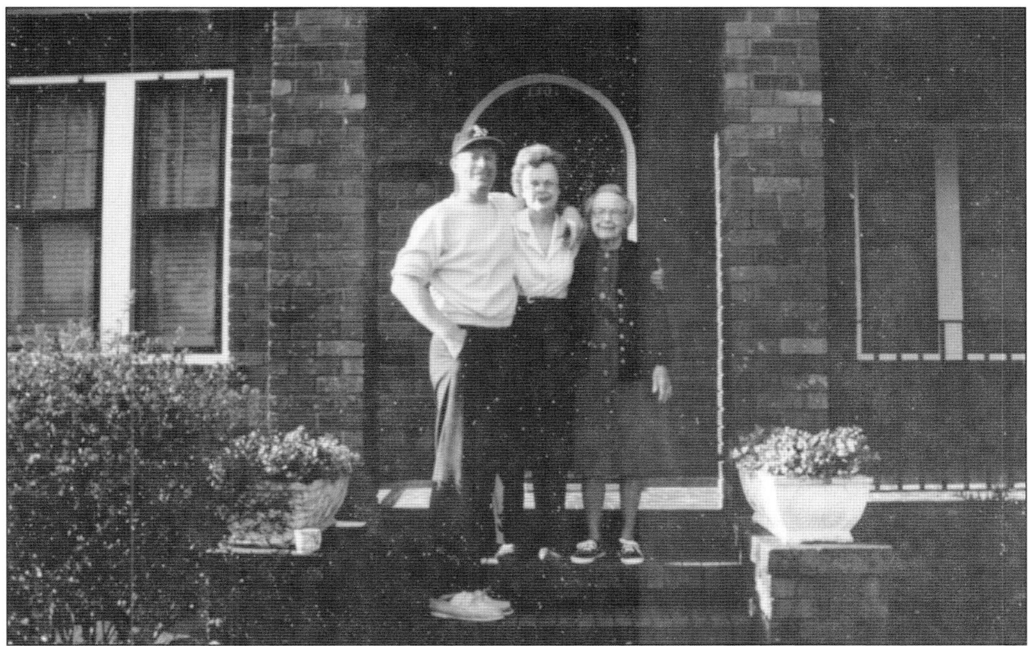

Buz Ellis, whose grandparents lived on Washington Avenue across from Daffin Park, has fond memories of playing in the park and attending games at Grayson Stadium with his father, Neal Ellis, who was sports editor for the *Savannah Morning News* in the early 1960s. Here he is shown in 1982 with his mother, Wilma Roesel Ellis, and his grandmother Kate Roesel. The house was in the family for more than 50 years. (Courtesy of Buz Ellis.)

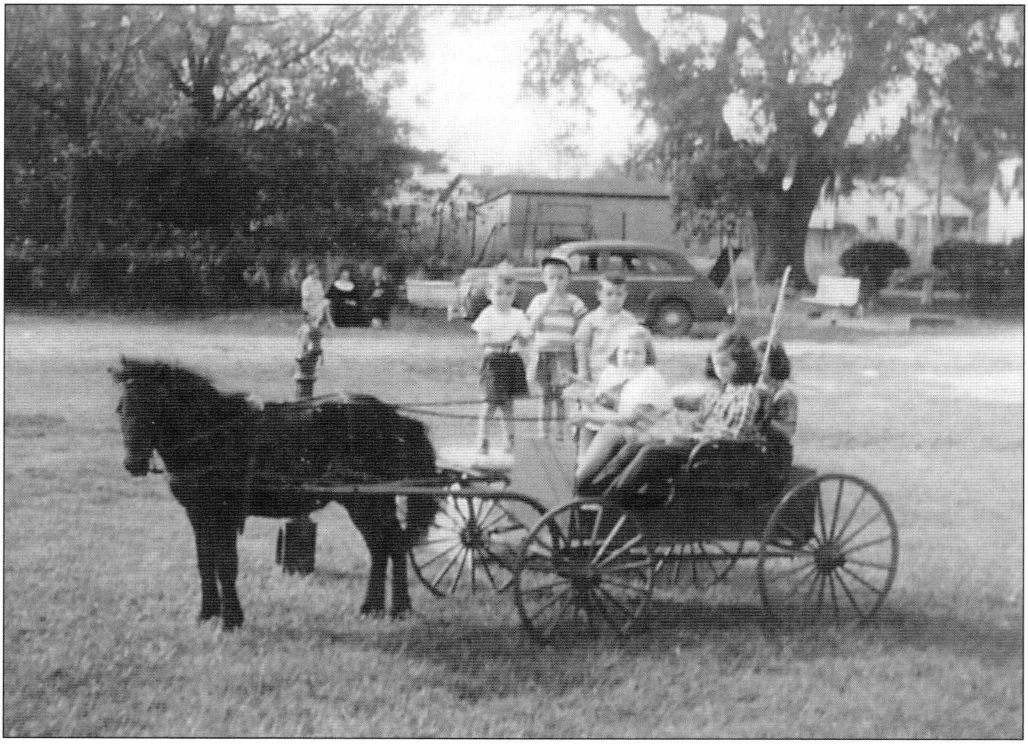

The Belford family welcomed visitors of all ages to see the animals at their Bee Road home. In the background of this photograph are two women sitting on a bench with a nun. Three little boys watch as Barbie Little (the blonde in the cart) prepares to tell Beauty the pony to giddy-up. The old Georgia Hussars building on Bee Road is behind the car. The Hussars were a troop of mounted rangers organized in 1736 by Gen. James Oglethorpe. They saw action in several wars and remained a horse cavalry until 1940 and are still an active unit in the Georgia Army National Guard. (Courtesy of the Belford family.)

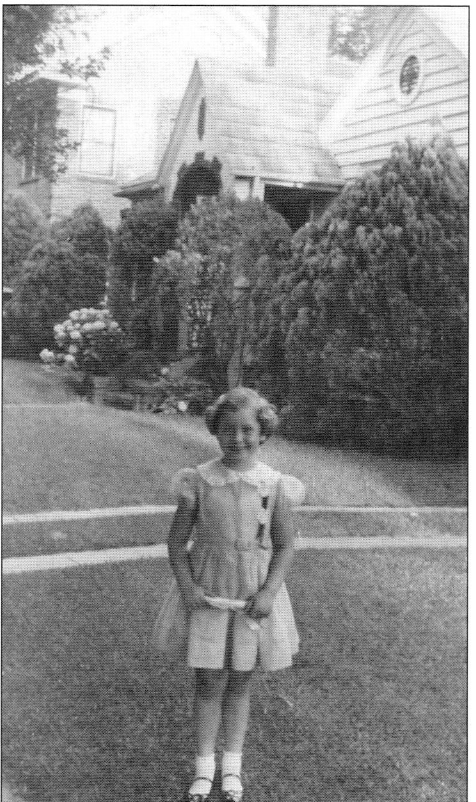

Like many Parkside and Ardsley Park children, Linda Calhoun attended kindergarten at nearby St. Michael's Episcopal Church. Here she is in 1954 holding her diploma and standing on the lawn of her Fiftieth Street home. In the background is the residence of Mr. and Mrs. Parker Dewberry. (Courtesy of Linda Calhoun Lynes.)

In the 1940s, Mary Orsini is standing beside her baby stroller. A sparse-looking Fiftieth Street near Bee Road is in the background. (Courtesy of the Orsini family.)

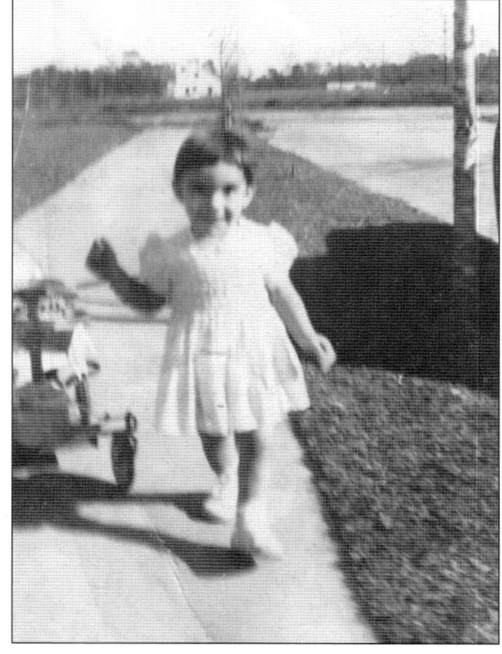

Charles Skinner and his family lived at 1207 East Forty-Ninth Street, and he and his older brother John made fast friends with many boys in the neighborhood. Charles and a few of his pals are shown here. They spent many an afternoon and weekends playing in each other's backyards and at nearby Daffin Park. (Courtesy of the Skinner family.)

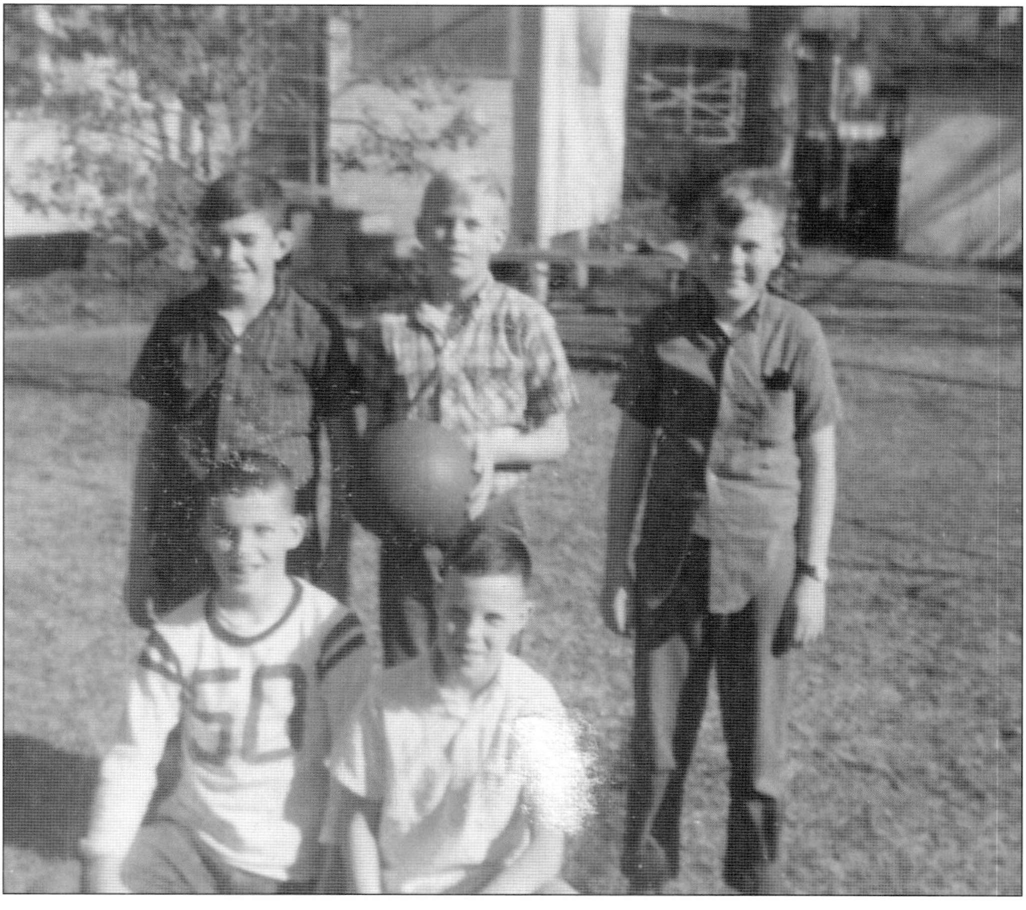

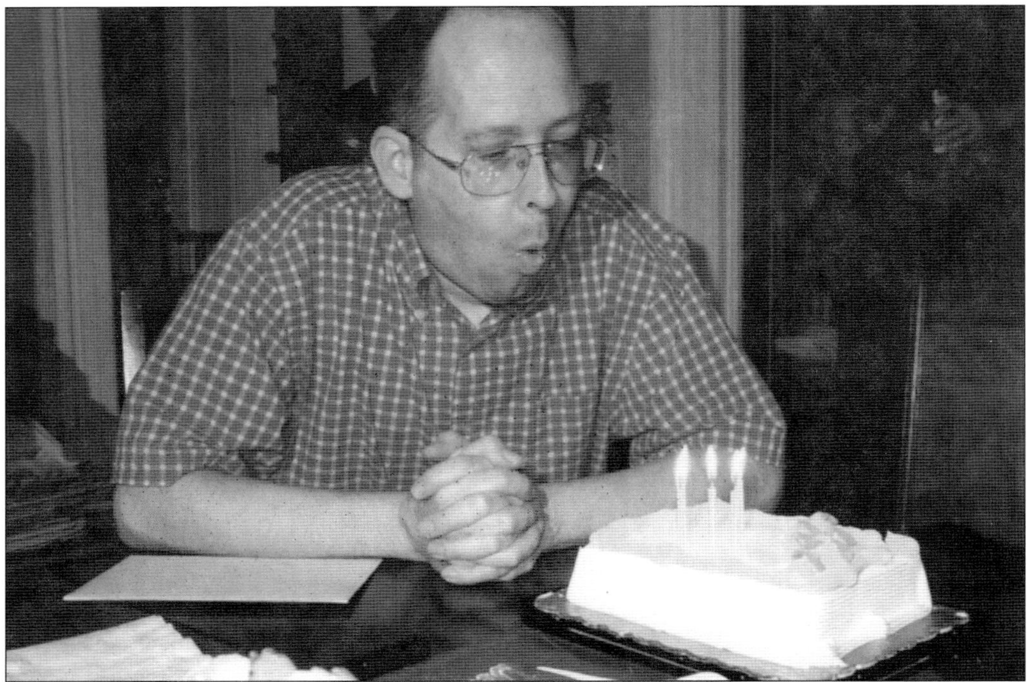

John DeLorme grew up on Forty-Ninth Street in Parkside and was instrumental in the effort to have Daffin Park and Parkside listed in the National Register of Historic Places. Here he is in 2006 celebrating his birthday. The park on the northeast corner of East Forty-Ninth Street was donated to the city by the Parkside Land Company in 1922 and likely was named Brinkman Park after Henry Christian Brinkman, who served as a city alderman for several terms between 1925 and 1935. It was renamed Brinkman-DeLorme Park in honor of John DeLorme. (Courtesy of the DeLorme family.)

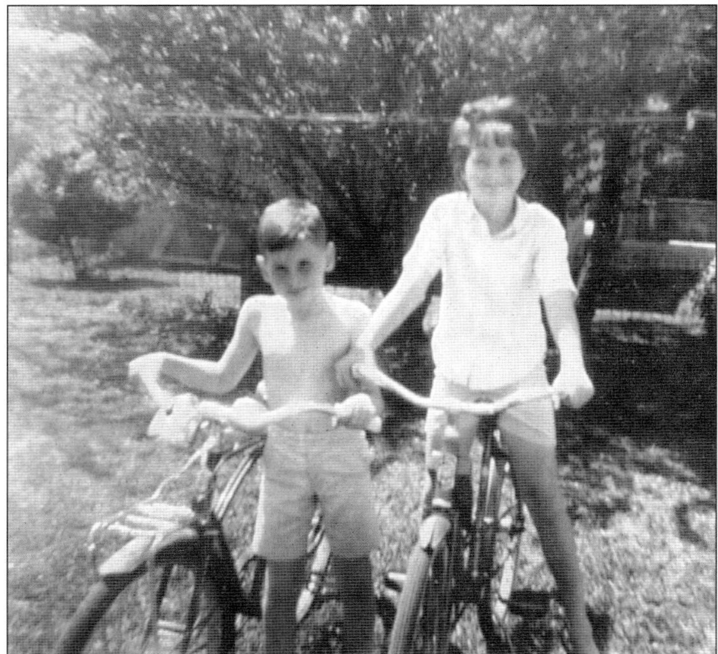

Like many neighborhood children, Jean "Cissy" Toole and her nephew Bobby Goff loved to ride bicycles throughout Parkside and beyond. Many people who grew up in Parkside remember being outside practically from dawn to dusk playing with their friends. They rode bikes, climbed trees, and played ball in the streets, among other activities. (Courtesy of Shirley Toole Reckling.)

Nine

MEMORABLE BUSINESSES

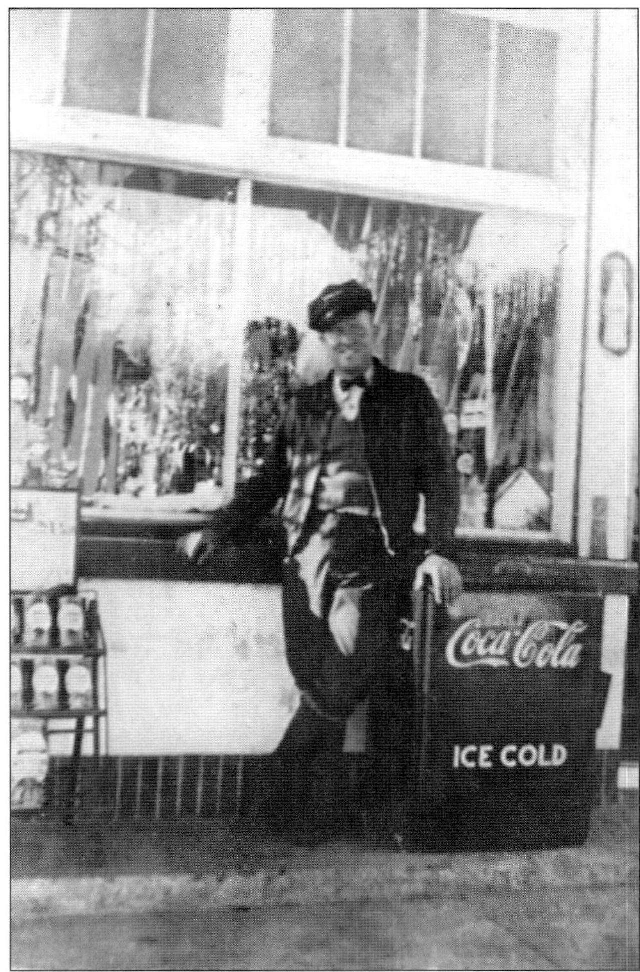

At one time, full-service gas station personnel wore uniforms. Rueben Ward "Red" Lariscy offered service with a smile at his service station on Waters Avenue between Forty-Ninth and Fiftieth Streets. (Courtesy of the Lariscy family.)

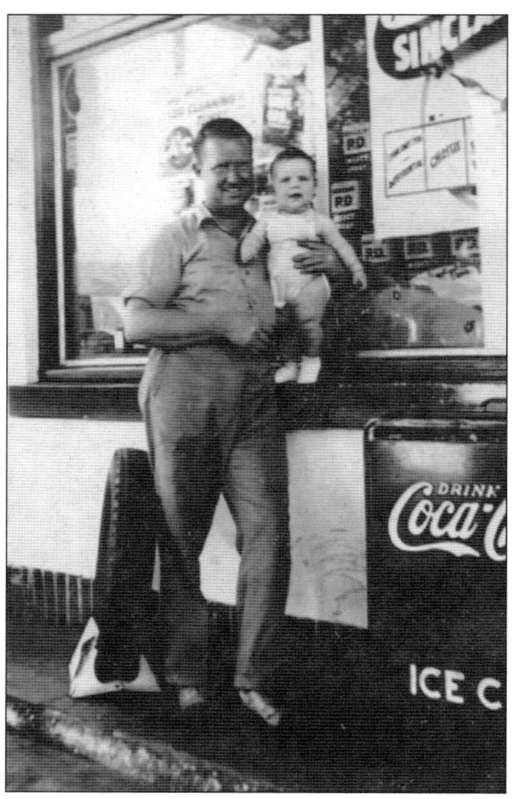

Red Lariscy opened his service station on Waters Avenue in the late 1930s. A few years later, he held his son Reuben Ward Lariscy Jr. in front of a Coca-Cola cooler at his station. The station was a fixture for Parkside residents, many of whom had house charge accounts long before the advent of credit cards. (Courtesy of the Lariscy family.)

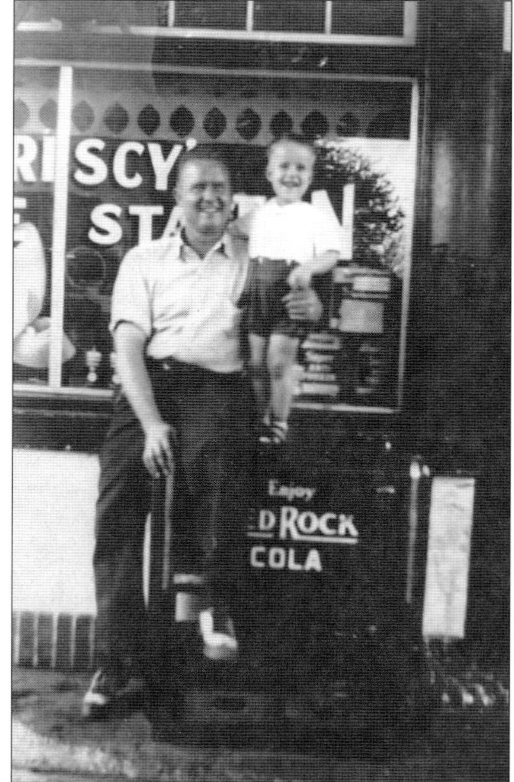

The backdrop for an older picture of toddler Ward Lariscy (in dad Red's arms) was a Red Rock Cola cooler. Note the bottle crates at lower right. (Courtesy of the Lariscy family.)

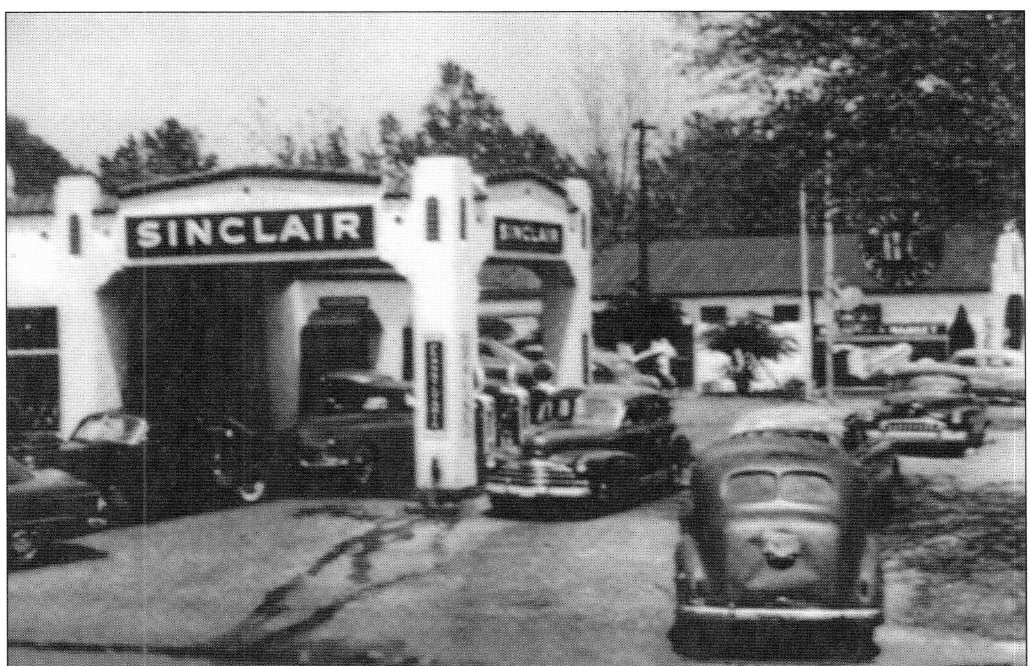

When Red Lariscy was drafted for World War II, he hired his brother L.P. to run his busy service station. But while Red was at the induction center, he had his birthday and became too old to serve. Instead, he returned to Savannah to help many loyal customers of Lariscy's Service Station. This is a view of the station from Forty-Ninth Street. (Courtesy of the Lariscy family.)

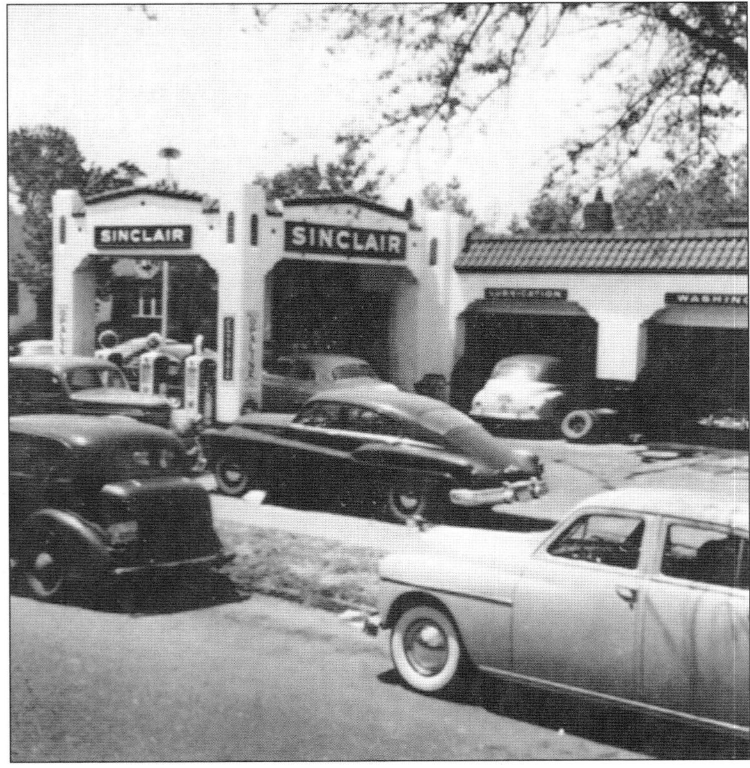

Red Lariscy's Sinclair Service Station was a bustling place in the 1940s and is where many Parkside residents took their cars for servicing or to fill up with gas, which included checking the vehicle's oil and washing the windshield. This is a view of the station from across Waters Avenue. (Courtesy of the Lariscy family.)

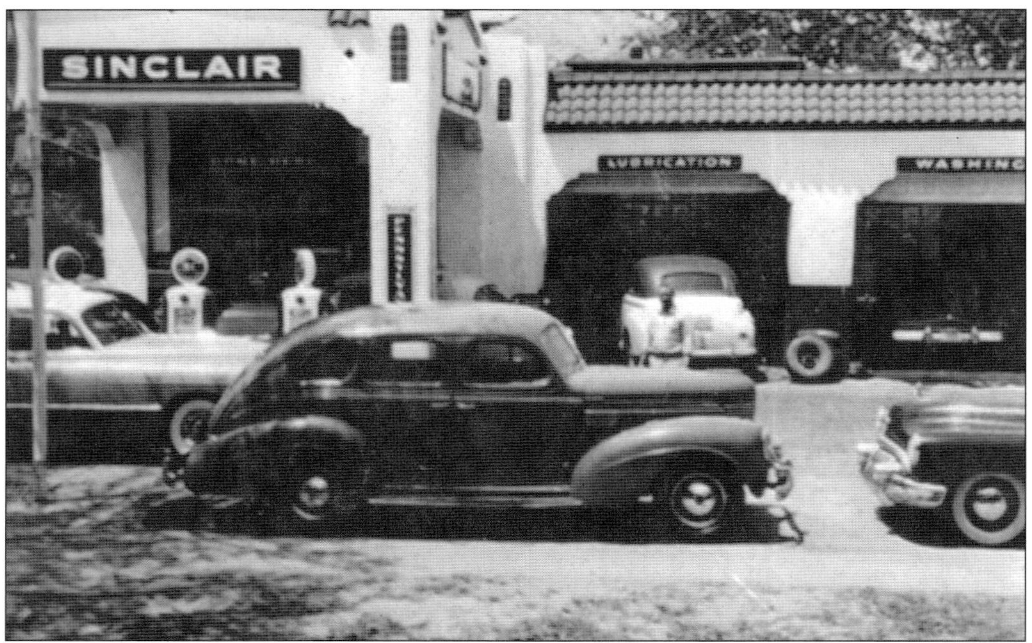

Red Lariscy and his station employees worked hard during the week, as seen in this photograph, but in his spare time, Red loved to fish. After he retired at age 65 in the early 1970s, he continued fishing in the saltwater at Bluffton, South Carolina, and in the freshwater of the Ogeechee River. (Courtesy of the Lariscy family.)

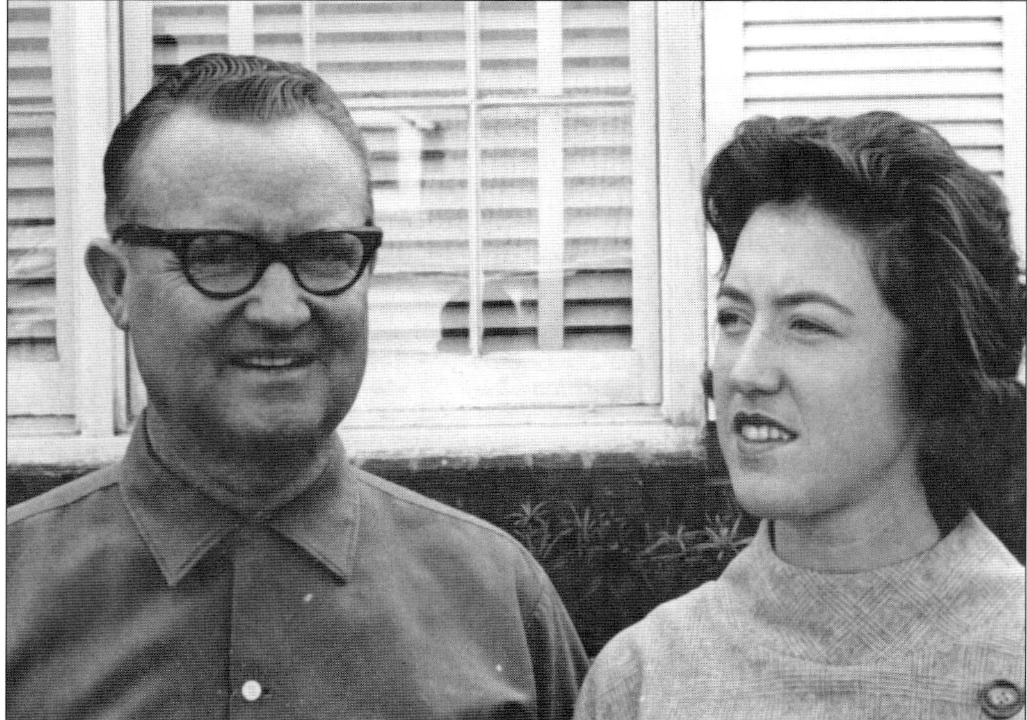

Here, Red Lariscy is pictured showing his unforgettable smile. With him is his daughter Harriett Lariscy, who sometimes helped do the books at the service station. (Courtesy of the Lariscy family.)

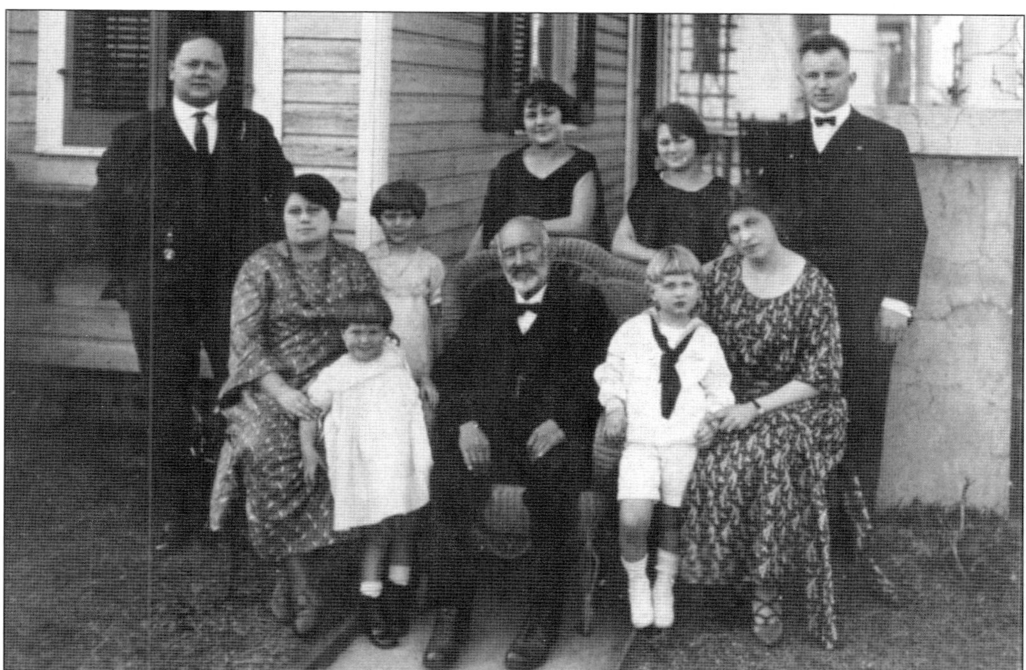

For more than two decades, Kleeman's Market on Waters Avenue between East Forty-Ninth and Forty-Eighth Streets was a familiar shopping spot for Parkside residents. This 1924 photograph includes the children and grandchildren of Leonard Kleeman, who was visiting from Germany. His son Carl George Kleeman Sr. and his wife, Betty Geffken Kleeman, had come to the United States around 1918. They chose Savannah because Betty had relatives in the local grocery business. Geffken's Market was on the northwestern corner of Broughton and Price Streets, where Carl Kleeman first worked. From left to right are (first row) Mary Elliott Kleeman, Veronica Kleeman, Leonard Kleeman, Carl George Kleeman Jr., and Betty Geffken Kleeman; (second row) Herbert Kleeman, Mary Kleeman, Anna Kleeman, Theresa Kleeman, and Carl George Kleeman Sr. (Courtesy of the Kleeman family.)

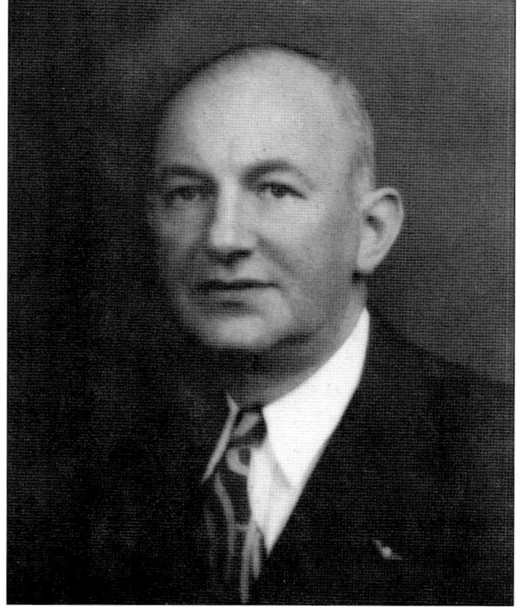

Carl George Kleeman Sr. owned and operated Kleeman's Market at 3205 Waters Avenue from 1934 to 1957. Though across Waters from the official western boundary of the Parkside neighborhood, Kleeman's catered to Parkside as well as Ardsley Park shoppers. The Waters location was the third market owned by Kleeman. The first one was on West Broad Street, and the second was off East Broad near Henry Street. (Courtesy of the Kleeman family.)

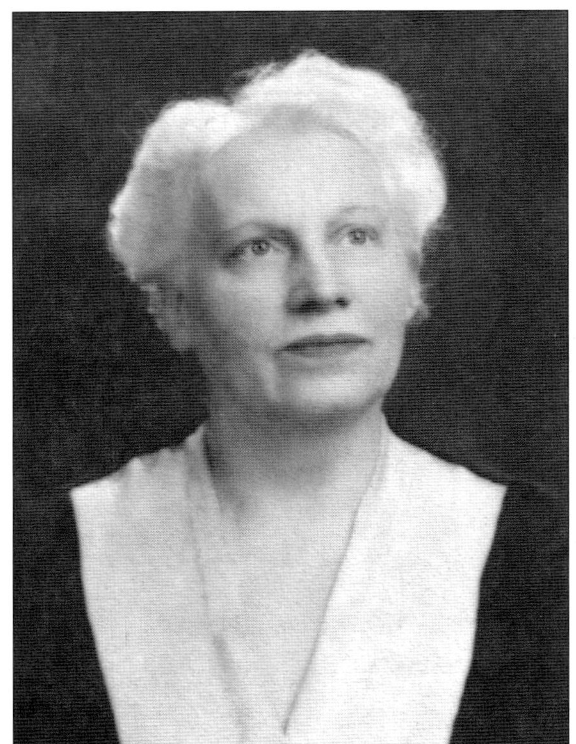

Kleeman's faced Waters Avenue, and Carl and Betty Kleeman (pictured) lived in the house next to it at the corner of East Forty-Eighth Street and Waters Avenue. Jan Bradley, whose grandparents lived in Parkside, remembers that her grandmother would call Kleeman's and place her grocery order. The groceries would come via bicycle ridden by a delivery man named Clifford. (Courtesy of the Kleeman family.)

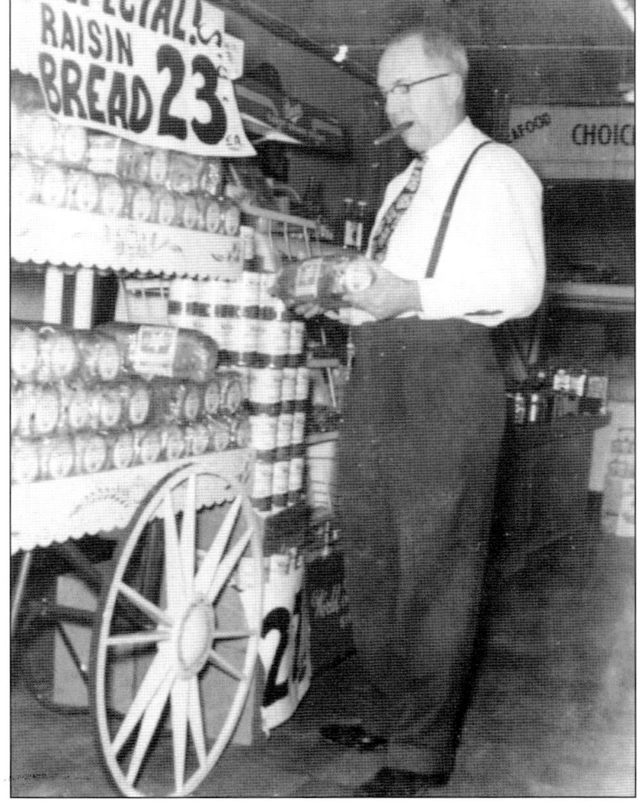

Al Orsini, pictured here inside his Waters Avenue market probably during the 1940s, owned several markets around town at different times. His daughter Mary remembers one on West Broad Street (now Martin Luther King Boulevard) and one off East Broad Street. In the late 1940s, Al Orsini was president of the Local Savannah Retail Food Dealers, an association comprised of 400 independent grocers. (Courtesy of the Orsini family.)

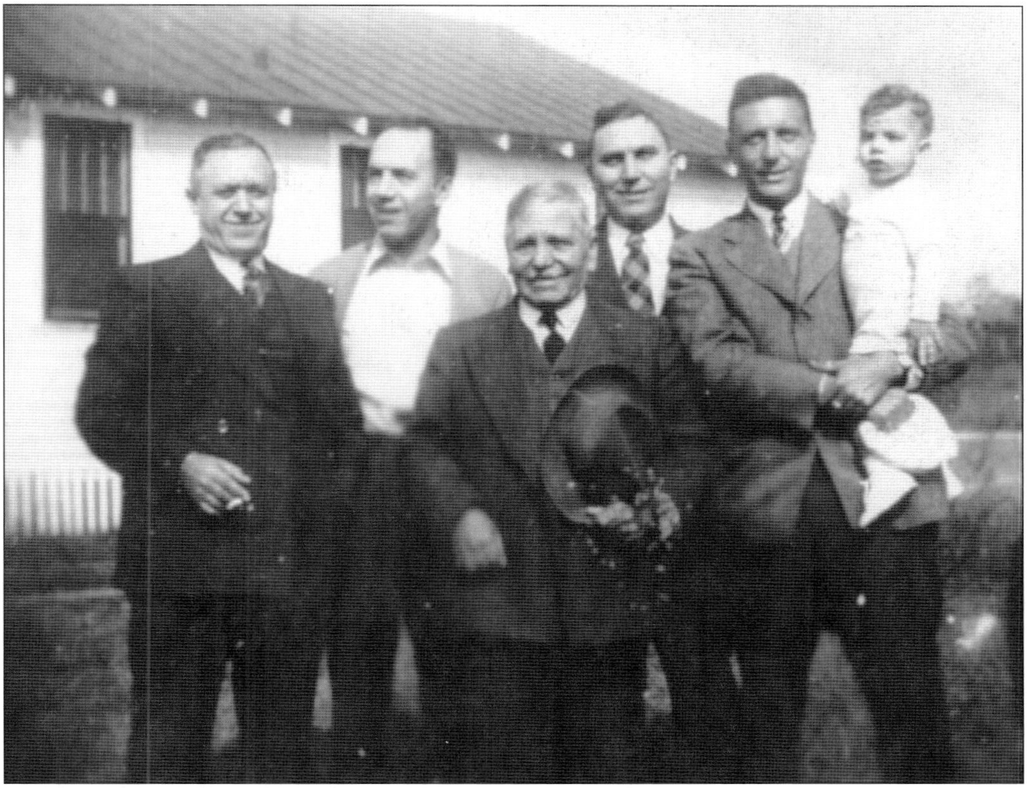

The Orsini brothers were all local grocers, including Al (second from left), who owned and operated Orsini's Market on Waters Avenue during the 1930s and 1940s. Shown here from left to right are Joe Rizza, Al, Marino Orsini (Al's father), Phil Orsini, and Iano Orsini (holding the baby). (Courtesy of the Orsini family.)

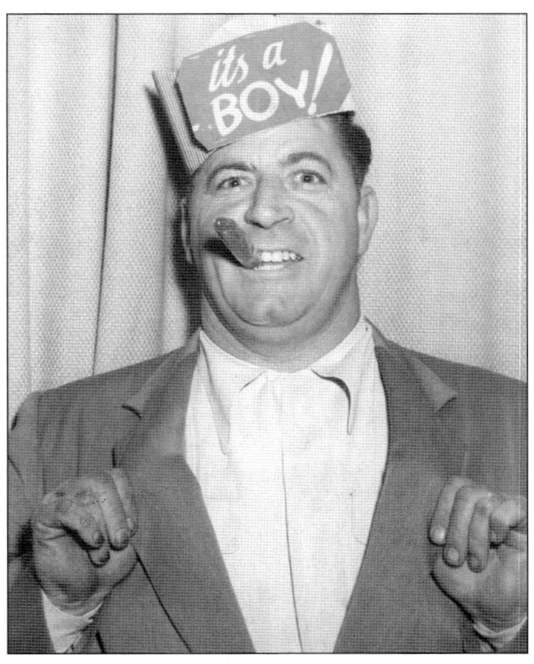

The late Carroll Burke was a former newspaper photographer who eventually opened his own studio in Savannah. For many years, he was the photographer for the Panther Athletic Club teams that practiced in Daffin Park. At the time of his death from cancer, the family was living with Burke's brother and family at 1125 East Forty-Eighth Street. After Carroll Burke's death, his widow and two sons stayed in the neighborhood and moved to 1219 Washington Avenue. (Courtesy of the Burke family.)

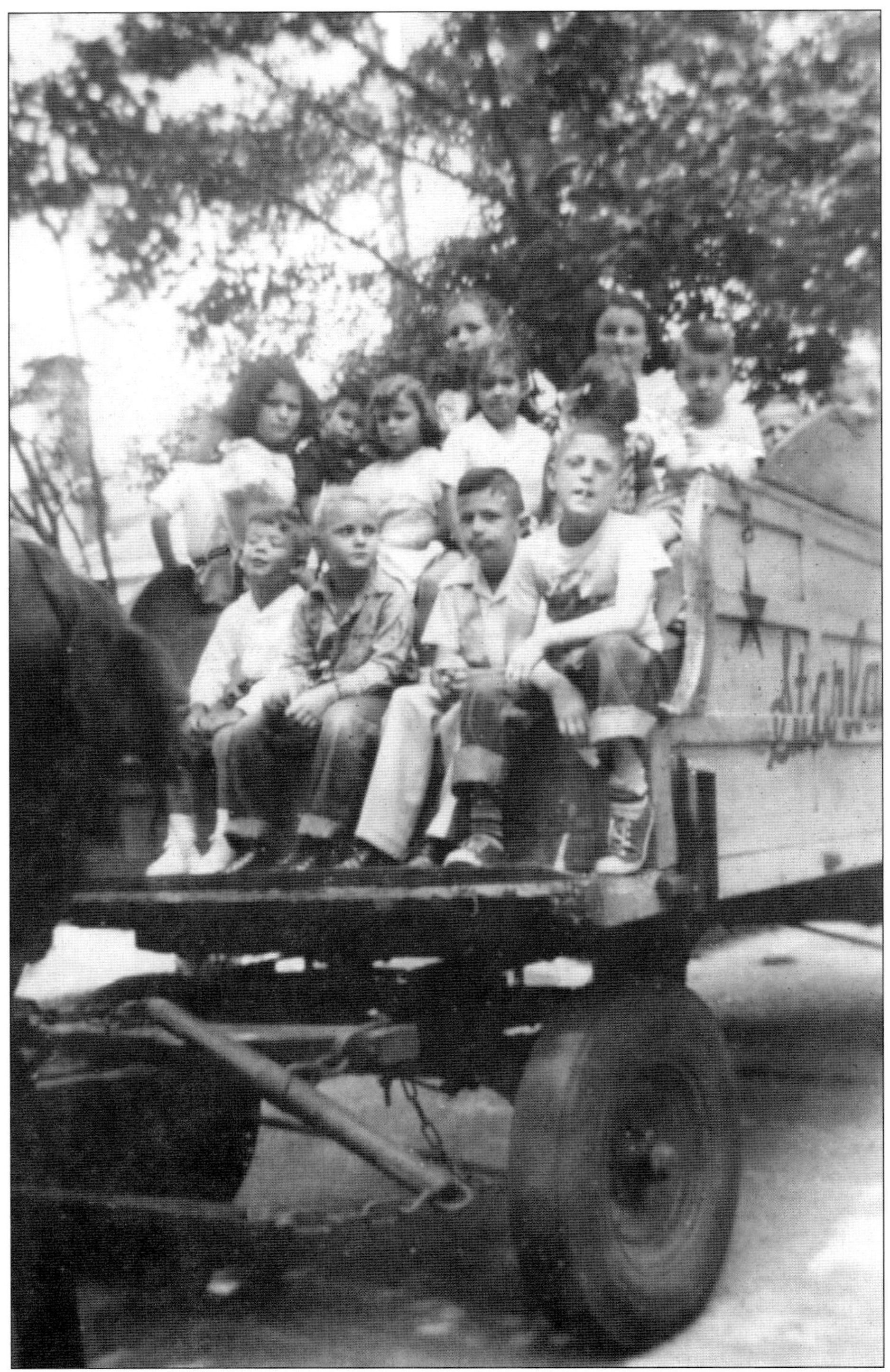

At one point in her childhood, Barbara Brown and her family lived at 1307 East Fiftieth Street. In the 1940s, when her birthday came around, Barbara's parents contacted Starland Dairies and hired the horse-drawn milk truck (turned hay wagon) for her special day. (Courtesy of Barbara Brown Wolling.)

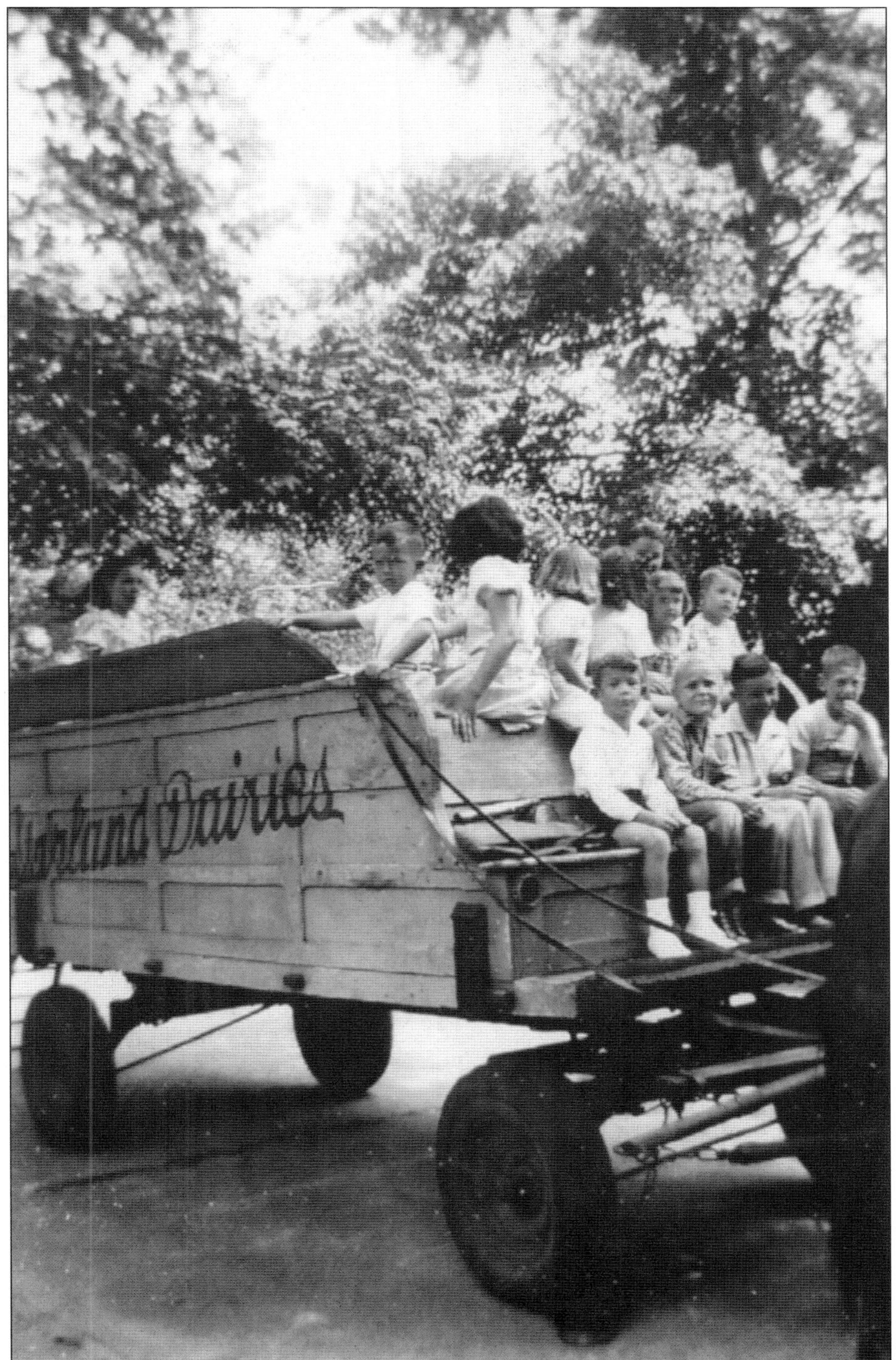

Shown in this picture is another angle of Barbara Brown's hayride birthday party. Starland Dairies was a Savannah institution from the early 1900s until the 1980s and had a processing plant on Bull Street north of Victory Drive. Today, the area is known as the Starland District and includes art and design boutiques, retail establishments, restaurants, and a collection of food trucks. (Courtesy of Barbara Brown Wolling.)

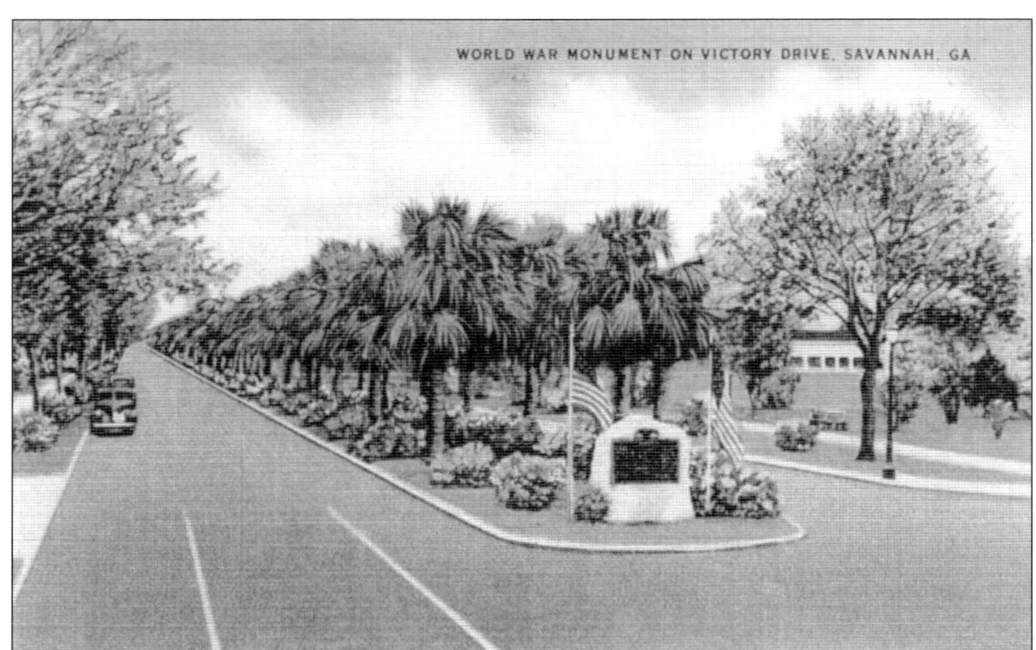

Businesses such as The Triple X Thirst Station on Victory Drive were just a short walk away for Parkside residents who might have wanted a Juicy Pig sandwich. In 1999, the World War I monument shown in this vintage postcard was moved just across the street to Daffin Park. The monument includes the names of Savannahians killed during World War I . Originally, Victory Drive was named Estill Avenue between Bull Street and Waters Avenue, and Dale Avenue from Waters Avenue eastward. The street was renamed Victory Drive in 1922 to honor those who died in the war. (Courtesy of Linda Wittish.)

This 1964 ad is for a barbershop that was located in the red brick building on Waters Avenue between Forty-Ninth and Fiftieth Streets. In the 1950s, the Savannah City Directory listed 49th Street Pharmacy, Manuel's Marketeria, Oglesbee's Barber Shop, and the DuCharme Beauty Parlor in the 3300 block of Waters. (Courtesy of Linda Calhoun Lynes.)

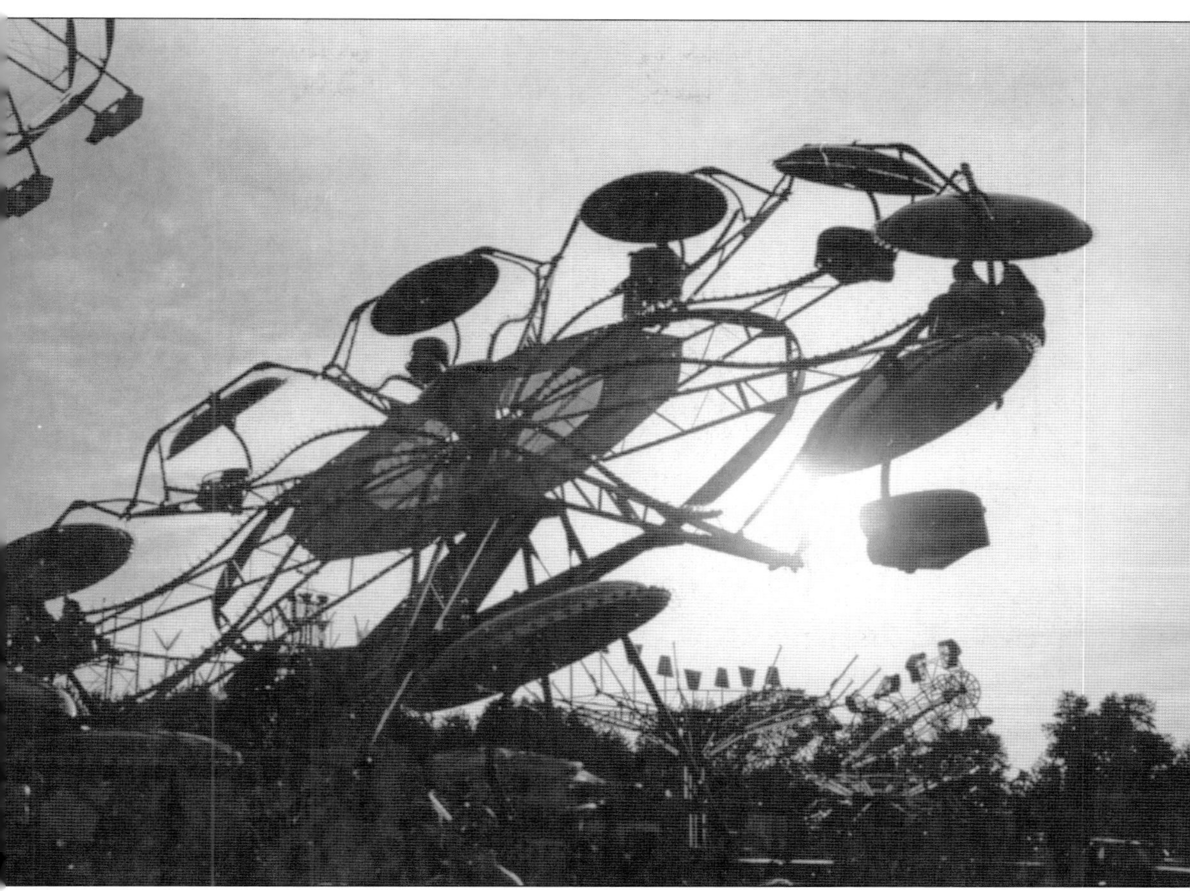

Many Savannahians cherish wonderful memories of Daffin Park, including New Year's Eve bonfires, time spent at the Jaycee Kiddie Fair, and other precious moments. The paratrooper ride was a favorite for both adults and children alike, including Parkside residents, who could walk to the fair. (Courtesy of the DeLorme family.)